As the Sun Has Risen

Scriptural Reflections on

C. S. LEWIS'

Life and Literature

H. DENNIS FISHER

Discovery House is affiliated with Our Daily Bread Ministries,
Grand Rapids, Michigan.

Request for permission to quote this book should be directed to: Permissions Department,
Discovery House, P.O. Box 3566, Grand Rapids, MI 49501,
or contact us by e-mail at permissionsdept@dhp.org.

All Scripture quotations, unless otherwise indicated, are from the
New King James Version®. Copyright © 1982 by Thomas Nelson.
Used by permission. All rights reserved.

Scripture quotations marked KJV are from the King James Version.

Scripture quotations marked NIV are taken from the Holy Bible, New International
Version®, NIV®. Copyright © 1973, 1978, 1984, 2011 by Biblica, Inc.™ Used by permission
of Zondervan. All rights reserved worldwide. www.zondervan.com. The "NIV" and "New
International Version" are trademarks registered in the United States Patent and Trademark
Office by Biblica, Inc.™

Interior design by Sherri L. Hoffman

Library of Congress Cataloging-in-Publication Data

Lewis, C. S. (Clive Staples), 1898-1963. [Works. Selections]
    As the sun has risen : scriptural reflections on C.S. Lewis' life and literature / [selected]
    by Dennis Fisher.
        pages   cm
    Includes index.
    ISBN 978-1-62707-348-6
    1. Lewis, C. S. (Clive Staples), 1898-1963—Quotations. 2. Lewis, C. S. (Clive
    Staples), 1898-1963—Religion. 3. Christianity—Quotations, maxims, etc.
    I. Fisher, Dennis (Hal Dennis) editor. II. Title.
    PR6023.E926A6 2015
    823'.912—dc23   2015009499

Printed in the United States of America
First printing in 2015

To my beloved wife, Janet, whose listening ear,
wise counsel, and persistent prayers have contributed
immeasurably to the content of this book.

May those who read it grow closer to Christ
as she and I have by exploring the world
of C. S. Lewis through the lens of Scripture.

———————⟫ • ⟪———————

FOREWORD

‒‒‒‒‒‒‒‒ ❯ ❮ ‒‒‒‒‒‒‒‒

By Walter Hooper

This is a book after my own heart. Dennis Fisher knows the works of C. S. Lewis so well that, like the fisherman in Our Lord's parable, he can cast his net into the sea and gather in some of every kind of Lewis' writings (Matthew 13:47–48). Thus, he enriches his own writings with Lewis' works, many of which will be unfamiliar to some readers. I am pleased he has chosen so many. Fifty-one years ago, when Lewis' brother, Warnie, encouraged me to edit C. S. Lewis' literary remains, I found his admirers eager to have any of his works they'd never seen. My job that last half century has been to find Lewis' writings and make them available to a very eager public. But while I hope I'm wrong, this seems to be changing.

I meet people almost every day who are passionate about *Mere Christianity* or passionate about the Chronicles of Narnia—but who are strangely indifferent to his other works. I come across people who purport to be "Lewis scholars" but who have never read Lewis' three interplanetary novels, beginning with *Out of the Silent Planet* (1938). Is it because they think of Lewis as several different writers, and they have chosen the one they like? Or is it that Lewis' books are so readily available that one thinks of reading the others "sometime"?

Until I met a man recently who claims to have read *Mere Christianity* twenty times, but who'd never read Lewis' *Miracles* (1947), I did not realise how fortunate I was in my introduction to the writings of C. S. Lewis.

It was 1953 and I was a senior at the University of North Carolina in Chapel Hill. This was the time of the Korean War and the draft board had promised to leave me alone for a few months. In that happy place during a happy time of my life, I was introduced to J. B. Phillips' *Letters*

to Young Churches: A Translation of the New Testament Epistles (1947).
It contained an introduction by C. S. Lewis. I'd never heard his name
before, and I read the introduction simply because it was there. It made
a total conquest of me. I've been trying ever since 1953 to explain to
others why that brief article—now published as "Modern Translations
of the Bible" in Lewis' *God in the Dock* (1970)—made such a powerful
impact on me. What came through the introduction was not simply
information about the Epistles but something about *Lewis.* I believe
now, and I think I sensed it in 1953, that I'd stumbled upon someone
whose faith was as confident as that of the apostles. Lewis believed—or
so it seems to me—with the certainty of Peter and those who had been
with Jesus.

After a number of deferments I finished my degree and went straight
into the army. Before leaving for Fort Jackson in South Carolina, I
visited what will always be sacred for me—Straughan's Book Shop in
Greensboro, North Carolina. The remarkable Straughan sisters, Mattie
and Alice, liked to put the right book in the right hands, and when
they discovered my interest in C. S. Lewis they produced a copy of his
Miracles, which they had in stock. The sisters promised to find me his
other books and send them to me wherever I was.

The next day I went to Fort Jackson with Lewis' *Miracles.* During
basic training I kept *Miracles* hidden beneath my shirt, which made
for a good deal of discomfort during calisthenics and bayonet practice. However, in those little ten-minute breaks between firing bazookas
and throwing grenades, I managed to read a page or so. If a book can
hold your interest during all that excitement, and while you're crawling
under barbed wire in a muddy trench, it is a very, *very* good book.

In a few months' time I was sent to Fort Bragg, North Carolina, and
the first people to know of my move were the Straughan sisters. They
knew I wanted not this or that kind of book from this author, but *any*
book by C. S. Lewis. I will be forever grateful for the higgledy-piggledy
way the books arrived. They sent me the books as they could get them,
and I think the order in which they arrived was something like *A Preface
to Paradise Lost* (1942) followed by *Mere Christianity* (1952) followed by

English Literature in the Sixteenth Century (1954) followed by *The Lion, the Witch and the Wardrobe* (1950).

I knew and loved John Milton's *Paradise Lost*, but until I read Lewis' *Preface* I realised I'd never understood what was involved in the fall of man or why Satan was not a hero but a mere egoist. *Mere Christianity* added immeasurably to what I'd learned from *Miracles*, and reading *English Literature in the Sixteenth Century* introduced me to the world of English literature in which Lewis was completely at home. (I wonder if Christian readers realise what a good introduction this work on sixteenth-century literature is to the Protestant Reformation.) I think I was a mature enough Christian to know that, while the gospel is everlasting, it must always be presented in a manner that will make it appear in its perpetual freshness. *The Lion, the Witch and the Wardrobe*—Lewis' "supposal" of what Christ would be like were the Son of God to become incarnate as a Lion in a world of talking animals—did exactly that. Lewis had found his way past those "watchful dragons" that prevent us from attending to the truth of the gospel and making it appear in its real potency.[1] Those who are uncertain about combining Lewis' theological works with his academic will appreciate what he said to one reader: "Work whose Christianity is latent may do quite as much good and may reach some whom the more obvious religious work would scare away."[2] During my remaining time in the army the Straughan sisters sent me all Lewis' other books for which I will be forever grateful.

Writing about one of his close friends, Lewis claimed that Owen Barfield "cannot talk on any subject without illuminating it."[3] I knew Owen Barfield over many years, and he would have agreed with me that this claim was equally true of Lewis. More than that, Mr. Barfield put his finger on something that may be unique in the writer Dennis Fisher

---

1. C. S. Lewis, "Sometimes Fairy Stories May Say Best What's to Be Said," in *Of This and Other Worlds,* ed. Walter Hooper (London: Collins, 1982), p. 59.

2. C. S. Lewis, *The Collected Letters of C. S. Lewis,* vol. 3, ed. Walter Hooper (London: HarperCollins, 2006), p. 502.

3. Ibid., p. 1329.

celebrates in this enjoyable book. Talking about the quality and structure of Lewis' thinking—and by extension, his books—Mr. Barfield believed that: "what he thought about everything was secretly present in what he said about anything."[4] Those who go from reading their favourite Lewis books to those they have never read will find a happy surprise waiting for them for this reason, and they will find themselves acquiring what I call Lewis' "Christian world view," which includes almost everything that went into his broad and capacious mind.

I congratulate Dennis Fisher on including in this book Lewis' *A Grief Observed* (1961), and I end by remembering a great lady who had read and enjoyed all Lewis' works. Because *A Grief Observed* dealt in part with the death of his beloved wife, Lewis published it under the pseudonym N. W. Clerk. After his death it was published under his own name.

It was my privilege to be Lewis' secretary during the last months of his life, and soon after he died he received a letter from a librarian in Kansas. It grieves me that her letter is lost, and that I cannot remember her name. But the *point* of her letter I will never forget. It went something like this. "Dear Mr. Lewis, I am very sad. I have read all your books, and for years I've considered you the best writer there is. But now you have a rival. I have just read Mr. N. W. Clerk's *A Grief Observed*, and it breaks my heart that he is as good a writer as you. I am torn between the two of you—and this makes me very unhappy."

I sent this perceptive lady a note saying that Mr. Lewis and Mr. Clerk had both died—but that she had reason to be cheerful—Mr. Lewis and Mr. Clerk were the *same* person.

WALTER HOOPER, Oxford, England

4. *Owen Barfield on C. S. Lewis*, ed. G. B. Tennyson (Middletown, CT: Wesleyan University Press, 1989), p. 122.

INTRODUCTION

C. S. Lewis is one of the most quoted authors in today's world. Yet critics in his own day predicted that his writings would have a very short shelf life. So why would C. S. Lewis have such name recognition today? Some might say that it was the skillful way the Oxford don integrated his Christian faith into so many different kinds of writing. It was his personal secretary Walter Hooper who said, "C. S. Lewis was the most thoroughly converted man I have ever met." What Hooper meant by this is that Lewis did not confine his Christian faith to a restricted area on Sunday morning worship or his private devotional time. Instead, Lewis was receptive to the spiritual light that Christ gives to every aspect of life. Of this Lewis said, "I believe in Christianity as I believe that the sun has risen: not only because I see it, but because by it I see everything else." *As the Sun Has Risen: Scriptural Reflections on C. S. Lewis' Life and Literature* is a daily devotional guide that attempts to make accessible the vast writing of this gifted and creative Christian author. It seeks to help us see different aspects of our lives through Christ's heavenly light.

Since so many other books on C. S. Lewis are on the market, what might be the distinguishing characteristic of this volume? Looking at one of our Lord's parables might provide an answer: "Again, the kingdom of heaven is like a dragnet that was cast into the sea and gathered some of every kind, which, when it was full, they drew to shore; and they sat down and gathered the good into vessels, but threw the bad away" (Matthew 13:47–48).

The dragnet mentioned here is unique in the New Testament. It was not the kind of net that the disciples used when Jesus told them to draw in a miraculous catch of fish (John 21:6–11). The parable's dragnet is a long draw-mesh that was spread wide and then drawn together.

This devotional book is a dragnet of sorts. But its purpose is not to divide the good from the bad in Lewis' writings. Instead, this volume helps spread a wide net in order to capture both the familiar and the less known in Lewis' writings. In so doing it is hoped that the reader will be both inspired and instructed in surprising new ways. This book includes familiar allusions to such classics as *Mere Christianity, The Screwtape Letters,* and The Narnia Chronicles. But the journey will not end there. We will also explore Lewis' science fiction, poetry, word studies, literary criticism, correspondence, and other less familiar works. In addition, we will reflect on the life Lewis led and those relationships that both blessed and frustrated him.

The book provides 365 daily devotional articles that follow a simple format. Under each date is listed a Scripture reading. A short devotional is then given with an insight from C. S. Lewis' life or literature that is related to a biblical text. "For Further Reading" gives us a place to go to explore the topic more fully in Lewis' writings. Finally, the theme is made memorable by an inspirational statement at the bottom of the page.

It is hoped that this devotional will appeal to those new to Lewis as well as to those familiar with this great Christian author. Above all, the purpose of this book is to link the works of C. S. Lewis with Scripture, which is the ultimate source of spiritual nourishment. In using this devotional guide, may we all experience what the prophet Jeremiah so eloquently expressed centuries ago: "Your words were found, and I ate them, and Your word was to me the joy and rejoicing of my heart; for I am called by Your name, O LORD God of hosts" (Jeremiah 15:16).

As the Sun Has Risen

READ: Job 38:1–7

Angel Praise

Who laid [the earth's] cornerstone, when the morning stars sang together, and all the sons of God shouted for joy?   —Job 38:6–7

In *The Magician's Nephew*, a young boy witnesses the creation of Narnia through the song of the great lion Aslan: "A voice had begun to sing. It was very far away and Digory found it hard to decide from what direction it was coming. Sometimes it seemed to come from all directions at once. Sometimes he almost thought it was coming out of the earth beneath them. Its lower notes were deep enough to be the voice of the earth herself. There were no words. It was hardly a tune. But it was beyond comparison, the most beautiful sound he had ever heard."

Most likely, C. S. Lewis drew his inspiration for this scene from the biblical record of God speaking to Job out of the whirlwind: "Where were you when I laid the foundations of the earth? . . . when the morning stars sang together, and all the sons of God shouted for joy?" (Job 38:4–7).

God's mighty act of creation was met with songs of praise and shouts of joy from angels—referred to in this passage as "the sons of God." When we behold His creative masterpiece, can we do anything less?

As you look at the wonders of creation today, why not sing a song of praise to the great Architect who made it possible?

For Further Reading: *The Magician's Nephew* by C. S. Lewis, chapter 9

Father's Discipline

My son, do not despise the chastening of the LORD, nor detest His correction; for whom the LORD loves He corrects, just as a father the son in whom he delights. —Proverbs 3:11–12

C. S. Lewis observed: "What would really satisfy us would be a God who said of anything we happened to like doing, 'What does it matter so long as they are contented?' We want in fact not so much a father in heaven as a grandfather in heaven—a senile benevolence who, as they say, 'liked to see young people enjoying themselves' . . . that it might be truly said at the end of the day, 'a good time was had by all.'"

In our families on earth we see how complete leniency in child rearing can create self-centered and destructive lives. The loving parent guides the moral development of the child by providing encouragement and discipline as necessary. So it is with our heavenly Father. Because He is interested in our sharing His own divine character, He uses painful circumstances to help us grow. "For whom the LORD loves He corrects, just as a father the son in whom he delights" (Proverbs 3:12). This means we need both instruction and training as we mature. God's major way of accomplishing this is through painful circumstances that test us and make us more like Him.

> *God sends testing our way to make*
> *us share in His own character.*

FOR FURTHER READING: *The Problem of Pain* by C. S. Lewis, chapter 2

READ: 2 Corinthians 5:14–15; Colossians 1:20; 1 John 2:1–2

Cosmic Reconciliation

By Him to reconcile all things to Himself, by Him, whether things on earth or things in heaven, having made peace through the blood of His cross. —Colossians 1:20

As Jesus Christ was hanging there—dying on the cross—He was thinking about you personally (Hebrews 12:2). Yet the impact of His death was also cosmic in scope. Not only those who believe the gospel will be reconciled to God, but someday all of intra-galactic space as well.

In Lewis' science fiction book *Perelandra*, here is how the Adam of another planet describes Christ's atoning work accomplished on our world.

> When He died in the Wounded World He died not for men, but for each man. If each man had been the only man made, He would have done no less. Each thing, from the single grain of Dust to the strongest eldil [angel], is the end and the final cause of all creation and the mirror in which the beam of His brightness comes to rest and so returns to Him. Blessed be He!

The day is coming when God will reconcile the entire universe— *whether things on earth or things in heaven* (Colossians 1:20). This will set the stage for a new heaven and a new earth, which will ring out with the rejoicing of the redeemed.

Let us praise God for the time when He will reconcile the entire universe to himself.

For Further Reading: *Perelandra* by C. S. Lewis, chapter 17

READ: John 11:38–44

Temporal or Eternal Reunion?

[Christ] cried with a loud voice, "Lazarus, come forth!" And he who had died came out bound hand and foot with graveclothes, and his face was wrapped with a cloth. —John 11:43–44

Have you had your heart broken by losing someone in death? Sometimes the desire for reunion in this present life is so great we don't want to wait for heaven. But this wished-for reunion would not solve all our problems.

In his book *Miracles*, C. S. Lewis writes: "The raising of Lazarus differs from the Resurrection of Christ Himself because Lazarus, so far as we know, was not raised to a new and more glorious mode of existence but merely restored to the sort of the life he had before. . . . He who will raise all men at the general resurrection here does it small and in a close . . . merely anticipatory fashion."

Certainly, there was a joyous reunion between Lazarus and his sisters Mary and Martha. But inevitably death would claim each of them and the grieving process would be experienced in a fresh way. Perhaps it would be Lazarus weeping at the tomb of Martha the next time.

This is why the resurrection—though future—brings such hope. All believers will live in eternal joy with one another and their Redeemer.

The loss of our believing loved ones to death will one day be replaced with an eternal and glorified fellowship with them.

FOR FURTHER READING: *Miracles* by C. S. Lewis, chapter 16

READ: Revelation 19:1–10

Married to Royalty

Let us be glad and rejoice and give Him glory, for the marriage of the Lamb has come, and His wife has made herself ready.
—Revelation 19:7

Near the end of his life, after C. S. Lewis had suffered a coma, he had trouble recognizing those who came to visit. But when Maureen Moore, who had been under his care when she was young, dropped by, she was surprised by his lucid response. "Jack, it is Maureen." He opened his eyes and said, "No, it is Lady Dunbar." "How did you know?" she asked in surprise. Lewis responded, "I never forget a fairy tale." Earlier in her life Maureen had inherited the title of baroness—thus making her Lady Dunbar—so she was exactly who Jack said she was.

Lewis loved the concept of the fairy tale, and he often built stories of people from common beginnings being elevated by marrying royalty. Amazingly, we who believe in Christ have each been called to a royal marriage in heaven. " 'Let us be glad and rejoice and give Him glory, for the marriage of the Lamb has come, and His wife has made herself ready.' And to her it was granted to be arrayed in fine linen, clean and bright, for the fine linen is the righteous acts of the saints" (Revelation 19:7–8).

Let us strive to live holy lives that are worthy of our future union with the King of Kings.

FOR FURTHER READING: *Jack* by George Sayer;
The Weight of Glory by C. S. Lewis, Introduction

READ: Genesis 1:20–25

Animal Friends

And God made the beast of the earth according to its kind, cattle according to its kind, and everything that creeps on the earth according to its kind. And God saw that it was good.

—Genesis 1:25

Are you an animal lover? Some of us have fond memories of a dog whose emotional connection with us made him almost a member of the family. Others like the genteel habits and purring of a house cat, while others prefer the mimics or chirps of birds. The special relationship pets have with us may lead us to treat them as if they were almost human. Although the Bible teaches there is a distinction between us as God's image-bearers and the animal kingdom, God did give animals to us for chores and as companions.

C. S. Lewis loved animals. While he was writing some of his most famous works, his pets—a dog and a cat—lived in peace under his roof. In *Mere Christianity*, Lewis writes: "The higher animals are in a sense drawn into Man when he loves them and makes them (as he does) much more nearly human than they would otherwise be." The Bible tells us, "And God made the beast of the earth according to its kind. . . . And God saw that it was good" (Genesis 1:25). God created the animal kingdom for human beings so they might celebrate the special bond between horse and rider, hunter and dog, and cat and home-dwellers.

God created animals to serve, to delight, and to fellowship with the human race.

FOR FURTHER READING: *Mere Christianity*
by C. S. Lewis, book 4, chapter 8

READ: 1 Corinthians 15:1–10

Just to Feel Good?

For this cause I was born, and for this cause I have come into the world, that I should bear witness to the truth. —John 18:37

For nearly seventy years a huge portion of the world's population ran a pilot project to see if Marxism was a viable social mechanism. Then in 1989 the wall separating West and East Germany came down and many communist countries lost faith in their atheistic philosophy. It was Marx who said that "religion is the opiate of the people." He believed that people turned to religion to feel better even if it weren't true.

In his pilgrimage from atheism to Christian faith, C. S. Lewis claimed the exact opposite of this. "I didn't go to religion to make me happy. I always knew a bottle of Port would do that." Repeatedly in his writings and sermons he proclaimed his conversion to the Christian faith was solely because it was true.

When Jesus stood before Pilate, He proclaimed: "For this cause I was born, and for this cause I have come into the world, that I should bear witness to the truth" (John 18:37).

We are not Christians because it makes us feel good. We experience God's joy and peace because it is based upon the truth that Christ died, rose again, and will make all things new (Revelation 21:5).

We serve Christ because He bears witness to the truth.

FOR FURTHER READING: *God in the Dock* by C. S. Lewis, "Answers to Questions on Christianity"

READ: Psalm 22:1–21

Feeling Forsaken

My God, My God, why have You forsaken Me?
—Matthew 27:46

In the book *The Screwtape Letters*, C. S. Lewis records an imaginary conversation between a senior devil and a junior one discussing the proper means of temptation for a Christian. Using reverse psychology, they conclude that "the Enemy" is God and what the two devils desire is to confound the believer's faith in Him. "Be not deceived, Wormwood, our cause is never more in jeopardy than when a human, no longer desiring but still intending to do our Enemy's will, looks round upon a universe in which every trace of Him seems to have vanished, and asks why he has been forsaken, and still obeys."

Sometimes we may think the Lord has let us down. For example, Abram thought God's promise of an heir had gone unheeded (Genesis 15:2–3). The psalmist in his trouble felt ignored (Psalm 10:1). Job's troubles were so great that he thought God might even kill him (Job 13:15). And Jesus cried out from the cross: "My God, My God, why have You forsaken Me?" (Matthew 27:46). Yet despite these internal struggles, faith and obedience still followed. And God was shown to be faithful (Genesis 21:1–7; Psalm 10:16–18; Job 38–42; Matthew 28:9–20).

God is delighted with our baby steps of obedience—
especially when we feel forsaken.

FOR FURTHER READING: *The Screwtape Letters* by C. S. Lewis, letter 8

READ: Psalm 71:17–18; Proverbs 16:31; Leviticus 19:32

The Autumn of Life

Now also when I am old and grayheaded, O God, do not forsake me, until I declare Your strength to this generation.

—Psalm 71:18

C. S. Lewis passed away when he was one week short of his sixty-fifth birthday. Interestingly, older age was the favorite season of his life. To a friend he wrote: "Yes, autumn is really the best of the seasons; and I'm not sure that old age isn't the best part of life. But of course, like autumn, it doesn't last."

In our youth-oriented culture, we might be tempted to think that reaching a more mature age is something to dread. But the Bible offers a very different perspective on growing old: Aging is important because it is part of the journey (Psalm 71:17–18). It has its own dignity and glory (Proverbs 16:31). It is a season sustained by God (Isaiah 46:4). It can bring wisdom if we trust God (Job 32:7). It often has earned the respect of others (Leviticus 19:32). And it can be an especially fruitful time (Psalm 92:14).

Both autumn and reaching a mature age have much for which we should be thankful.

*Truly, the autumn of life can be
among the best of life's seasons.*

FOR FURTHER READING: *The Collected Letters of C. S. Lewis,* volume 3

READ: John 15:1–16

Secret Master of Ceremonies

I have called you friends, for all things that I heard from My Father I have made known to you. You did not choose Me, but I chose you. —John 15:15–16

C. S. Lewis made and kept many friends during his lifetime. Indeed, Christian friendship was one of his most treasured possessions. Lewis believed that Christ was invisibly behind the scenes making Christian friendships thrive: "A secret master of ceremonies has been at work. Christ, who said to the disciples, 'Ye have not chosen me, but I have chosen you,' can truly say to every group of Christian friends, 'Ye have not chosen one another but I have chosen you for one another. The friendship is not a reward for our discriminating and good taste in finding one another out. It is the instrument by which God reveals to each of us the beauties of others.' "

Friends of faith feed our soul, stimulate our mind, and listen to our heart. Life-related insights are not far away as we encourage and challenge each other on our spiritual journeys. But as Lewis wisely observes, a third party—Christ—is there, revealing inner fruit that He is causing to grow, and He invites us to help in its cultivation. Jesus Christ is the secret master of ceremonies to Christian friendship.

Through friendship, Christ reveals to each of us the beauty of others.

FOR FURTHER READING: *The Four Loves* by C. S. Lewis, "Friendship"

READ: John 1:1–14; Colossians 2:1–10; Philippians 2:5–11

The Grand Miracle

In the beginning was the Word, and the Word was with God, and the Word was God. . . . And the Word became flesh and dwelt among us.   —John 1:1, 14

C. S. Lewis viewed the incarnation as the center of the Christian faith. In his view, all of the Old Testament led up to that one Grand Miracle, and the entire New Testament recorded its reality and its implications. In short, Lewis summarized it as follows: "The Christian assertion being that what is beyond all space and time, what is uncreated, eternal, came into nature, into human nature, descended into His own universe, and rose again, bringing nature up with Him."

The Scriptures support this view throughout. John tells us that Jesus, whom he called the Word, "was God . . . and . . . became flesh and dwelt among us" (John 1:1, 14). Paul declares that in Christ "dwells all the fullness of the Godhead bodily" (Colossians 2:9). Also, he eloquently describes how Christ, who was in the very form of God, laid aside His heavenly glory and became a man who would serve and suffer for our redemption (Philippians 2:5–11). The deity of Christ is central to our redemption. It is the hope of becoming glorified children of God for all of eternity!

Jesus Christ is perfect humanity and undiminished deity united in one person forever!

FOR FURTHER READING: *God in the Dock*
by C. S. Lewis, "The Grand Miracle"

READ: Deuteronomy 6:4–9; 2 Timothy 3:14–16

Value Rich Learning

You shall teach them diligently to your children, and shall talk of them when you sit in your house, when you walk by the way, when you lie down, and when you rise up. —Deuteronomy 6:7

C. S. Lewis' book *The Abolition of Man* lays the foundation for teaching children and youth on acquiring values derived not only from the Bible but also from other traditions that reflect similar ethics. Lewis wrote, "Aristotle says that the aim of education is to make the pupil like and dislike what he ought. When the age for reflective thought comes, the pupil who has been thus trained in 'ordinate affections' . . . will easily find the first principles in Ethics; but to the corrupt man they will never be visible at all."

Old Testament Jewish parents were commanded to teach virtue to their children. And they understood godly living ultimately sprang from the wellspring of the Word of God. "You shall teach them diligently to your children, and shall talk of them when you sit in your house, when you walk by the way, when you lie down, and when you rise up" (Deuteronomy 6:7).

As our world becomes more global and diverse, we should celebrate cultural differences and values of shared agreement. Yet Christian virtues are ultimately grounded upon the Word of God. For there we find "a lamp to [our] feet and light to [our] path" (Psalm 119:105).

We should celebrate diversity, support agreed-upon values, and grow deep in the truth of Scripture.

FOR FURTHER READING: *The Abolition of Man* by C. S. Lewis, chapter 1

READ: Revelation 8:1–4

Incense Prayers

*The smoke of the incense, with the prayers of the saints, ascended
before God from the angel's hand.*   —Revelation 8:4

C. S. Lewis carried in his library writings by Jeremy Taylor, a seventeenth-century clergy in the Church of England. He has been called the "Shakespeare of Divines" for his poetic style of expression. Taylor, although from a religious tradition that did not use incense, recognized the visual power of ascending incense smoke to illustrate the prayers of believers.

Of this Taylor wrote: "The temple itself is the heart of man; Christ is the High Priest, who from there sends the incense of prayers, and joins them in intercession, and present all together to his Father, and the Holy Ghost, by his dwelling here, has also consecrated it into a temple."

Taylor linked Old Testament temple worship to our prayers in Christ. In Exodus 30, God gave instructions about the role of incense in worship. The priest was to burn it daily (Exodus 30:7). Ancient incense carried a wonderful fragrance that helped believers more fully enter into a sweet experience of intercession.

The metaphor appears again in the New Testament book of Revelation concerning the prayers of the saints (Revelation 8:1–4). Paul also used the idea of incense to describe the spiritual aroma believers exude to unbelievers through witness in word and deed (2 Corinthians 2:14–16). We are to be the "pleasing aroma of Christ" among others (2 Corinthians 2:15 NIV).

*As you pray today why not picture your intercession as a
sweet smoke ascending in heavenly petition and praise?*

FOR FURTHER READING: Jeremy Taylor, *From the Library of C. S. Lewis*
compiled by James Scott Bell

Partnering with God

Elijah was a man with a nature like ours, and he prayed earnestly that it would not rain; and it did not rain on the land for three years and six months. And he prayed again, and the heaven gave rain, and the earth produced its fruit. —James 5:17–18

Some Bible teachers place so much emphasis on the sovereignty of God that we wonder if it is appropriate to ask God for anything. But C. S. Lewis believed that God partners with us through prayer. Lewis writes: " 'God,' said Pascal, 'instituted prayer in order to lend to His creatures the dignity of causality.' But not only prayer; whenever we act at all He lends us that dignity . . . They have not advised or changed God's mind—that is, His over-all purpose. But that purpose will be realized in different ways according to the actions, including the prayers, of His creatures."

James uses an Old Testament prophet as a case study on how God answers prayer (James 5:17–18). Elijah had the same emotions and frailties as we. Yet, being led of God, he interceded to affect weather conditions for God's purposes in Israel (1 Kings 17:1; 18:20–46). Because of one man's prayers, a terribly long drought was followed by a wonderfully fruitful rain. Most certainly God is sovereign in His orchestrating of events in heaven and earth. But He also invites us to partner with Him in prayer.

*God invites you today to partner with Him
in prayer to accomplish His purposes.*

FOR FURTHER READING: *The World's Last Night and Other Essays*
by C. S. Lewis, "The Efficacy of Prayer"

Brimful

I have come that they may have life, and that they may have it more abundantly. —John 10:10

Some people think of God as an impersonal energy force that animates the universe. This philosophy gives them a religious connection with nature, and it does not trouble them with the moral accountability of a holy and sovereign Creator. But the Bible does not hold this view of God. C. S. Lewis captured the dynamic nature of the Christian God in this way: "[God] is so brim-full of existence that He can give existence away, can cause things to be, and to be really other than Himself, can make it untrue to say that He is everything."

Once in the history of our world, this Creator who is "brim-full of existence" became human. He taught about His Father's kingdom, worked miracles, forgave sins, died, and rose from the grave. And it was this God-man Jesus Christ who could give life abundantly (John 10:10). In the original Greek, *abundance* implies "a super surplus of all that sustains life such as love, joy, peace and lasting satisfaction for eternity." Jesus Christ is brimful of all we need for our satisfaction!

The God-man Jesus Christ is brimful with abundant life for all who trust Him.

FOR FURTHER READING: *Miracles* by C. S. Lewis, chapter 11

READ: Romans 11:25–36

The Wise and Good God

Oh, the depth of the riches both of the wisdom and knowledge of God! How unsearchable are His judgments and His ways past finding out! —Romans 11:33

In Romans 11:33, Paul reflects on how God's chosen people of Israel could have rejected the promised Messiah when He appeared in Jesus Christ. Yet through the inspiration of the Spirit, Paul is given insights into God's wisdom and goodness, which leads him to a doxology of praise: "Oh, the depth of the riches both of the wisdom and knowledge of God! How unsearchable are His judgments and His ways past finding out!" (Romans 11:33).

Only a God who sees all in eternal perspective and whose nature is perfectly love and righteousness could bring a higher good out of Israel's national rejection of Jesus Christ. Their rejection had the effect of providing salvation for all in the broader Gentile world who believe in Him.

In reflecting on God's workings, C. S. Lewis insightfully wrote, "God's will is determined by His wisdom which always perceives, and His goodness which always embraces the intrinsically good." The lesson for us today is that although God's will may seem a mystery to us at times, His wise perspective and intrinsic goodness guarantee the best possible outcome.

> *The sovereign guidance of the world by a loving and all-powerful God brings peace of mind.*

FOR FURTHER READING: *The Problem of Pain*
by C. S. Lewis, chapter 6

READ: 1 John 1:1–10; 3:20–21

Feeling Forgiven

For if our heart condemns us, God is greater than our heart, and knows all things.   —1 John 3:20

In the book *Letters to an American Lady,* Lewis answers a letter in which the correspondent does not feel forgiven. He cites 1 John 3:20: "For if our heart condemns us, God is greater than our heart, and knows all things." Then Lewis follows with this advice: "The feeling of being, or not being, forgiven and loved, is not what matters. One must come down to brass tacks. If there is a particular sin on your conscience, repent and confess it."

Lewis' point is well taken. John tells us: "If we confess our sins, [God] is faithful and just to forgive us our sins and to cleanse us from all unrighteousness" (1 John 1:9). The Greek word for *confess* is literally, "to say the same things as." When we agree with God about a sin and repent—in other words, turn from it—we are promised forgiveness.

Although we may still struggle with feelings of guilt, the reality is that God's gaze is on the finished work of Christ. God sees us through the lens of Christ taking our sins on the cross and giving us His own righteousness in return (2 Corinthians 5:21).

> *The basis for our forgiveness is not how we feel but faith in Christ's atoning work on the cross for us.*

FOR FURTHER READING: *Letters to an American Lady* by C. S. Lewis

READ: 1 Peter 5:5–7; James 4:4–10

Foolish Pride

Pride goes before destruction, and a haughty spirit before a fall.
—Proverbs 16:18

In C. S. Lewis' children's book *The Horse and His Boy*, a boy named Shasta flees north to Narnia with a talking horse called Bree. A former warhorse, the stallion brags about his past heroism. When a mild-tempered mare named Whin joins their party, however, she becomes the brave one, while Bree gallops away in fear.

When encountering the great lion Aslan, Bree repents of his pride. The great lion king dialogues with the humbled horse as follows: " 'Now Bree,' he said, 'you poor, proud, frightened Horse, draw near. Nearer still my son. Do not dare not to dare . . .' 'Aslan,' said Bree in a shaken voice, 'I'm afraid I must be rather a fool.' 'Happy the horse who knows that while he is still young,' " Aslan responds.

Bree illustrates the truth: "Pride goes before destruction, and a haughty spirit before a fall" (Proverbs 16:18). In the Old Testament, *pride* often meant "arrogance or cynical insensitivity to the needs of others." *Haughty* is a word used of tall trees connoting a person who is looking down on others. Both attitudes have negative consequences. This is why we are admonished to humble ourselves under the mighty hand of God (1 Peter 5:6).

Arrogant pride is often destructive, but
humility under God is constructive.

FOR FURTHER READING: *The Horse and His Boy*
by C. S. Lewis, chapter 14

READ: John 16:19–24; 1 Peter 1:3–9

Elusive Joy

Therefore you now have sorrow; but I will see you again and your heart will rejoice, and your joy no one will take from you.
—John 16:22

As a young man, C. S. Lewis published the narrative poem *Dymer* under the pseudonym Clive Hamilton. The poem tells the story of a young man's adventures after fleeing a future totalitarian state. At one point Dymer reflects on how fleeting joy is: "Can it be possible / That joy flows through and, when the course is run / it leaves no change, no mark on us to tell / its passing? . . . / Joy flickers on / The razor-edge of the present and is gone."

Of course, Lewis wrote *Dymer* when he was still an atheist. In his autobiography *Surprised by Joy*, Lewis explains how from childhood his life had been characterized by the quest for lasting joy. Even in an epic poem written in his young adulthood, Lewis reveals his sadness at the elusiveness of joy.

After his conversion, Lewis experienced the lasting joy he had been looking for—a "joy no one will take from you" (John 16:22). Because Christian joy is derived from union with Christ himself, it is accessible now and for all eternity. Later, in reflecting on this, Lewis would write: "joy is the serious business of heaven."

Temporal joy is elusive, but spiritual joy in Christ is accessible for eternity.

FOR FURTHER READING: *C. S. Lewis: A Companion and Guide* by Walter Hooper, "Narrative Poems"

READ: 1 Samuel 16:1–7

Looking on the Heart

The LORD said to Samuel, . . . "For the LORD does not see as man sees; for man looks at the outward appearance, but the LORD looks at the heart."   —1 Samuel 16:7

In his lesser-known scholarly work *A Preface to Paradise Lost,* C. S. Lewis gives us some insight into human nature. Often we think of people of other historic periods as different from ourselves. But Lewis did not hold this assumption. In this work Lewis wrote: "The things which separate one age from another are superficial. Just as, if we stripped the armour off a medieval knight . . . we should find beneath . . . an anatomy identical with our own . . . the Unchanging Human Heart, and on this we concentrate."

Often we categorize people based on a superficial impression. When Samuel was called to select the next king of Israel, he too had first impressions. But Samuel was not to anoint any of the older sons of Jesse; instead he was to anoint David, the youngest, who looked least like a king. "Do not look at his appearance or at his physical stature . . . . For the LORD does not see as man sees; for man looks at the outward appearance, but the LORD looks at the heart" (1 Samuel 16:7). From David's time to the present, the heart of a person is what matters to God. And that is what should matter to us.

Ask God to help us see the heart of those we know in the present and those we read about from another age.

FOR FURTHER READING: *A Preface to Paradise Lost* by C. S. Lewis, chapter 9

READ: Ephesians 3:14–19

Is Christ Getting Bigger?

[That you] may be able to comprehend with all the saints what is the width and length and depth and height—to know the love of Christ which passes knowledge."   —Ephesians 3:18–19

In *Prince Caspian*, Lucy is initially the only one of the Pevensie children who can see the great lion Aslan. Interestingly, he appears to have grown in size from the first time she saw him until the second: " 'Aslan,' said Lucy. 'You're bigger.' 'That is because you are older, little one,' answered he. 'Not because you are?' 'I am not. But every year you grow, you will find me bigger.' "

In this way, C. S. Lewis paints a marvelous picture about growing in our understanding about the reality of Christ. As we pursue spiritual intimacy with the Savior (Philippians 3:10) and grow in heart-felt obedience (John 14:21), our grasp of how wonderful He is grows exponentially.

Paul's overwhelming desire was that all believers would grow in their comprehension of the love of God in Christ Jesus. To the church at Ephesus he wrote: "[That you] may be able to comprehend with all the saints what is the width and length and depth and height—to know the love of Christ which passes knowledge" (Ephesians 3:18–19). In reality, God's love is infinite. And for this reason the believer will never fully comprehend Christ's love.

> *As our spiritual lives deepen, so does our*
> *perception of the Lord Jesus.*

FOR FURTHER READING: *Prince Caspian* by C. S. Lewis, chapter 9

READ: Matthew 18:21–30

Repetitive Forgiveness

"Lord, how often shall my brother sin against me, and I forgive him? Up to seven times?" Jesus said to him, "I do not say to you, up to seven times, but up to seventy times seven."
—Matthew 18:21–22

In his book *Reflections on the Psalms*, C. S. Lewis writes: "There is no use in talking as if forgiveness were easy. We all know the old joke, 'You've given up smoking once; I've given it up a dozen times.' In the same way I could say of a certain man, 'Have I forgiven him for what he did that day? I've forgiven him more times than I can count.' For we find that the work of forgiveness has to be done over and over again."

Lewis' point is a vital one to consider. Some people we encounter make a habit of insensitive, harmful behavior. But just as we go to God with confession of the same sin—asking over and over for forgiveness—we should do the same with those who harm us. This does not mean we lower all defenses and let an abusive person do damage whenever he or she feels like it. There is a place for setting boundaries on the abuser. But what repeated forgiveness does mean is that we seek to have the same gracious attitude God has for us in our repeat offenses. Only by God's grace is this even possible.

Forgiving repeat offenders reflects the gracious pattern of God's heart through Christ.

FOR FURTHER READING: *Reflections on the Psalms* by C. S. Lewis, chapter 3

READ: Psalm 119:35–37

Becoming Others-Oriented

Behold, how good and how pleasant it is for brethren to dwell together in unity! —Psalm 133:1

The "me generation" was a popular social term coined in the United States in the 1970s. But in reality the self-centered life has been around much longer than that. It has been a characteristic of the human race since the fall of mankind (Genesis 3). Today entire magazines are devoted to "self," "you," and "success." Although there is nothing wrong with seeking self-improvement, an independent path of disregard for God and others will lead only to misery. In *The Weight of Glory*, C. S. Lewis wisely condensed some important principles that touch our personal lives, daily attitudes, and relationship with others. He said, "Obedience is the road to freedom, humility the road to pleasure, unity the road to personality."

To follow Christ in today's culture requires walking to a different drumbeat. As we seek to obey God, a growing sense of freedom comes from aligning ourselves with His purpose for our lives (Psalm 119:35). Humbly serving the interests of others brings a spiritual satisfaction in the imitation of Christ, who has been rightly called the One who lives for others (Philippians 2:3–4). Also, by cultivating positive relationships with other believers, we find ourselves becoming more authentic in who we are and what we are becoming (Psalm 133:1).

It is more blessed to give than to receive. —Acts 20:35

FOR FURTHER READING: *The Weight of Glory* by C. S. Lewis, "Membership"

READ: Revelation 22:1–5

The Theater of Imagination

In the middle of its street, and on either side of the river, was the tree of life, which bore twelve fruits, each tree yielding its fruit every month. The leaves of the tree were for the healing of the nations. —Revelation 22:2

Before the invention of the printing press or film, the art of storytelling thrilled countless generations with words, not visual images. In ancient Greece the traveling teller of tales was known as the *rhapsode,* who would recite great epics such as the *Iliad* and the *Odyssey.* In open-air theaters, the minds of the members of the audience would fill with vivid pictures of epic battles, star-crossed lovers, and heartbreaking tragedies. Little could be seen on the stage, but great emotions were stirred through the imagination of the listeners.

In his book *Studies in Words*, C. S. Lewis observes this phenomenon by saying, "The poet's route to our emotions lies through our imaginations." This is certainly true of the rich imagery we find in Scripture. In the Hebrew oral tradition, many inspired stories were told and retold for generations before being written down.

What kinds of pictures come into your mind as you read Revelation 22 and John's inspired description of heaven? "In the middle of its street, and on either side of the river, was the tree of life, which bore twelve fruits, each tree yielding its fruit every month. The leaves of the tree were for the healing of the nations" (Revelation 22:2). Use the theater of your imagination to visualize the grandeur God has in store for us!

As we meditate on the Word of God, the Spirit illuminates our imagination to picture truths that access our heart.

FOR FURTHER READING: *Studies in Words* by C. S. Lewis, chapter 12

READ: Revelation 21:1–4

Life's Contradictions

For now we see in a mirror, dimly, but then face to face. Now I know in part, but then I shall know just as I also am known.
—1 Corinthians 13:12

C. S. Lewis' first great apologetic work was *The Problem of Pain*. It showed remarkable insight into the problem of evil, which asks, "Why do bad things happen to good people?" However, years later when Lewis lost his wife, Joy, to cancer, his private diary recording the experience was deeply personal. Later published as *A Grief Observed*, Lewis' diary expressed the raw emotions of anguish—even going so far as to question God. Eventually, Lewis did begin to experience comfort and renewed faith again. Reflecting on eternity, he wrote: "Heaven will solve our problems, but not, I think, by showing us subtle reconciliations between all our apparently contradictory notions. The notions will all be knocked from under our feet. We shall see there never was any problem."

Paul tells us that right now our human perspective is at best limited. But in eternity our view will be opened up to a very wide lens (1 Corinthians 13:12). In heaven we will know God and ourselves with the big picture of divine perspective. Once in the glorified state, the apparent life contradictions we now experience will make sense in God's love and providence (Revelation 21:1–4).

Life's contradictions reflect our limited understanding of God's purposes.

FOR FURTHER READING: *A Grief Observed* by C. S. Lewis

READ: Revelation 21:1–13

Temporary or Permanent?

Now I saw a new heaven and a new earth, for the first heaven and the first earth had passed away. Also there was no more sea.
—Revelation 21:1

In the first novel in his Space Trilogy, *Out of the Silent Planet*, C. S. Lewis provides the reader with the Christian perspective that our world is temporary until God remakes it into a permanent one. An inhabitant on Malacandra (Mars) tells the earth man Ransom: "A world is not made to last forever, much less a race; that is not Maleldil's [God's] way."

The Bible's view of the future acknowledges this reality. John tells us, "Now I saw a new heaven and a new earth, for the first heaven and the first earth had passed away. Also there was no more sea" (Revelation 21:1).

The Greek word used for a new heaven and new earth is *kainos*, which means, "something new but based upon a former prototype or design." Certain models of automobiles are revised and improved, but their signature name and appearance are still recognizable. Similarly, those persons and objects we see in the new heaven and new earth will be recognized as those we have known before but with a glorious new remaking. This world of ours will be remade with some exciting improvements.

This world is only a prototype that will be refashioned as our permanent home.

FOR FURTHER READING: *Out of the Silent Planet*
by C. S. Lewis, chapter 16

READ: Jeremiah 20:1–9; 1 Corinthians 9:1–16

Every Believer a Witness

"Woe is me if I do not preach the gospel!"   —1 Corinthians 9:16

In his essay "Modern Theology and Biblical Criticism," C. S. Lewis defends the trustworthiness of the Christian Scriptures. As he does so, Lewis' own passion for the faith comes to the surface: "Woe to you if you do not evangelize," he says, quoting the apostle Paul.

The passion to proclaim the Word of God amidst opposition has a twin echo from the Old and New Testaments. Jeremiah, who suffered terrible persecution for proclaiming an unpopular message, tells us he could not remain silent: "Then I said, 'I will not make mention of Him, nor speak anymore in His name.' But His word was in my heart like a burning fire shut up in my bones; I was weary of holding it back, and I could not" (Jeremiah 20:9).

Centuries later, Paul, a former Pharisee who had been captured by the grace of God, shared a similar conviction about being compelled to preach: "For if I preach the gospel, I have nothing to boast of, for necessity is laid upon me; yes, woe is me if I do not preach the gospel!" (1 Corinthians 9:16). A passion for telling others is one trait of a dedicated believer.

Not all believers have the gift of evangelist, but each of us is called to serve as a witness wherever God has placed us.

FOR FURTHER READING: *Christian Reflections* by C. S. Lewis, "Modern Theology and Biblical Criticism"

READ: Galatians 5:13; Colossians 3:16; 1 Thessalonians 4:18; Hebrews 10:24–25

The Inner Ring

And let us consider one another in order to stir up love and good works, not forsaking the assembling of ourselves together, as is the manner of some, but exhorting one another, and so much the more as you see the Day approaching. —Hebrews 10:24–25

At Oxford University, C. S. Lewis was something of an outsider. The academic community never allowed him to become a professor at Oxford—only a tutor. Many think this was due to his popular writing on Christian themes.

Lewis wrote about the darker side of elite politics in his sermon "The Inner Ring." "The quest of the Inner Ring will break your hearts unless you break it. But if you break it, a surprising result will follow. If in your working hours you make the work your end, you will presently find yourself all unawares inside the only circle in your profession that really matters. You will be one of the sound craftsmen, and other sound craftsmen will know it."

In contrast to the Inner Ring, C. S. Lewis and his friend and fellow writer J. R. R. Tolkien organized the Inklings, a small group of scholarly friends who took turns critiquing and encouraging individual member's writing projects.

Rather than seeking a group known for status and upper mobility, Lewis counseled students to become part of a circle where mutual growth could be encouraged (Romans 12:10; 1 John 3:23; 1 Peter 4:9).

Christian small groups are to be inviting and to encourage growth.

FOR FURTHER READING: *The Weight of Glory*
by C. S. Lewis, "The Inner Ring"

READ: Genesis 2:1–15

Tending Our Garden

Then the LORD God took the man and put him in the garden of Eden to tend and keep it. —Genesis 2:15

The Hebrew word *eden* means, "enchantment, pleasure, or delight." At creation, man was placed in a perfect environment, which would yield fruit easily and abundantly from his labors. In order to lead man to full moral and spiritual development, God gave him clear commands and a specific prohibition to govern his behavior. He also gave him the power of choice and set before him the privilege of growing in divine favor. Thus began the moral discipline of the human race. God would cultivate man's heart as man tended His garden.

In reflecting on this biblical text, C. S. Lewis saw a parallel between our own hearts and the need for cultivation: "When God planted a garden, He set a man over it and set the man under Himself. When He planted the garden of our nature and caused the flowering loves to grow there, He set our will to dress [tend] them. . . . And unless His grace comes down, like the rain and the sunshine, we shall use this tool to little purpose." Through redemption, God is once again at work cultivating our hearts as we tend to our respective daily duties.

The heart and mind need cultivating just as a garden does.

FOR FURTHER READING: *The Four Loves* by C. S. Lewis, chapter 6

READ: 1 John 4:1–10

God's Delight

In this is love, not that we loved God, but that He loved us and sent His Son to be the propitiation for our sins. —1 John 4:10

In one of his letters that has been preserved for us to read, C. S. Lewis reflected on God's overwhelming love for us. Knowing the dark side that we all possess, Lewis made this observation about God's care that reaches out to us in spite of our foibles and follies: "God loves us: not because we are lovable but because He is love, not because He needs to receive but because He delights to give." The starting point for God's love is His character, not our intrinsic lovability.

Pagans in the ancient world worried about displeasing the gods. They would often bring some kind of gift to offer at the altar to appease a god's anger for wrong conduct and to win future blessing. Do we do something similar? Do we come to God fearing His rejection because of our weaknesses and sins? His love for us is not like that. It is inexhaustible!

Genuine guilt does bring the fear of punishment. But Jesus Christ took the wrath of God against sin upon himself in our place (1 John 4:10). Confession and repentance will open the way to experience again God's delight in us as His beloved creatures.

God delights in us because of who He is and what His Son has done for us.

FOR FURTHER READING: *The Four Loves* by C. S. Lewis, "Charity"

READ: Revelation 20:1–6

Reigning with Christ

Blessed and holy is he who has part in the first resurrection. Over such the second death has no power, but they shall be priests of God and of Christ, and shall reign with Him a thousand years.
—Revelation 20:6

In *The Lion, the Witch and the Wardrobe*, when four Pevensie children are put on the four thrones in the castle of Cair Paravel, Aslan makes this eloquent pronouncement: "To the glistening eastern sea, I give you Queen Lucy the Valiant. To the great western woods, King Edmund the Just. To the radiant southern sun, Queen Susan the Gentle. And to the clear northern skies, I give you King Peter the Magnificent. Once a king or queen of Narnia, always a king or queen of Narnia. May your wisdom grace us until the stars rain down from the heavens."

Although the Chronicles of Narnia are fantasy, Lewis often used them to describe spiritual realities that are concrete and eternal. In the New Testament, believers in Christ are promised that they will reign with Jesus Christ—and Lewis' portrayal of the thrones of Cair Paravel seem to be a picture of that future event. One Bible commentary describes reigning with Christ in this way: "A shout of triumph goes up in heaven. The air is full of sound—the din of a great multitude, the roar of rushing waters and loud peals of thunder. The cry is, 'Hallelujah!'—'Praise the Lord!' The triumph of God over the beast is celebrated in the wedding of the Lamb. His bride is the church, in all her purity and beauty."

The future for the believer includes the promise of gloriously reigning with Christ.

FOR FURTHER READING: *The Lion, the Witch and the Wardrobe* by C. S. Lewis, chapter 17

READ: Genesis 1:25; Habakkuk 3:19; Psalm 42:1–2

Elegant Animals

As the deer pants for the water brooks, so pants my soul for You, O God. My soul thirsts for God, for the living God. —Psalm 42:1–2

George Sayer, a former student of C. S. Lewis, became a lifelong friend. In his book *Jack*, Sayer describes an outdoor excursion they took when Lewis' health had begun to fail. "We walked with some hesitation along a narrow path through a wood and suddenly found ourselves in a glade surrounded by a number of miniature deer. Jack was entranced. 'You know, while I was writing the Narnia books, I never imagined anything as lovely as this,' he said. We sat on a fallen trunk, and Jack gazed radiantly at the elegant little animals and adored the God who had created them."

Often we can be moved by a sunset or the stars on a clear night to praise our Creator. But like Lewis we also need to rejoice in our Creator for the elegant animals He has made. Indeed, biblical authors sometimes use animals to teach us lessons about our strength from God and our spiritual hunger for God (Habakkuk 3:19; Psalm 42:1–2). We too, like Jack, should take time to gaze "radiantly at the elegant little animals" and adore the God who created them.

Today, watch for God's elegant animals; learn lessons from their ways and praise the God who created them.

For Further Reading: *Jack: A Life of C. S. Lewis* by George Sayer, chapter 22

READ: Proverbs 21:31; Jeremiah 6:16; Matthew 11:28–29

Rest for the Soul

Stand at the crossroads and look; ask for the ancient paths, ask where the good way is, and walk in it, and you will find rest for your souls. —Jeremiah 6:16 (NIV)

Years before serving as C. S. Lewis' personal secretary, Walter Hooper had been in basic training for the U.S. Army at Fort Jackson, South Carolina. Hooper tells how during a lull between practicing firing a bazooka, he would pull Lewis' book *Miracles* from under his shirt and read a few pages. When asked why he read on the firing range, he answered that at the end of the day he was too exhausted and fell immediately to sleep.

Wisely, Hooper had found a place of rest in the midst of a hectic schedule. Proverbs tells us where our true rest lies: "Stand at the crossroads and look; ask for the ancient paths, ask where the good way is, and walk in it, and you will find rest for your souls" (Jeremiah 6:16 NIV). Many of us have daily pressures that make us stressed. But looking to God for the "good way" can bring rest for our souls.

What conflict are you facing today? Take time to find a place of spiritual connection and find a place of peace in the midst of conflict. There you will find "rest for your [soul]" (Matthew 11:29).

> *God can bring rest for the soul in the midst of stressful circumstances.*

FOR FURTHER READING: *Miracles* by C. S. Lewis, chapter 16

READ: Psalm 119:1–24; Colossians 2:1–3; 2 Timothy 3:15–16

Percolating with Life

The Father and . . . Christ, in whom are hidden all the treasures of wisdom and knowledge. —Colossians 2:2–3

In *The Allegory of Love*, C. S. Lewis wrote: "There is nothing in literature which does not, in some degree, percolate into life." Certainly this is true in those inspired books that make up our Bible. Not only are they the Word of God but they are also recognized as great literature.

The Bible's historical books contain ancient narrative that reveals the gracious beginnings and rebellious ways of the human race. The poetic books paint marvelous word pictures that capture the joys and tears of life's journey. The wisdom books of the Bible distill the philosophical reflections of man's sojourn on earth and what they mean in light of eternity. The gospel accounts provide narrative about God becoming man and His redemptive death and resurrection. The Epistles give wonderful reflections on what that redemption means. Finally, the book of Revelation paints a picture of what our future will be with God.

But the unique aspect of what makes Scripture percolate into life is the central actor in the drama it describes: Jesus Christ himself "in whom are hidden all the treasures of wisdom and knowledge" (Colossians 2:3).

God's Word is a rich collection of inspired literature that percolates with spiritual life.

FOR FURTHER READING: *Allegory of Love* by C. S. Lewis, chapter 3

READ: Romans 2:14–15; Psalm 119

Traditional Values

For when Gentiles, who do not have the law, by nature do the things in the law, these, although not having the law, are a law to themselves, who show the work of the law written in their hearts, their conscience also bearing witness, and between themselves their thoughts accusing or else excusing them. —Romans 2:14–15

Have you ever watched people go through a Chinese food buffet line? You find those who load their plate up with breaded meats dripping with sauce while others choose limited portions of seafood and vegetables. It's all a matter of preference and choice.

People take a similar approach to ethical choices—they become items of personal preference. Sexual behavior, for instance, is no longer under the guidelines of church and family but open to whatever feels right to the individual. In *The Abolition of Man*, C. S. Lewis skillfully argues for objective values. In other words, certain behaviors are right and others are wrong. Of this Lewis writes: "The human mind has no more power of inventing a new value than of imagining a new primary colour, or indeed, of creating a new sun and a new sky for it to move."

Lewis cites many ancient civilizations to support his point, including the cultures of the Babylonians, Greeks, Romans, and Chinese. Their cultures' codes of conduct reflected a commonality of ethical principles with those of the Ten Commandments of the Old Testament. Indeed, it appears that these ancient cultures observed the objective ethical code built into human nature (Romans 2:14–15).

The law of God written on our hearts can be seen in other cultures from ancient times.

FOR FURTHER READING: *Abolition of Man* by C. S. Lewis, chapter 2

READ: Psalm 14:1–3; Romans 1:18–25

The Question of God

The fool has said in his heart, "There is no God." —Psalm 14:1

The Question of God: C. S. Lewis and Sigmund Freud Debate God, Love, Sex, and the Meaning of Life by Armand Nicholi is a fascinating read. The author explores the worldview of these two men and asks which view best explains the world we live in and provides meaning and hope for human existence.

Originally designed as a course taught at Harvard University, *The Question of God* has enjoyed success as a popular book and PBS television program. The author makes interesting comparisons and contrasts between the two men's backgrounds, family connections, and life orientation. At one point both Lewis and Freud could be seen as the person described in Psalm 14:1. But then Lewis was converted to Christianity, and because of his former atheism he was well-suited to answer skeptical objections to faith.

What astonished Lewis as he recounted his journey from atheism to faith was how his worldview was utterly transformed. Lewis had moved away from denying God and found that "the fear of the LORD *is* the beginning of wisdom" (Psalm 111:10). The life trajectory of Lewis, who started out as an atheist, shows the life-transforming power of the gospel.

*A worldview centered on Christ satisfies
the longing of the human heart.*

FOR FURTHER READING: *The Question of God:
C.S. Lewis and Sigmund Freud Debate God, Love, Sex,
and the Meaning of Life* by Armand Nicholi

READ: John 20:1–22

The Breath of God

He breathed on them, and said to them, "Receive the Holy Spirit."
—John 20:22

C. S. Lewis believed in the doctrine of the triune God: Father, Son, and Holy Spirit. Some scholars have wrongly concluded that Lewis left out the person and work of the Spirit in the Narnia Chronicles, but this is not so. If someone were to reexamine the ways in which Aslan's breath appears, he or she would see the mighty activity of the Holy Spirit illustrated.

After Aslan rises from the dead, he breathes on the statues at the Witch's castle, thus restoring them to life. In many other instances in different Narnia Chronicles, Aslan's breath instills courage, builds faith, and moves people to their mission. It even takes part in the creation of the Narnian world.

Lewis' allusion to Aslan's breath may have been adapted from John 20:22: "[Christ] breathed on them, and said to them, 'Receive the Holy Spirit.'" In the garden of Eden, God breathed life into the first man (Genesis 2:7). In John 20, God the Son—crucified and risen from the dead—breathes life into His disciples. Forty days later the Holy Spirit would be given to the church on the Day of Pentecost (Acts 2).

The Christian life is not to be lived by human willpower but by the mighty power only the Holy Spirit can provide.

FOR FURTHER READING: *Companion to Narnia*
by Paul F. Ford, "Aslan's Breath"

READ: John 14:1–6

Who Is Jesus Christ?

Jesus said to him, "I am the way, the truth, and the life. No one comes to the Father except through Me."   —John 14:6

C. S. Lewis' classic *Mere Christianity* was originally a series of talks given on the British Broadcasting Corporation (BBC) during World War II. *Focus on the Family* has developed a wonderful Radio Theatre program called *C.S. Lewis at War: The Dramatic Story Behind Mere Christianity.*

The talks Lewis gave were not based on inspirational slogans that encouraged people to be courageous for king and country. Nor did they vilify the enemy. Instead, Lewis built the case for the reality of a Sovereign Creator who has placed a sense of right and wrong in each human heart, and this serves as a clue to the meaning of the universe. As his arguments built upon conscience and the witness of creation, Lewis put the spotlight on the historic figure of Jesus of Nazareth, who made the shocking claim to be God.

Lewis then suggested that his listeners respond to the truth claims of Jesus Christ: "Either this man was, and is, the Son of God, or else a madman or something worse." The continued relevance of *Mere Christianity* is the call to make a decision about who Jesus Christ claimed to be.

*Amidst the struggles of life, the gospel of
Jesus Christ is eternally relevant.*

FOR FURTHER LISTENING: *C. S. Lewis at War: The Dramatic
Story Behind Mere Christianity* (Audio CD)

READ: Philemon 1:1–25

Being Middle Aged

Being such a one as Paul, the aged. —Philemon 1:9

In one of *The Screwtape Letters*, the senior tempter advises his young field operative about the temptations of middle age: "The long, dull, monotonous years of middle-aged prosperity or middle-aged adversity are excellent campaigning weather." Screwtape goes on to describe how to wear down the "patient" either through broken dreams and ongoing resentments or by tying him to the world through earthly success. In this way we see how mature years carry their own kinds of temptations.

In Philemon 1:9 the apostle Paul refers to himself as "Paul, the aged." Interestingly, some scholars believe Paul was only in his late forties or early fifties when he wrote this letter. By today's standards, Paul would not be considered a senior. Life expectancy in the first century, however, was much shorter than it is today. Despite his awareness of aging, Paul was surprisingly productive in the years that followed. Paul preached the gospel, wrote inspired letters, and planted and nurtured young churches. While some limitations may impede us as we age, we can still strive to serve the Lord until He calls us home.

*Middle age can be a great launching pad for
productivity in service of the King.*

For Further Reading: *The Screwtape Letters* by C. S. Lewis, letter 28

READ: Psalm 119:97–104

Is the Map Right?

Through Your precepts I get understanding; therefore I hate every false way. —Psalm 119:104

In *Yours, Jack: Spiritual Direction from C. S. Lewis*, we find a wonderful collection of correspondence rich in devotional insight. In one letter Lewis addresses how believers sometimes find difficulty in following the Bible during life's journey. After a painful circumstance, feelings of spiritual doubt may set in. Before long those believers are actually wondering if God's Word is providing the right directions at all.

About this quandary, Lewis writes: "As foolish people on a walk, when by their own errors they are off the course, think the map was wrong, so, when we do not find in ourselves the fruits of the Spirit which all our teachers promise, it is not that the promise was false, but that we have failed to use the Grace we have been given. The 'map' can be found in almost any Christian teaching."

Because our world is fallen, we should expect sometimes to encounter baffling contradictions not only in circumstances but also in our own hearts and minds. When we do, the way out is to see trouble as an opportunity to seek God's grace in the situation.

We may not see the big picture, but the inspired map of God's redemptive love is fully adequate for the journey of faith.

FOR FURTHER READING: *Yours, Jack: Spiritual Direction from C. S. Lewis,* 1951 Letters

READ: Joshua 1:1–8

Rereading and Meditating

This Book of the Law shall not depart from your mouth, but you shall meditate in it day and night, that you may observe to do according to all that is written in it. For then you will make your way prosperous, and then you will have good success. —Joshua 1:8

In a letter to his friend Arthur Greeves, C. S. Lewis talked about one of the tests of a book's greatness. In referring to *The Faerie Queene*, he wrote: "It must be a really great book because one can read it as a boy in one way, and then re-read it in middle life and get something very different out of it—and that to my mind is one of the best tests."

Certainly, the reading of excellent books will yield fresh insights with each reading. But the Word of God stands in a category all its own. Supernaturally inspired by God, Scripture can yield inexhaustible truths and help for those who take time to reflect on it. God commanded Joshua to meditate upon God's Word day and night (Joshua 1:8).

The Hebrew word for *meditate* can mean "to utter in a low sound" like the cooing of a dove (Isaiah 38:14), and it can mean "to be preoccupied with." The word *meditate* has also been used of a cow chewing her cud. Altogether this means we should enjoy the sound of, be preoccupied with, and carefully digest the Word of God as a way of life.

Reading, rereading, and meditating on the Word of God can yield divine dividends in life transformation.

FOR FURTHER READING: *The Letters of C. S. Lewis to Arthur Greeves,* edited by Walter Hooper

READ: Ephesians 2:14; 1 Timothy 2:5

The Great Bridge Builder

Jesus said to him, "I am the way, the truth, and the life. No one comes to the Father except through Me." —John 14:6

In *The Voyage of the Dawn Treader*, the great Aslan inspires courage by saying: "But I will not tell you how long or short the way will be; only that it lies across a river. But do not fear that, for I am the great Bridge Builder." Lewis' insight into the awe-inspiring power of Jesus Christ to bridge seemingly impossible barriers is remarkable.

Jesus Christ is able to bridge the gap between a holy God and sinful men because of His atoning death and the transfer of righteousness to those who believe (1 Timothy 2:5). Yet we are also told that He breached the terrible and ancient barrier between Jew and Gentile. The Scriptures proclaim that through faith in Jesus Christ the wall of separation between former pagans and the children of Abraham has been removed for all time (Ephesians 2:14). Now each can receive a new identity, which joins them together as part of the family of God. The work of Jesus Christ has the power to build bridges both vertically and horizontally.

Jesus Christ is the great bridge builder between God and man and between Jew and Gentile.

FOR FURTHER READING: *The Voyage of the Dawn Treader* by C. S. Lewis, chapter 16

READ: 2 Corinthians 1:1–10

Ministering Out of Our Wounds

Blessed be the God and Father of our Lord Jesus Christ, the Father of mercies and God of all comfort, who comforts us in all our tribulation, that we may be able to comfort those who are in any trouble, with the comfort with which we ourselves are comforted by God. —2 Corinthians 1:3–4

In *Letters to an American Lady*, we read of C. S. Lewis trying to get his focus off his own struggles so he could provide empathy and encouragement to one of his correspondents: "I must try not to let my own present unhappiness harden my heart against the woes of others! You too are going through a dreadful time. Ah well, it will not last forever. There will come a day for all of us when 'it is finished.' God help us all."

So often we can become so preoccupied with our own hurts that we ignore the pain of others. The apostle Paul reminds us, however, that the very wounds God has allowed us to suffer can be a marvelous means of ministry to others in pain. A spirit of exaltation and praise punctuates Paul's recognition that God can use our afflictions to help others: "Blessed be the God and Father of our Lord Jesus Christ, the Father of mercies and God of all comfort" (2 Corinthians 1:3).

Are you struggling with some painful wound today? Be encouraged. As you seek God for consolation, He can give your suffering meaning by helping you to use it to comfort others.

Through the God of all comfort, we can minister to others out of our own woundedness.

FOR FURTHER READING: *Letters to an American Lady* by C. S. Lewis

READ: Romans 15:1–7

Lewis' Library

For whatever things were written before were written for our learning, that we through the patience and comfort of the Scriptures might have hope. —Romans 15:4

What if you could spend a day perusing the personal library of C. S. Lewis? If his writings have given *you* special help, what kind of books provided *him* with spiritual insight?

A book was written to answer that question. It is called *From the Library of C. S. Lewis: Selections from Writers Who Influenced His Spiritual Journey.* Of it editor James Stuart Bell writes: "I believe that from these readings we can obtain clearer insight into C. S. Lewis as well as feed our imaginations and intellects upon those whose talents produced works of theology and literature that contain timeless standards."

George MacDonald, Boethius, John Bunyan, Augustine, G. K. Chesterton, Thomas Aquinas, and Blaise Pascal are just a few of the names found in the Lewis library. Some of these Christian writers may not impact you the way they did Lewis. But the sheer breadth and depth of these authors should compel us to become students of the past—as was Lewis. We are encouraged to learn from the writings of those who came before us (Romans 15:4). Christian writers of long ago can most certainly enrich our lives.

*Learning from others on the path of faith in
Christ can give us strength for the journey.*

FOR FURTHER READING: *From the Library of
C. S. Lewis,* compiled by James Stuart Bell

READ: Song of Solomon 2:10–17

Being in Love

My beloved spake, and said unto me, Rise up, my love, my fair one, and come away. —Song of Solomon 2:10 (KJV)

When C. S. Lewis lost his wife, Joy, to cancer, he recorded his thoughts and feelings of grief in a journal. Published later as *A Grief Observed*, this short book contains reflections not only on loss but also on romantic love: "For those few years [Joy] and I feasted on love, every mode of it—solemn and merry, romantic and realistic, sometimes as dramatic as a thunderstorm, sometimes as comfortable and unempathetic as putting on your soft slippers."

Lewis understood that the romantic high of love should also make room for the reality of imperfections. Yet there is always a residue of wonder in looking upon the beloved. Lewis commented, "This is one of the miracles of love; it gives—to both, but perhaps especially to the woman—a power of seeing through its own enchantments and yet not being disenchanted."

The Bible also exalts the blessing of romantic love within marriage. In Song of Solomon we read beautiful imagery that celebrates the emotional, physical, and spiritual joys of wedded bliss. It showcases the joyous union that God designed for man and woman in the state of their innocence (Genesis 2:18–24).

God has designed romantic love to lead to a lasting commitment within marriage.

FOR FURTHER READING: *A Grief Observed* by C. S. Lewis, chapter 4

READ: Luke 1:1–4; Acts 1:1–3

Life Map

*The former account I made, O Theophilus, of all that Jesus began
both to do and teach.*   —Acts 1:1

C. S. Lewis and his brother Warnie were lifelong friends. Certainly they
had their ups and downs, but from early childhood until the day of
Jack's death, the relationship remained intact. One interesting contrast
between the brothers was that Warnie was an avid diary keeper while
Jack—after some initial journaling in his youth—gave up the practice.

Brothers & Friends: The Diaries of Major Warren Hamilton Lewis
provides the reader with different glimpses into Lewis family life. In
one entry we read: "Today the family paid its long projected visit to
Whipsnade Zoo. . . . At about quarter past eleven J told me that the
plan now was that he and I should make a start in the Daudel [motor-
cycle]." Later Warnie would learn that it was while traveling to the zoo
that his brother Jack began believing that Jesus Christ was the Son of
God.

Keeping a journal is not for everyone. But for some, journaling can
bring to mind past life experiences that give a different perspective to
our present walk. Try it. You may find yourself recording unexpected
workings of God in your life.

> *Writing down our story can be a way of
> reminding us of God's faithfulness.*

FOR FURTHER READING: *Brothers & Friends:
The Diaries of Major Warren Hamilton Lewis,* edited
by Clyde S. Kilby and Marjorie Lamp Mead

READ: Genesis 3:3–4:26

Walking Away from God

Then Cain went out from the presence of the LORD and dwelt in the land of Nod on the east of Eden. —Genesis 4:16

In C. S. Lewis' space trilogy *Perelandra,* Tinidril, the "Eve" of another world, is tirelessly tempted to step out of the will of God by a demon-possessed physicist named Weston. Finally, she tells the tempter that she will not do this, for she understands: "To walk out of [God's] will is to walk into nowhere."

Walking away from God is a terrible choice. Indeed, at the beginning of our world the first mother and son can illustrate this. Both Eve and Cain gave in to the temptation to sin, suffered initial alienation from God, and experienced unintended consequences for their disobedience. But Eve accepted God's direction about how to restore the relationship. In contrast, Cain went out from the presence of the Lord and set up a way of life with himself at the center (Genesis 3:3–4:26).

Sometimes we may become so disappointed with our life's direction that we are tempted to no longer live a committed life of faith. But we would do well to see how the Eve of Scripture chose to stay in relationship with God while her son Cain went away from His presence.

Come what may, the best place for the believer is in the presence of God.

FOR FURTHER READING: *Perelandra* by C. S. Lewis, chapter 9

READ: Hebrews 11:1–7

Meeting Saints in Heaven

*By faith Abel offered to God a more excellent sacrifice than Cain,
through which he obtained witness that he was righteous, God
testifying of his gifts; and through it he being dead still speaks.*
—Hebrews 11:4

Who is your favorite Bible character or Christian author? Within the
pages of Scripture or through a favorite Christian book, these believers
continue to help us draw nearer to God and give us practical help in
life's journey—even those who have gone on to heaven.

In one of his letters, C. S. Lewis marveled about feeling connected to
someone who had already gone on to glory. That relationship was made
possible through another's writing. Lewis wrote: "If one had not experienced it, it would be hard to understand how a dead man out of a book
can be almost a member of one's family circle—still harder to realize,
even now, that you and I have a chance of someday really meeting him."

The author of Hebrews holds a similar view of life change through
the written Word (Hebrews 11:4). We will meet these saints in a new
world, and what we might learn from them is for now unknown. But
one thing is certain: They will joyously bear witness to the praise of the
glory of God's grace (Ephesians 1:1–21). This will be a shared theme
with all believers, and it will be the background for our shared relationships there.

*God uses the words of saints already in heaven
to give us strength for the journey, and someday
we will meet those saints in person!*

For Further Reading: *The Collected Letters of C. S. Lewis*, volume 2

READ: Isaiah 6:1–7

A Sense of Awe

*"Woe is me, for I am undone! . . . For my eyes have seen the King,
the LORD of hosts."*   —Isaiah 6:5

In his book *Into the Region of Awe*, David Downing traces the spiritual
life of C. S. Lewis. In this insightful book we are introduced to a term
often used by Lewis. It is the word *numinous*. Taken from the Latin
term for "divine presence or will," the word took on the meaning of a
divinity making its presence known. In more modern times the word
began to refer to the deep emotion of fear and wonder experienced in
God's presence.

Sometimes we can adopt too casual an approach to our interactions
with God. Because the grace of God reached down into our brokenness
for restoration, a sense of reverence should accompany our access to
Him. Remember, we have been told: "Our God is a consuming fire"
(Hebrews 12:29). When Isaiah was brought into the presence of God,
he was stunned by God's holiness and his own sin (Isaiah 6:5).

God has provided free access to the throne of grace (Hebrews 4:16).
But in view of God's holiness and the costly price Christ paid for our
redemption, adoration and awe should set the stage for our response to
being in His presence.

*Spiritual intimacy with Christ means reverential
worship, not coarse familiarity.*

FOR FURTHER READING: *Into the Region of Awe*
by David Downing, chapter 5

READ: Ecclesiastes 2:1–11; 12:1–14

Dissatisfaction

You will show me the path of life; in Your presence is fullness of joy; at Your right hand are pleasures forevermore. —Psalm 16:11

When Solomon asked God to give him wisdom to rule His people, God also blessed him with riches. Yet the book of Ecclesiastes reveals how Solomon's many pursuits left him feeling empty: "Then I looked on all the works that my hands had done, and on the labor in which I had toiled; and indeed all was vanity and grasping for the wind. There was no profit under the sun" (Ecclesiastes 2:11). It would appear that the initial desire to acquire something might lead to dissatisfaction when it is finally obtained.

Similarly, in *The Pilgrim's Regress* by C. S. Lewis the main character John discovers that his desires are frustrated: "If it is what I wanted, why am I so disappointed when I get it? If what a man really wanted was food, how could he be disappointed when the food arrived?" Temporal objects or wants cannot satisfy the eternal desires of the human heart.

John's quest for satisfaction, however, is eventually rewarded when he comes into relationship with the "land owner" who allegorically represents God. Likewise, Solomon understood that lasting joy and satisfaction would only be found in a relationship with God (Ecclesiastes 12:13).

Only a relationship with God through Christ can provide lasting satisfaction.

FOR FURTHER READING: *The Pilgrim's Regress* by C. S. Lewis, book 3

READ: John 16:22–33

The Right to Happiness

Peace I leave with you, My peace I give to you; not as the world gives do I give to you. Let not your heart be troubled, neither let it be afraid. —John 14:27

During the early days of the Revolutionary War, a young Virginia statesman in the 13 Colonies of America wrote, "We hold these truths to be self-evident, that all men are created equal, that they are endowed by their Creator with certain unalienable Rights, that among these are Life, Liberty and the pursuit of Happiness."

In today's popular culture, some seem to think that "the pursuit of happiness" is a personal right. C. S. Lewis questioned this. To him this "right to happiness" could be shown to be ridiculous just by suggesting unrealistic expectations such as "a right to be six feet tall, or . . . to get good weather whenever you want to have a picnic."

So much of what we think would make us happy lies outside the sphere of our control. So what should be our response? A wise Christian professor once told his student: "We are not promised happiness in this world. But we are promised supernatural joy and peace in the midst of tribulation" (John 14:27; 16:22). This side of heaven lasting happiness will always be just out of our reach. But Christ will be with us providing joy and peace in life's journey.

Happiness in this world is fleeting, but dependence upon Christ brings peace and joy.

FOR FURTHER READING: *God in the Dock* by C. S. Lewis, "We Have No 'Right to Happiness'"

READ: 1 Chronicles 6:32; Habakkuk 2:1–3;
Luke 14:28–30; 1 Corinthians 14:40

Getting Organized

*For which of you, intending to build a tower, does not sit down first
and count the cost, whether he has enough to finish it.*

—Luke 14:28

The theme of preparation and planning runs through both the Old and New Testament. The prophet Habakkuk was commanded to implement a plan (Habakkuk 2:2). Levites were expected to carefully plan music for worship (1 Chronicles 6:32). Jesus gave a parable about finishing a task with appropriate resources (Luke 14:28–30). And Paul exhorted the Corinthian believers to maintain church order (1 Corinthians 14:40).

Similarly, being organized was central to the medieval mind. In his book *The Discarded Image*, C. S. Lewis tells us: "At his most characteristic, medieval man was not a dreamer nor a wanderer. He was an organiser, a codifier, a builder of systems." Medieval persons believed in the order of creation, which caused them to relish orderliness and meaning. Lewis went on to say: "There was nothing medieval people liked better, or did better, than sorting out and tidying up. Of all our modern inventions I suspect that they would most have admired the card index."

Some of us are better at managing details than others. But the reality is that without some kind of organization very important tasks just won't get done. It's an idea found throughout the Bible: Count the cost and be prepared.

*God is ready to help you organize your day. All you need
do is still your heart and ask for His direction.*

FOR FURTHER READING: *The Discarded Image* by C. S. Lewis, chapter 1

READ: Hebrews 6:1–10

Gains and Losses

One thing I do, forgetting those things which are behind and reaching forward to those things which are ahead.

—Philippians 3:13

Life is a series of gains and losses. When we cling to that which must be surrendered, feelings of loss overpower us. In *An Experiment in Criticism*, C. S. Lewis wrote: "The process of growing up is to be valued for what we gain, not for what we lose." The apostle Paul understood this when he wrote: "One thing I do, forgetting those things which are behind and reaching forward to those things which are ahead, I press toward the goal for the prize of the upward call of God in Christ Jesus" (Philippians 3:13–14).

By today's standards, Lewis died relatively young. He was just one week shy of his sixty-fifth birthday. In his correspondence, we learn of health setbacks that limited his physical stamina. Yet Lewis was remarkably productive up until the end of his life. All of us who live a normal life span will one day lose the physical appearance and stamina of youth. But what really matters in the process of gains and losses is keeping productive in the present with an eye on God's upward call of the future.

The glory of the Christian journey is being productive in the present with an eye on a glorious future.

FOR FURTHER READING: *An Experiment in Criticism*
by C. S. Lewis, chapter 7

READ: Matthew 14:22–33

Leap of Faith

And immediately Jesus stretched out His hand and caught him,
and said to him, "O you of little faith, why did you doubt?"
—Matthew 14:31

Near the end of C. S. Lewis' allegory *The Pilgrim's Regress,* the main character John meets Mother Kirk, who represents the Christian church. "Reason" will not let John free from his influence until Mother Kirk tells John to dive into a pool and come up on the other side. When John tells her he does not know how to dive, she says, "The art of diving is not to do anything new but simply to cease doing something. You have only to let yourself go." Some might call this a "leap of faith."

Later, in a letter to Arthur Greeves, Lewis explained how Owen Barfield taught him to dive. What Lewis concluded about his first successful dive was that it required getting rid of the instinct for self-protection. Lewis then quoted St. Augustine: "*Securus te projice,*" which translates, "Throw yourself away without care."

For the Christian, trusting God is not a blind leap into the unknown. It is releasing self-protection and then shifting our trust to the Christ of Scripture. When Peter came walking to Jesus, doubt quenched his initial faith, and he began to sink. But Jesus was there to catch him (Matthew 14:28–31). The same thing is true for us in our walk of faith. Circumstances may threaten us, but "underneath are the everlasting arms" (Deuteronomy 33:27).

The Christian's leap of faith requires the transfer
of trust from self to the Christ of Scripture.

FOR FURTHER READING: *C. S. Lewis: A Companion and Guide* by Walter Hooper, "The Pilgrim's Regress"

READ: 2 Corinthians 10:1–5

Taking Thoughts Captive

Casting down arguments and every high thing that exalts itself against the knowledge of God, bringing every thought into captivity to the obedience of Christ. —2 Corinthians 10:5

Some have wrongly concluded that C. S. Lewis simply took out a pen and paper and made up the Narnia Chronicles out of his head. But this is certainly not the case. Those who have literary backgrounds have shown how Lewis drew heavily from Irish, Welsh, Greek, Roman, and mythic traditions.

Still others have struggled with Lewis' use of clearly pagan characters like tree spirits, witches, and river gods to play roles in the Narnian world. Why would he do this? Didn't pagan myths lead the human race away from the living God (Romans 1:18–25)?

Lewis drafted pagan mythology into a different kind of service. Indeed, he was remarkably gifted at taking mythic figures and reworking them to retell the Christian story of redemption. Like the apostle Paul, Lewis was skilled at "bringing every thought into captivity to the obedience of Christ" (2 Corinthians 10:5).

Both J. R. R. Tolkien and Lewis believed that great spiritual truths could sometimes be more clearly seen within the context of fairy tale. We see this when Aslan comes back to life in the imaginary world of Narnia, which deftly illustrates Christ's historic victory over death.

The Christian is to make every thought obedient to Christ.

FOR FURTHER READING: *Companion to Narnia*
by Paul L. Ford, Introduction

Feeding on the Word

This Book of the Law shall not depart from your mouth, but you shall meditate in it day and night, that you may observe to do according to all that is written in it. For then you will make your way prosperous, and then you will have good success. —Joshua 1:8

C. S. Lewis is not known as a famous Bible teacher. Instead, he is remembered for his creative writing and his apologetics for the faith. Nonetheless, Lewis regularly fed upon the Word of God. He once wrote: "A man can't be always defending the truth; there must be a time to feed on it."

The Bible itself contains many examples of people who fed on Scripture. In resisting temptation, Jesus said, "It is written, 'Man shall not live by bread alone, but by every word that proceeds from the mouth of God'" (Matthew 4:4). While Job endured terrible trials, he proclaimed, "I have treasured the words of His mouth more than my necessary food" (Job 23:12). And in Berea we see a community of faithful people who were commended for regular study of the Word: "These were more fair-minded than those in Thessalonica, in that they received the word with all readiness, and searched the Scriptures daily to find out whether these things were so" (Acts 17:11). Only through being nourished by the Word can we remain strong for the arduous journey of faith.

We too should set aside quality time each day to devour and digest the nourishing message of the Word of God.

*Daily reading of the Word strengthens our
faith; neglect of the Word weakens it.*

FOR FURTHER READING: *Reflections on the Psalms*
by C. S. Lewis, Introduction

READ: 2 Corinthians 5:1–17

A New Creation

Therefore, if anyone is in Christ, he is a new creation; old things have passed away; behold, all things have become new.
—2 Corinthians 5:17

In *The Magician's Nephew*, a cabby's horse named Strawberry is not only given the gift of speech by Aslan but is also turned into a winged horse like the mythical Pegasus. The boy Digory is then sent on a mission to acquire enchanted fruit for the protection of the newly created Narnia. He soars high into the sky and over the mountains to his destination on the back of the mighty winged horse.

The image of a winged horse also appears in Lewis' description of the glorification of the believer in Christ. In *Mere Christianity*, Lewis writes: "Christ's work of making New Men [is like] . . . turning a horse into a winged creature. . . . It is not mere improvement but Transformation."

The apostle Paul speaks of this transformation as becoming a "new creation" in Christ (2 Corinthians 5:17). But what does this mean? When we are born again in the Spirit (John 3:3; Titus 3:5), we are placed in spiritual union with Christ (Ephesians 1). The old life of enslavement to sin has been replaced by a new freedom to grow in Christlikeness (Romans 6:6–14; 2 Corinthians 5:14–15; Ephesians 4:23–5:2). We have a new nature and a new destiny.

Being "in Christ" does not mean mere improvement but spiritual transformation.

FOR FURTHER READING: *Mere Christianity* by C. S. Lewis, book 4, chapter 11

READ: Ecclesiastes 1:14; Matthew 6:43; Psalm 118:22–24

Living in the Present

This is the day the Lord has made; we will rejoice and be glad in it.
—Psalm 118:24

In *The Screwtape Letters*, we see how enemies of the faith would like to keep the believer from living in the present: "For the Present is the point at which time touches eternity . . . in it alone freedom and actuality are offered." In other words, we cannot change the past nor can we predict the future. But living by faith in the present is the place where we can experience God's grace and direction.

Depending upon unique temperaments and life experiences, each of us relates to time differently. Some with a more melancholy bent may find themselves vividly reliving past circumstances. For example, King Solomon in the book of Ecclesiastes repeatedly deemed much of his past experience as futile (1:14).

Still others have a tendency to worry about possible threats the future holds. Our Lord observed this tendency and addressed it in His famous Sermon on the Mount: "Therefore do not worry about tomorrow, for tomorrow will worry about its own things" (Matthew 6:34).

The biblical way of relating to time is to live by faith in the present. We are told: "This is the day the Lord has made; we will rejoice and be glad in it" (Psalm 118:24).

Regret springs from living in the past.
Anxiety springs from living in the future.
Contentment springs from living by faith in the present.

For Further Reading: *The Screwtape Letters* by C. S. Lewis, letter 15

READ: Romans 7:18–25; Galatians 5:16–17

Not Yet Perfect

I say then: Walk in the Spirit, and you shall not fulfill the lust of the flesh. For the flesh lusts against the Spirit, and the Spirit against the flesh; and these are contrary to one another, so that you do not do the things that you wish. —Galatians 5:16–17

In *The Voyage of the Dawn Treader*, we are told of a spoiled and selfish boy named Eustace Scrubb. He turns into a dragon and then is transformed back into a boy through a painful process initiated by Aslan. Although Eustace had been redeemed from his terrible fate, it did not mean he had become perfect: "It would be nice and fairly nearly true, to say that 'from that time forth, Eustace was a different boy.' To be strictly accurate, he began to be a different boy. He had relapses. There were still many days when he could be very tiresome. But most of those I shall not notice. The cure had begun."

When Jesus Christ takes over a life, there is often a dramatic, positive change. But that is not the whole story. Old habits and besetting weaknesses can return to plague the new believer in the walk of faith. For all of us, the need for daily dependence on God's Spirit is our only hope for gaining victory over the sins that plague us. We are not yet perfect, but some day we will be—in glory.

The goal of the believer's life is progress in Christlikeness, not perfection.

FOR FURTHER READING: *The Voyage of the Dawn Treader* by C. S. Lewis, chapter 7

READ: Matthew 23:37–39

Love Involves Risk

"O Jerusalem, Jerusalem, . . . How often I wanted to gather your children together, as a hen gathers her chicks under her wings, but you were not willing!   —Matthew 23:37

In C. S. Lewis' *The Four Loves*, we are told that opening our hearts can make us vulnerable to possible hurt: "To love at all is to be vulnerable. Love anything, and your heart will certainly be wrung and possibly broken. If you want to make sure of keeping it intact, you must give your heart to no one, not even an animal." Lewis would experience this pain when his wife, Joy, the love of his life, was taken from him through cancer.

In Scripture we see how God himself, through sacrificial love, has also risked a wounded heart for the beloved. When the long-awaited Messiah appeared in the person of Jesus Christ, He was rejected by national Israel. Here is Christ's anguished response: "O Jerusalem, Jerusalem, the one who kills the prophets and stones those who are sent to her! How often I wanted to gather your children together, as a hen gathers her chicks under her wings, but you were not willing!" (Matthew 23:37).

Yet despite the rejection of some, Christ has become the Savior to far more. Because Christ risked sacrificial love for the beloved, we now respond back to Him—and others—with love.

God asks us to take the risk of loving others as He has loved us.

FOR FURTHER READING: *The Four Loves* by C. S. Lewis, Introduction

READ: Psalm 19:1–6

Heavenly Sunshine

The heavens declare the glory of God; and the firmament shows His handiwork. —Psalm 19:1

Several years ago I was sitting at home preparing an academic paper on the concept of heaven in "Aslan's Country." As I worked, the sunlight broke through the tree branches and into my room with golden shafts of light. I was overwhelmed with its beauty. A spiritual rush flooded my soul, and I called out to my wife, Janet, who was in the next room, "Honey, I haven't felt this close to God in years!" The theme of heaven I was studying and the signpost of God's beauty in nature had come to sing a duet in my soul.

As King David reflected upon the glories of heaven during both night and day, he was struck with how they point to the Creator. Every day and all around the world the handiwork of God bears witness to His eternal power and Godhead (Romans 1:18–22). C. S. Lewis wrote: "If we find ourselves with a desire that nothing in this world can satisfy, the most probable explanation is that we were made for another world." The Bible teaches that the God of glory has provided a future dwelling place perfectly suited for our glorified nature and His holy and loving presence.

Let what you see in the sky today act as a signpost pointing to a future heavenly home.

READ: Deuteronomy 18:9–14; 1 Corinthians 15:25;
Colossians 2:15; 1 John 4:4

Greater Is He . . .

Greater is he that is in you, than he that is in the world.
—1 John 4:4 (KJV)

In his book *The Most Reluctant Convert*, author David Downing devotes an entire chapter to C. S. Lewis' interest in the occult before converting to Christianity. As an atheist, Lewis was torn between two worlds. The logical demands of his mind believed that ultimate reality was to be found in the meaningless dance of atoms in the material world. But his longing for "something more" drew him to wonder about another world claimed by spiritism.

When Lewis became a Christian, he then understood the grave error of the twin seductions of materialism and spiritism. "Lewis concludes that fallen spirits 'are equally pleased by both errors and hail a materialist and a magician with the same delight.'"

The follower of Christ is prohibited from experimenting with any occult activities (Deuteronomy 18:9–14). Jesus Christ defeated the powers of darkness at the cross (Colossians 2:15) and will ultimately bring all spiritual enemies under His authority (1 Corinthians 15:25). In the meantime, the Christian has nothing to fear from our adversary the devil, because we are assured that "greater is he that is in you, than he that is in the world" (1 John 4:4 KJV).

*Christianity best explains the material world we live
in and satisfies the desire for spiritual reality.*

Suggested For Further Reading: *The Most Reluctant Convert*
by David C. Downing, chapter 6

READ: Psalm 119:99–104; John 17:17; Romans 2:14–15

Windows on the World

Sanctify them by Your truth. Your word is truth. —John 17:17

An amusing story is told of several blind men who each examined a different part of an elephant such as the trunk, tail, ears, and legs. Because each man focused on only part of the animal, each was wrong about its identity. James Sire has written the fascinating book *The Universe Next Door.* In it we see how the scientist, the pantheist, and people with other worldviews fall into different errors by taking only part of the truth and making it into the whole. The Bible is then shown to be the great source of complete truth.

C. S. Lewis also saw how competing views of the world stole their values from the common source of God's truth. Lewis believed that "new ideologies" are only fragments of God's truth "arbitrarily wrenched from their context in the whole and then swollen to madness in their isolation, yet still owing to [it] and to it alone such validity as they possess."

Lewis found within Christianity the most consistent window on the world. As Jesus told His Father in prayer, "Your word is truth" (John 17:17).

God's Word is the complete tapestry of truth, and competing ideologies are only fragments torn from it.

FOR FURTHER READING: *Windows on the World: a Comparison of Major Worldviews,* available from Our Daily Bread Ministries

READ: Colossians 3:1–5

A Way Station

For here we have no continuing city, but we seek the one to come.
—Hebrews 13:14

In *The Magician's Nephew*, we read of Digory and Jill, who are traveling to a mysterious place called "the Wood Between the Worlds." It is a stopping-off place between different worlds like Earth, Charn, and Narnia. In fantasy, "The Wood Between the Worlds" would be considered part of a "multiverse," in other words, another reality existing on its own and a way station to other realities.

Sometimes we may feel that we live in a way station just on the edge of another world. And certainly the Christian does. The day is coming when our current world will melt away and be remade into a glorious new dwelling place with God (John 14:1–4; Revelation 21–22). This reality should affect the way we live. Paul exhorts us: "If then you were raised with Christ, seek those things which are above, where Christ is, sitting at the right hand of God" (Colossians 3:1). Until that day, we are to live as citizens of heaven obeying our Redeemer until He returns for us and takes us from this temporary way station to our eternal home (2 Corinthians 4:18; Philippians 3:20).

Although we live in a temporal world,
we are to focus on an eternal one.

SUGGESTED FOR FURTHER READING: *The Magician's Nephew*
by C. S. Lewis, chapter 3

READ: Proverbs 27:17; 1 Corinthians 4:15; Titus 2:3–5

Spiritual Mentors

For though you might have ten thousand instructors in Christ, yet you do not have many fathers; for in Christ Jesus I have begotten you through the gospel. —1 Corinthians 4:15

After his conversion, C. S. Lewis felt a special connection with George MacDonald. It was reading *Phantastes* that initially baptized Lewis' imagination, and later Lewis wrote MacDonald into *The Great Divorce* as a central character. In his introduction to *George MacDonald: An Anthology—365 Readings,* Lewis wrote: "I have never concealed the fact that I regarded [MacDonald] as my master; indeed I fancy I have never written a book in which I did not quote from him." Although MacDonald lived a generation before Lewis, MacDonald's writings mentored Lewis throughout his life.

Many believers today are hungry for the attention and counsel a spiritual mentor can provide. Not surprisingly, this need is addressed in the Word of God. Paul exhorts Timothy to teach faithful men who can then teach others (2 Timothy 2:2). And through Titus, Paul gives advice to older women in the church to provide encouragement to younger women (Titus 2:4–5). It is in the mentoring process that "As iron sharpens iron, so a man sharpens the countenance of his friend" (Proverbs 27:17). C. S. Lewis had a spiritual mentor in George MacDonald. Who is yours?

Through a spiritual mentor we can receive wise counsel, correction, and encouragement to help us grow.

FOR FURTHER READING: *George MacDonald: An Anthology—365 Readings,* edited by C. S. Lewis

READ: John 1:1–14; 8:1–12; Matthew 5:14–16

Let Your Light Shine

Let your light so shine before men, that they may see your good works and glorify your Father in heaven. —Matthew 5:16

At the funeral of C. S. Lewis, lifelong friend George Sayer mentioned the theme of spiritual illumination: "We clustered around to see the coffin lowered into the grave. It was the sort of day Jack would have appreciated, cold but sunny. It was also very still. A lighted church candle was placed on the coffin, and its flame did not flicker. For more than one of us, that clear, bright candle flame seemed to symbolize Jack. He had been the light of our lives, ever steadfast in friendship. Yet, most of all, the candle symbolized his unflagging pursuit of illumination."

The divine reality of holy love dwelt undiminished in the person of Jesus Christ, who is "the light of the world." The Scriptures tell us "God is light and in Him is no darkness" (1 John 1:5). Like a candle shining during a moonless night, His spiritual truth shines forth in a dark world of sin. But our Lord has also given us a role to play. In the Sermon on the Mount, Jesus proclaimed: "You are the light of the world" (Matthew 5:14).

Each of us is called to reflect the light of Christ to others.

For Further Reading: *Jack* by George Sayer, chapter 22

READ: 1 Timothy 5:1–10

Relationship Challenges

"Honor your father and mother," which is the first commandment with promise.   —Ephesians 6:2

In *Surprised by Joy*, C. S. Lewis chronicles how he had a lifelong struggle relating to his dad. Looking back on his frustrations, Lewis later wrote: "With the cruelty of youth I allowed myself to be irritated by traits in my father which, in other elderly men, I have since regarded as lovable foibles."

When Paul was instructing Timothy, a young pastor, in dealing with different relationships in the church, he had this to say: "Do not rebuke an older man, but exhort him as a father, younger men as brothers, older women as mothers, younger women as sisters, with all purity" (1 Timothy 5:1–2). Paul's inspired admonition bridged between both generational and gender issues.

Paul is surprisingly inclusive and realistic in his advice to Timothy. Even though Timothy was a younger pastor, this did not prevent him from the responsibility of correcting elders when it was necessary. Yet adopting the attitude of a respectful son, Timothy was to be gentle. Similarly, older women were to be related to as beloved mothers and younger women were to be treated with purity.

Every relationship has its challenges, but God's grace is available to minister to each one.

FOR FURTHER READING: *Surprised by Joy* by C. S. Lewis, chapter 10

READ: Psalm 8:1–5; Job 38:1–7

Starlit Signposts

When I consider Your heavens, the work of Your fingers, the moon and the stars, which You have ordained, what is man that you are mindful of him?
                                                            —Psalm 8:3–4

As he looked at the animated objects in the night's sky, C. S. Lewis used the word *heaven* in a double sense: "Run your mind up heaven by heaven to Him who is really the centre, to your senses the circumference, of all; the quarry whom all these untiring huntsmen pursue, the candle to whom all these moths yet are not burned." The stars serve as illuminated signposts pointing the way to the Creator.

As David gazed skyward at the wonders of creation, he wondered why God would care about such a small and imperfect thing as man. "When I consider Your heavens, the work of Your fingers, the moon and the stars, which You have ordained, what is man that You are mindful of him, and the son of man that You visit him?" (Psalm 8:3–4). These tiny points of light bear testimony to the center of all—the living God. But when God became a man in Jesus Christ, He became the "light that lights every man." Little did David know that one day God would visit man by becoming one of his descendants.

Christ is the ultimate signpost pointing the way to redemption and eternal fellowship with the Creator and Redeemer.

FOR FURTHER READING: *Planet Narnia* by Michael Ward, chapter 2

READ: 1 Samuel 2:1–30

True Honor

The LORD says: "Far be it from Me; for those who honor Me I will honor, and those who despise Me shall be lightly esteemed."
—1 Samuel 2:30

C. S. Lewis admits that as a young man he was self-absorbed and had a consuming ambition to gain glory as a writer of great poetry. When his first published work in poetry received little accolade, he was disappointed. In contrast, when Lewis came to faith in Christ, his lust for vainglory seemed to disappear. Instead, he began to focus on gaining glory for the One who had redeemed him.

In 1951 Lewis received a letter from Prime Minister Winston Churchill offering to recommend him for Commander of the British Empire. This was just one step below being knighted. It was in recognition of the morale boost Lewis' radio talks had provided for the British people during World War II. Lewis was touched by the offer but politely turned it down. He believed he had only done his duty with the gifts given him by God at a time when his country needed him. Of this attitude our Lord said: "He who speaks from himself seeks his own glory; but He who seeks the glory of the One who sent Him is true, and no unrighteousness is in Him" (John 7:18).

*Righteous believers seek to glorify their
Redeemer and not themselves.*

READ: Proverbs 31:10–31

Solid Folk

Who can find a virtuous wife? For her worth is far above rubies.
—Proverbs 31:10

After C. S. Lewis survived trench warfare in World War I, he published a book of poetry entitled *Spirits in Bondage*. At its writing Lewis was an atheist who believed that deep human desires were doomed to frustration in a painful and meaningless world. This collection of poems reflected the idea that the human spirit was in bondage to unrealizable desires.

But his poem "In Praise of Solid People" is not entirely negative in tone. One optimistic part of the poem refers to a humble and virtuous group of people he calls "solid folk": "Thank God that there are solid folk . . . who feel the things that all men feel and think in well-worn grooves of thought . . . Yet not unfaithful nor unkind with work-day virtues surely staid. Theirs is the sane and humble mind."

Proverbs 31 describes this same quality within the context of a godly wife and mother. Her virtue and industry are so productive and consistent as to cement a solid reputation for her both at home and in the community. The "solid folk" are those who earn our trust because they can be depended upon. Certainly, we should emulate their way of life to God's glory.

As we grow in Christlikeness, our character
becomes more solid and dependable.

FOR FURTHER READING: *Spirits in Bondage* by Clive Hamilton, "In Praise of Solid People," part 2, poem 24

READ: 1 Peter 2:1–10

Outliving Galaxies

You also, as living stones, are being built up a spiritual house, a holy priesthood, to offer up spiritual sacrifices acceptable to God through Jesus Christ. —1 Peter 2:5

Have you been on a temporary assignment somewhere and were reluctant to form friendships? Shortness of stay often means surface relationships.

In an address to the Society of St. Alban's and St. Sergius, Oxford, C. S. Lewis made a statement that can alter our perception of Christian relationships: "As organs in the Body of Christ, as stones and pillars in the temple, we are assured of our eternal self-identity and shall live to remember the galaxies as an old tale."

What a remarkable perspective this statement makes on investing in relationships with other believers. The immortal congregation of believers in Christ has been given many different names. The apostle Peter likens the community of Christians to a sacred building and an order of service: "You also, as living stones, are being built up a spiritual house, a holy priesthood, to offer up spiritual sacrifices acceptable to God through Jesus Christ" (1 Peter 2:5).

Scientific advances in astronomy have multiplied our awe at the size and shapes of the countless galaxies that decorate our universe. Yet Lewis reminded us that our redeemed community will outlast them all. What a thought!

Christian friendships will outlast the material universe.

FOR FURTHER READING: *The Weight of Glory* by C. S. Lewis, "Membership"

READ: Colossians 3:1–13

Hard to Get Along With

Bearing with one another, and forgiving one another, if anyone has a complaint against another; even as Christ forgave you, so you also must do. —Colossians 3:13

Have you ever had a roommate or family member who was hard to live with? Those of differing temperaments and ways of relating can become a real challenge. But we all have our weaknesses, and each of us is in need of the grace and forgiveness of God. No one is exempt.

In one of his letters, C. S. Lewis wisely generalized on the human condition: "We are all fallen creatures and all very hard to live with." But in Paul's letter to Colossi, we are given a remedy for dealing with troubling people: "Bearing with one another, and forgiving one another, if anyone has a complaint against another; even as Christ forgave you, so you also must do" (Colossians 3:13).

The New Testament Greek term translated *bearing with* means "to be patient and tolerant in working with others." The word *complaint* carries with it the idea of "finding fault with someone and pinning blame on them." Yet in this verse we see that all of us need forgiveness. When a brother or sister in Christ asks for forgiveness, we should grant it. After all, we have been forgiven by Jesus.

All of us are imperfect and are in need of grace and forgiveness from God and others.

FOR FURTHER READING: *Letters to an American Lady* by C. S. Lewis

READ: Jeremiah 31:27–34

Beloved Pessimist

Oh, that my head were waters, and my eyes a fountain of tears,
that I might weep day and night. —Jeremiah 9:1

Fred Paxford was the loyal gardener and handyman at The Kilns, C. S. Lewis' home. He possessed an almost lovable but negative attitude toward life. Many believe that it was Paxford's gloomy temperament that provided inspiration for the character Puddleglum in *The Silver Chair*. Eustace and Jill are often frustrated by his pessimistic view of life. Puddleglum admits openly: "I'm a chap who always liked to know the worst and then put the best face I can on it." Nonetheless, Puddleglum's loyalty to Aslan eventually reveals his admirable character.

In the real world of Christian faith, we find that God calls people with a wide range of temperaments into His service, and some are like Puddleglum. Old Testament Jeremiah, for example, has been called "the weeping prophet." Indeed Jeremiah 9:1 records his anguish: "Oh, that my head were waters, and my eyes a fountain of tears, that I might weep day and night" (Jeremiah 9:1).

Jeremiah's message was not a popular one, and his view of the future was less than optimistic. But his loyalty to the God of Israel revealed his godly character, and his message would eventually include the promise of a brighter day (Jeremiah 31:27–34). Even this beloved pessimist had a positive message from God!

Pessimists who yield their hearts to God can experience
strengthened character and hope for the future.

FOR FURTHER READING: *The Silver Chair* by C. S. Lewis, chapter 12

READ: Psalm 78:1–6

Preserving to Pass On

We will not hide them from their children, telling to the gener-
ation to come the praises of the LORD, and His strength and His
wonderful works that He has done.   —Psalm 78:4

C. S. Lewis' *English Literature in the Sixteenth Century: Excluding Drama*
is a scholarly work that touches both mind and heart. In it Lewis warns
of the consequences if we do not preserve and pass on valuable things to
others: "What is vital and healthy does not necessarily survive . . . . An
art, a whole civilization, may at any time slip through men's fingers in a
very few years and be gone beyond recovery."

God promises His Word will survive into eternity (Isaiah 40:8). But
what if we neglect to read it to others, especially to our own families?
How will its message continue to influence the younger generations?

In Psalm 78 we read a passage that stresses passing on the message of God's love. The psalmist writes, "He established a testimony in
Jacob, and appointed a law in Israel, which He commanded our fathers,
that they should make them known to their children; that the generation to come might know them, the children who would be born, that
they may arise and declare them to their children" (Psalm 78:5–6).

The eternal, life-giving message of God's Word
must be passed on to each new generation.

FOR FURTHER READING: *English Literature in the*
Sixteenth Century: Excluding Drama by C. S. Lewis

READ: Proverbs 3:1–20

God's Guidance

*Trust in the L*ORD *with all your heart, and lean not on your own understanding; in all your ways acknowledge Him, and He shall direct your paths.* —Proverbs 3:5–6

The Scriptures are clear that God leads us as believers through the Holy Spirit as He provides us with guidance through the Word of God (Psalm 119:105; John 16:13). But is that the only way God might direct us?

In addressing how God the Holy Spirit leads the believer, C. S. Lewis mentioned in one of his letters that it would be a mistake to limit divine guidance purely to a subjective experience. "In reality," he said, "He speaks also through Scripture, the Church, friends, books, etc."

Is Lewis correct in suggesting that we can find additional ways of sensing God's leading? Acts 15 shows the importance of seeking advice from church leadership when needed, and Proverbs uplifts the counsel of those we trust (Proverbs 11:14).

God's Word and the direction of the Holy Spirit are the primary ways in which God leads. But we can also seek additional means of guidance in the journey of faith—as long as they do not contradict Scripture. Let's look for God's clear guidance.

> *God gives us guidance through the Spirit's prompting, the inspired Word, church leadership, personal friends, and books.*

FOR FURTHER READING: *The Collected Letters of C. S. Lewis,* volume 3

READ: Revelation 20:10–15

A Troubling Doctrine

And anyone not found written in the Book of Life was cast into the lake of fire. —Revelation 20:15

There is no more unpopular Bible doctrine than that of hell. Despite this aversion, the teaching in Roman Catholic, Eastern Orthodox, and Protestant traditions have continued to uphold a belief in a literal hell. Among the reasons for this would be the authority of Christ's own teaching and the support of the apostles (Matthew 10:28; 16:26–27; John 3:16; Romans 6:23; 2 Thessalonians 1:3-10; Revelation 20:10–15).

Recently, some efforts have been made to explain away the doctrine of hell. Some say that divine punishment is not eternal but only refers to the annihilation of the soul. Still others have tried to argue that all will eventually be saved due to the relentless love of God. As much as we would like to accept either alternative, neither is authentically biblical.

But C. S. Lewis offers fresh insights on hell and human free will. In *The Great Divorce*, Lewis stresses that an unrepentant sinner will refuse to submit to God even in the afterlife. Instead, that person chooses eternal separation: "There are only two kinds of people in the end: those who say to God, 'Thy will be done,' and those to whom God says, in the end, 'Thy will be done.' All that are in Hell, choose it."

Unredeemed fallen angels and unrepentant humans dwell in a state alienated from God by their own choice.

READ: Psalm 139:1–24

Being Authentic

O LORD, You have searched me and known me. You know my sitting down and my rising up; You understand my thought afar off.
—Psalm 139:1–2

C. S. Lewis collaborated with his wife, Joy, in writing the novel *Till We Have Faces: A Myth Retold.* The book retells the story of Psyche and Cupid from the older sister Orual's point of view.

Orual spends much of her time in the frustrated pursuit of love and accuses the gods of injustice. At the end of the story, however, Orual realizes that the gods really cannot meet with her unless she has established an authentic identity and admits her own felt needs. In the final line of the book she says, "How can they meet us face to face till we have faces?"

In the Christian life, we can sometimes come to God while putting on a false face. Part of this may come from the reality that we are not the perfect person we would like to be. But God wants us to be transparent and open to Him with our real needs, sins, and hurts. Only when we are authentic can we experience a satisfying connection with the Source of love and reality himself. The Scriptures tell us that God knows what we are like already (Psalm 139:1–2). We honor our Savior best when we come to Him with authenticity.

God wants to meet with the real you and hear what you think and feel today.

FOR FURTHER READING: *Till We Have Faces* by C. S. Lewis, chapter 4

READ: 2 Corinthians 2:14–17

Aroma of Christ

Now thanks be to God who always leads us in triumph in Christ, and through us diffuses the fragrance of His knowledge in every place.   —2 Corinthians 2:14

In *The Lion, the Witch and the Wardrobe*, the Pevensie children have accepted Mr. and Mrs. Beaver's hospitality and are enjoying a wonderful fish dinner. When Mr. Beaver says, "They say that Aslan is on the move," a variety of unexpected delights fill the hearts of the children: "Susan felt as if some delicious smell or some delightful strain of music had just floated by her." In contrast to this, Edmund, who has fallen under the spell of the White Witch, is repelled by the name Aslan.

Susan and Edmund's contrasting responses to the name of Aslan have a parallel in Scripture. When the apostle Paul mentions "the fragrance of Christ," he refers to two different reactions that depend upon the spiritual condition of those who come in contact with it. "For we are to God the fragrance of Christ among those who are being saved and among those who are perishing. To the one we are the aroma of death leading to death, and to the other the aroma of life leading to life" (2 Corinthians 2:15–16). How can we make the message of Christ a pleasant "aroma" to those around us?

Christ exudes a spiritual aroma that
speaks of life or of death depending on
the heart of the one encountering it.

FOR FURTHER READING: *The Lion, the Witch and the Wardrobe*
by C. S. Lewis, chapter 7

READ: Galatians 1:1–24

Before and After

"He who formerly persecuted us now preaches the faith which he once tried to destroy." And they glorified God in me.
—Galatians 1:23–24

On the cover of a short biographical booklet entitled *C. S. Lewis: The Story of a Converted Mind,* a striking contrast can be seen. Graphic artists placed a picture of the young Lewis next to one of him as an older man. The "before" photo shows an almost cocky Lewis dressed in a smart suit with bow tie and hands in his pockets. By contrast, the older Lewis has a relaxed smile and is walking with the aid of a cane past the stained-glass window of a country church.

What a marvelous contrast these photos have captured! Lewis admits that when he was a young man he was self-absorbed and filled with pride. But after his conversion, Lewis says he was "taken out of himself" and began to focus on God and the needs of others.

A similar "before and after" picture can be seen in Paul's conversion. The former Pharisee who had persecuted the church now proclaimed the gospel he once opposed (Galatians 1:23–24). When Jesus Christ invades a life, He has a way of creating a powerful contrast between the person before and after conversion. How does your "before and after" portrait look?

God takes self-centered people and transforms them into individuals who live for others.

FOR FURTHER READING: *C. S. Lewis: The Story of a Converted Mind* by Dennis Fisher, Discovery Series, Our Daily Bread Ministries

READ: 1 Samuel 17:1–51

Good and Bad Giants

Then all this assembly shall know that the LORD does not save with sword and spear; for the battle is the LORD's, and He will give you into our hands. —1 Samuel 17:47

Often in the Chronicles of Narnia, giants are sinister and evil creatures. But there are exceptions. In *The Lion, the Witch and the Wardrobe*, we encounter Rumblebuffin. Brought back to life by Aslan after being turned into a statue by the White Witch, this gentle giant aligns himself with good Narnians in the great battle to free their country from the evil forces of the White Witch. Rumblebuffin's slow mental capacities are offset by his innocence of heart and desire to do good.

Interestingly, the Bible also speaks of giants. In Genesis 6:4 we are told of a race of giants that existed at a particularly depraved time in human history. But perhaps the most memorable giant in biblical history is Goliath of Gath. Goliath stood more than nine feet tall and was armed with a huge javelin and spear (1 Samuel 17:1–7). The unprotected shepherd boy David went out to face him with only a sling and five smooth stones. But the living God gave him the power to defeat this fearful enemy.

In life's journey we sometimes face people and circumstances that may seem like giants. Yet with faith and perseverance we can overcome them by God's grace.

There is no giant so big that it cannot be overcome by the power of God.

FOR FURTHER READING: *The Lion, the Witch and the Wardrobe* by C. S. Lewis, chapter 16

READ: Isaiah 55:1–13

Majestic Music

The mountains and the hills shall break forth into singing before you, and all the trees of the field shall clap their hands.

—Isaiah 55:12

C. S. Lewis wrote to his friend Arthur Greeves about the healing effect music had upon him: "How tonic Beethoven is, and how festal—one has the feeling of having taken part in the revelry of giants."

Music does have a way of stirring the soul. And the Word of God applies the majesty of music to nature itself (Isaiah 55:12). All one needs do is walk down the beach and hear the thunder of waves or listen to the symphony of birds just before the first shafts of light at dawn. The sounds of the ocean, rivers, and hills exalt in praise to the Creator, Sovereign Lord, and Redeemer.

Yet the Scriptures also recognize that nature, as it now is, has been corrupted by the fall of man (Romans 8:19–22). One day, however, we will see the natural world redeemed and brought into harmony with God and man. Although our fallen world will occasionally produce discord, the future will feature a marvelous symphony incorporating both heaven and earth. And we will have front row seats.

Until that cosmic day of redemption, the believer can continue to praise God in a fallen world.

FOR FURTHER READING: *The Letters of C. S. Lewis to Arthur Greeves*, edited by Walter Hooper

READ: Matthew 28:1–6; 1 Corinthians 15:20–28

Chocolate Eggs

But the angel answered and said to the women, "Do not be afraid, for I know that you seek Jesus who was crucified. He is not here; for He is risen, as He said." —Matthew 28:5–6

Sometimes the emphasis on things like Easter bunnies and Easter eggs can be a major distraction on the special Sunday when we celebrate our Lord's resurrection from the dead. Indeed for some young children the anticipation of getting a chocolate bunny or hunting for Easter eggs is greater than the prospect of going to church that day. Yet by the grace of God kids can and often do pick up on the spiritual message of Easter. C. S. Lewis wrote: "I have been told of a very small and very devout boy who was heard murmuring to himself on Easter morning a poem of his own composition which began 'Chocolate eggs and Jesus risen.' This seems to me, for his age, both admirable poetry and admirable piety."

We cannot completely remove the secular distractions that bombard our families around Eastertime. But we can keep the message of resurrection clear and accessible to our children by repeating often and well the story describing this cosmic event. We must never lose the wonder of the angel's proclamation at the empty tomb: "He is not here; for He is risen, as He said" (Matthew 28:6).

Worldly distractions should take a backseat to the story of the Bible.

For Further Reading: *Reflections on the Psalms* by C. S. Lewis, chapter 5

READ: Matthew 26:36–45; 2 Corinthians 12:7–10

When God Says "No"

*A thorn in the flesh was given to me . . . . Concerning this thing I
pleaded with the Lord three times that it might depart from me.
And He said to me, "My grace is sufficient for you, for My strength
is made perfect in weakness."* —2 Corinthians 12:7–10

When our petitions to heaven seemingly go unheeded, we can become
discouraged and weakened in our faith. But what if God were to say
"yes" to our every prayer?

If Paul's request to be delivered from his "thorn in the flesh" had
been granted, it seems likely that Paul would have been less dependent
on God's grace. The apostle himself admits this trouble was given to
keep him from pride. The divine "no" led to a greater life transformation, which resulted in glory to God.

What if God had said, "Yes" to Jesus' prayer that He might be spared
dying on the cross (Matthew 26:36–45)? We would still be in our sins
and under the judgment of God—destined to eternal separation from
Him. But when Jesus yielded His will to the Father, His obedience to
the cross provided redemption for all who believe.

When God says "no" to our prayers, it is for our own good. C. S.
Lewis wisely reflected: "I must often be glad that certain past prayers
of my own were not granted." Our wise Father does not grant every
request His children make—and for good reason.

> *When God says "no" to a prayer, He does so from
> a divine perspective that we do not have.*

FOR FURTHER READING: *Christian Reflections*
by C. S. Lewis, chapter 12

The Latest Book

The grass withers, the flower fades, but the word of our God stands forever. —Isaiah 40:8

Think of the most popular book you can think of from five years ago. Is it still enjoying the same attention from those who raved about it? Is that book even still in print? Sometimes we can fall into the "latest book fad" without realizing it. C. S. Lewis had a decided preference for old books that had stood the test of time. He once commented: "The more 'up to date' the book is, the sooner it will be dated."

Does this mean that we should never be on the lookout for a recently printed book that has gotten a lot of positive reviews? Of course not. But if our motivation is to be in the know on the "latest thing," we might want to reconsider.

Solid truth has the quality of staying power. Isaiah tells us that this is certainly a characteristic of the Word of God (Isaiah 40:8). And the psalmist also tells us: "Forever, O LORD, Your word is settled in heaven" (Psalm 119:89). While being informed on the latest books, we should maintain our grounding in those that last—especially the one that lasts forever!

The Word of God is eternally relevant to the human condition.

FOR FURTHER READING: *Letters to Malcolm: Chiefly on Prayer*
by C. S. Lewis, chapter 2

READ: Ephesians 2:1–10

You *Are* Special

For we are His workmanship, created in Christ Jesus for good works, which God prepared beforehand that we should walk in them. —Ephesians 2:10

In seeking to address the pride that comes from thinking *I'm special,* Lewis put it another way. We should not think *I'm no more special than anyone else,* but . . . *everyone is as special as me.*

Some believers suffer from self-reproach because of their weaknesses and sins. Still others may have an inflated view of themselves. But the biblical balance is to see that you are valuable enough for Jesus Christ to shed His blood and die for you. For the present you are still a work in progress. The best way of assessing self-esteem is to remind ourselves that each believer is deeply valuable to God.

In Paul's wonderful letter to the church at Ephesus, we find this statement about all believers in Christ: "We are His workmanship, created in Christ Jesus for good works, which God prepared beforehand that we should walk in them" (Ephesians 2:10). The actual word translated *workmanship* is *poema,* from which we get our English word *poem.* In context it gives us a picture of something valuable and beautiful but still a work in progress. That means we are indeed special in God's eyes.

*Jesus Christ died for each believer bestowing
upon each a priceless value.*

FOR FURTHER READING: *The Collected Letters of C. S. Lewis,* volume 3

READ: Romans 1:8–17

Circulating the Gospel

I am a debtor both to Greeks and to barbarians, both to wise and to unwise. So, as much as is in me, I am ready to preach the gospel to you who are in Rome also. —Romans 1:14–15

Writing of the great Bible translator William Tyndale, C. S. Lewis cited his tenacity of purpose to get the gospel out in spite of royal opposition: "To an emissary of his opponent King Henry, Tyndale said, 'If God spare my life, ere many years I will cause a boy that driveth the plough to know more of the scriptures than thou dost.'" Lewis goes on to reflect "and the fulfillment of that vaunt [boast] is the history of his life. . . . Every line he wrote was directly or indirectly devoted to the same purpose: to circulate the 'gospel.'"

Since the fateful day when Saul encountered Christ, the apostle Paul became a tireless herald of the message of redemption. His ministry target extended to the educated and the uneducated, the Jew and the Gentile—and to the regions beyond (Romans 1:14–15).

Each of us has been entrusted with the good news that Christ's atoning death and resurrection from the dead can save from sin all who repent and believe. Accordingly, we have our own sphere of influence where we can share that good news. What can you do today to "circulate the gospel"?

Each of us has a unique circle of friends who need to hear the gospel through what we say and how we live.

FOR FURTHER READING: *English Literature in the Sixteenth Century: Excluding Drama* by C. S. Lewis, book 2

READ: Matthew 8:5–13

Pagan Signposts

Assuredly, I say to you, I have not found such great faith, not even in Israel! 　　　　　　　　　　　　　　　—Matthew 8:10

As young atheist C. S. Lewis interacted with his friends about the truth claims of Christianity, he found his love for pagan myths pointing him to a historic event. In a letter to his friend Arthur Greeves, Lewis wrote: "My dear Arthur, I . . . was mysteriously moved [by the pagan idea of a god sacrificing himself] . . . providing I met it anywhere except in the Gospels . . . . Now the story of Christ is . . . working on us in the same way as the others, but *with this tremendous difference that it really happened.*"

Pagan mythologies can link to the story of Christ as "redemptive analogies." Indeed, missionaries report that tribal beliefs can lay a foundation for understanding the person and work of Christ. In the first century, a Roman centurion most likely from a religious background of pagan gods encountered Jesus of Nazareth. When the Roman saw the reality of Jesus' power to heal, he asked the Master to have mercy on his sick servant. Before granting him his request, Jesus responded "Assuredly, I say to you, I have not found such great faith, not even in Israel!" (Matthew 8:10). A "pagan" had found redemption!

Pagan beliefs can become signposts to the reality of Jesus Christ.

FOR FURTHER READING: *The Collected Letters of C. S. Lewis,* volume 1

READ: 2 Timothy 3:10–17

Learning from Your Mistakes

All Scripture is given by inspiration of God, and is profitable for doctrine, for reproof, for correction, for instruction in righteousness, that the man of God may be complete, thoroughly equipped for every good work. —2 Timothy 3:16–17

In answering a child's request for feedback on a writing project, C. S. Lewis showed kindness and sensitivity: "I hope you don't mind me telling you all this. One can learn only by seeing one's mistakes."

Lewis understood that hindsight is often one of the best teachers. And for the Christian, the Word of God is always there to advise our attempts to make progress in the school of Christian growth.

In Paul's mind, learning from our mistakes is intimately tied up with the Word of God: "All Scripture is given by inspiration of God, and is profitable for doctrine, for reproof, for correction, for instruction in righteousness" (2 Timothy 3:16).

But what does this mean? "Doctrine" might better be translated "teaching," and it refers to God's supernatural revelation of truth. "Reproof" has to do with the conviction of sin and the sense of guilt that comes with this. "Correction" has the idea of the restorative power that God provides to turn someone to the right direction in life. And "instruction" refers to God's road map for life's journey. God has provided everything we need to learn from our mistakes. Are we willing to learn?

Grace is the means by which we learn from our mistakes and become more disciplined in the walk of obedience.

FOR FURTHER READING: *C. S. Lewis: Letters to Children,* edited by Lyle Dorsett

READ: John 14:1–11

One Way

Jesus said to him, "I am the way, the truth, and the life. No one comes to the Father except through Me." —John 14:6

Because of the vast number of people who inhabit our planet and the diverse religions to which they adhere, it is easy to see that the exclusive claims of Jesus Christ can cause some to struggle. Undoubtedly, our Lord claimed He is the only way to God when He said: "I am the way, the truth, and the life. No one comes to the Father except through Me" (John 14:6).

How could He make such inclusive claims? The answer lies in the nature of a holy God and the spiritual condition of fallen man. The Bible tells us that human beings have chosen to live independently from God through sin. This act of transgression carries the penalty of death. By giving His life on the cross, the Lord Jesus provided the means of payment for sin. Now all who repent and believe in Christ's atoning death and resurrection can be given forgiveness and placed on the road to heaven. As Lewis' character John in *The Pilgrim's Regress* says, "One road leads home and a thousand roads lead into the wilderness." Only Jesus Christ is the true way home.

Jesus Christ is the way to God, the ultimate source of reality, and the wellspring of eternal life.

FOR FURTHER READING: *The Pilgrim's Regress* by C. S. Lewis, book 8

READ: Ezekiel 34:11–26

Contrasting Colleges

I will make them and the places all around My hill a blessing; and I will cause showers to come down in their season; there shall be showers of blessing. —Ezekiel 34:26

For more than three decades, C. S. Lewis had a demanding workload as a tutor at Magdalen College at Oxford University. Yet his peers never elected him professor. However, academicians at Cambridge University appreciated Lewis' academic and popular writing. In fact, they created a Chair of Medieval and Renaissance Literature and recruited Lewis to take it. Ironically, his new college had the same name as his old one but with a different spelling. Here is what he wrote about the two colleges: "Did I tell you I've been made a professor at Cambridge? . . . It means rather less work for rather more pay. And I think I shall like Magdalene [Cambridge] better than Magdalen [Oxford]. It's a tiny college (a perfect cameo architecturally) and they're so old fashioned, and pious, and gentle and conservative—unlike this leftist, atheist, cynical, hard-boiled, huge Magdalen."

Sometimes the Lord will move us from a place of testing to a place of blessing where "there shall be showers of blessing" (Ezekiel 34:26). In Lewis' case that place had the same name, but with a different spelling—and a different spiritual environment.

God can lead from blessing into trial and trial into blessing, but He is always sovereign.

FOR FURTHER READING: *Letters to an American Lady* by C. S. Lewis

READ: 1 Corinthians 15:1–20

Spiritual Spring

Christ has indeed been raised from the dead, the firstfruits of those who have fallen asleep. —1 Corinthians 15:20 (NIV)

Sometimes winter can drag on so long that we feel like spring will never arrive. C. S. Lewis, who loved the change of seasons, drew from his longing for spring an insight on Christ's resurrection from the dead as a promise of new life to come. "To be sure," he wrote in *God in the Dock*, "it feels wintry enough still: but often in the very early spring it feels like that. Two thousand years are only a day or two by this scale. A man really ought to say, 'The Resurrection happened two thousand years ago' in the same spirit in which he says, 'I saw a crocus yesterday.' Because we know what is coming behind the crocus."

In God's timing "Spiritual Spring" did not take place that long ago. When Christ rose from the dead, the renewal of heaven and earth began: "Christ has indeed been raised from the dead, the firstfruits of those who have fallen asleep" (1 Corinthians 15:20 NIV). Sometimes living in this fallen world can feel like a painful season to endure. But a joyous time of "Spiritual Spring" is coming soon for those who trust Christ.

Today, let nature's signs of spring remind you of Christ's resurrection and the new life it will bring.

FOR FURTHER READING: *God in the Dock* by C. S. Lewis, chapter 9

READ: Genesis 3:1–7; Romans 6:12–14; 1 John 2:15–17

Turkish Delight

So when the woman saw that the tree was good for food, that it was pleasant to the eyes, and a tree desirable to make one wise, she took of its fruit and ate. —Genesis 3:6

In *The Lion, the Witch and the Wardrobe*, the White Witch offers Edmund enchanted candy called Turkish Delight. In his desire to get more of the coveted candy, Edmund betrays his siblings and aligns himself with the wicked witch. Later, only Aslan can redeem the boy from his sinful choices.

Where did C. S. Lewis get his idea for Turkish Delight? Authors Leland Ryken and Marjorie Mead in their helpful book *A Reader's Guide Through the Wardrobe* give us some background on this tasty treat: "[It has its] origins in eighteenth century Turkey during the time of the Ottoman Empire . . . . This popular sweet . . . is primarily made from sugar and starch and often includes small pieces of various nuts (e.g., pistachios, hazelnuts or almond), as well as flavorings such as rose-water, lemon or other fruits . . . . In Lewis' childhood, it would have been traditionally offered as a special Christmas treat."

Lewis skillfully uses an addiction to sweets to illustrate a central biblical theme of temptation, sin, and its consequences. In reading of the fall of the human race, we see how physical appetite was central (Genesis 3:1–7). The Scriptures warn of different kinds of temptation (1 John 2:15–17) and tell us how the power of God enables us to resist them (Romans 6:12–14).

*Feeding addictions leads to slavery, while
walking in the Spirit leads to liberty.*

FOR FURTHER READING: *A Reader's Guide Through the Wardrobe*
by Leland Ryken and Marjorie Lamp Mead

READ: 2 Timothy 4:1–4; Titus 1:9

Feelings or Doctrine?

Holding fast the faithful word as he has been taught, that he may be able, by sound doctrine, both to exhort and convict those who contradict. —Titus 1:9

In *Mere Christianity*, Lewis tells the story of a "hard bitten" Royal Air Force Officer who objected to theology. But the serviceman said he did believe in God. When alone in the desert he had felt the presence of God and considered this a great mystery. Lewis goes on to observe that in one sense the officer was right. When we see the beauty of the Atlantic Ocean from shore and then look at a map of the Atlantic, our feelings seem more real. But we need the map because a great many before us have sailed the Atlantic and it is useful in finding our way around on it.

This is the difference between God's Word and spiritual experience. Theology begins with God's divine revelation the Bible and then it is cross-checked by committed believers through the centuries to establish truths about God to instruct us. A growing and vibrant relationship with God will occasionally result in experiences of God's power, love, and reality. But these feelings should be directed by the road map the Word of God provides (Titus 1:9).

Spiritual experiences should be guided by sound doctrine based on Scripture.

FOR FURTHER READING: *Mere Christianity* by C. S. Lewis, chapter 11

READ: Romans 12:3–16; Philippians 2:1–4

Different Minds

Fulfill my joy by being like-minded, having the same love, being of one accord, of one mind. —Philippians 2:2

In *Studies in Words*, C. S. Lewis spends considerable time studying the origin of the English word *wit*. Today we understand the term as "an ability to say or write things that are clever and usually funny." But in the fourteenth century during Chaucer's time, *wit* had a much different meaning. Lewis explains that "Each man's wit [had] . . . its own cast, bent, or temper." Lewis then applies this to our own way of thinking: "You could once speak of wits to mean types of mind, or 'mentalities,' or the people who have them."

In other words, a person's wit means his or her unique thought process. Some people require considerable time to process ideas, while others arrive at conclusions almost on the spot. Still others think in very abstract ideas, while others prefer to reflect in terms of the concrete and specific examples. Interestingly, Jesus taught the people in humble parables while Paul expounded theology in lofty abstract ideas. Because each of us thinks with different minds, we should celebrate each other's "wit" and the richness this brings to life.

We all have our own "wit," which gives us insights others might not have.

FOR FURTHER READING: *Studies in Words* by C. S. Lewis, chapter 4

READ: Ruth 1:16–17; Proverbs 17:17; 18:24

Loyalty in Misfortune

A friend loves at all times, and a brother is born for adversity.
—Proverbs 17:17

In *Prince Caspian*, we meet the talking badger Trufflehunter, among C. S. Lewis' most well-drawn characters. One of his distinguishing characteristics is his loyalty. He explains to others that as a "beast he does not change and being a badger he holds on." In difficult times Trufflehunter has a stabilizing effect on those around him, especially with the potentially disloyal and impulsive dwarfs.

One of the most striking examples of loyalty in the Bible can be seen in the story of Ruth. Her mother-in-law Naomi has lost her sons and husband in death. As Naomi, overwhelmed with bad times, seeks to return home to Israel, Ruth demands to go with her. Ruth's words are moving in their steadfastness: "Entreat me not to leave you, or to turn back from following after you; for wherever you go, I will go; and wherever you lodge, I will lodge; your people shall be my people" (Ruth 1:16–17). Ruth serves as a sterling example of loyalty in the midst of adverse times. And in the changing circumstances we all face, the loyalty of true friends is a great comfort (Proverbs 17:17).

> *Sometimes it is when life seems hardest that*
> *we discover who our true friends are.*

READ: John 14:1–16

The Promise of Comfort

And I will pray the Father, and He will give you another Helper,
that He may abide with you forever. —John 14:16

The correspondence between C. S. Lewis and his friend Don Giovanni Calabria has been preserved in what is now known as *The Latin Letters*. The reason for this is that both men were so fluent in written Latin that they did not need to bridge the gap between English and Italian, their native languages. In one sad letter Lewis reflected upon his wife, Joy, and her untimely death: "Has [Christ] not promised comfort to those who mourn?"

Devastated by this great loss, Lewis struggled with his grief. Yet the reality of Christ and His promise was there as a life preserver in the tempest-tossed seas of sadness. Truly our Lord's Sermon on the Mount affirms not only the inevitability of mourning but the hope of solace in its wake. For the Christian this comfort has its source in God the Holy Spirit. The word translated *helper* is the Greek word *parakaleo*. It means "someone called alongside to help." Many Christians report having gone through terrible tragedies and yet were carried along by a powerful sense of God's peace and joy.

The Holy Spirit is the ultimate promise of
comfort for the believer who suffers.

FOR FURTHER READING: *Latin Letters of C. S. Lewis*

READ: 2 Thessalonians 3:1–17

Called to Correspond

The salutation of Paul with my own hand, which is a sign in every epistle; so I write. —2 Thessalonians 3:17

When his brother Warren was not available to help Jack Lewis with answering letters, Jack felt the strain of answering them all himself. In a letter to Arthur Greeves, he wrote, "No more now: the daily letter writing without W. [Lewis' brother Warren] to help me is appalling— an hour and a half or two hours every morning before I can get to my own work."

Some authors might have their secretaries answer their mail, but C. S. Lewis did not. Why? Lewis felt that God had given him a position of Christian influence. If people came to him with questions or needed advice, he felt he was called of God to correspond.

What if Paul had not written to the many churches he and his followers had planted? Would the church at Corinth have become defeated by their carnality (1 Corinthians 3:1–23)? Might the believers at Galatia have fallen back into legalism (Galatians 3:1–29)? Or would the church at Colosse have adopted a heretical view of Jesus Christ (Colossians 1:15–23)? Thankfully Paul felt called to correspond to those in spiritual need. Who do you know that might benefit from an e-mail, text, or letter today?

Spiritual help can often take the form of correspondence to those in need.

FOR FURTHER READING: *The Letters of C. S. Lewis to Arthur Greeves,* edited by Walter Hooper

READ: Deuteronomy 6:4–9; Matthew 19:13–14;
Ephesians 6:4; Colossians 3:21

Little Adults

You shall teach them diligently to your children, and shall talk of them when you sit in your house, when you walk by the way, when you lie down, and when you rise up. —Deuteronomy 6:7

When C. S. Lewis gained a reputation for his Narnia Chronicles, he was asked to give his advice on writing for children. In the essay "On Three Ways of Writing for Children," he provides helpful insights on treating children as people:

> Once in a hotel dining-room I said, rather too loudly, "I loathe prunes." "So do I," came an unexpected six-year-old voice from another table. Sympathy was instantaneous. Neither of us thought it funny. We both knew that prunes are far too nasty to be funny. That is the proper meeting between man and child as independent person-alities. Of the far higher and more difficult relations between child and parent or child and teacher, I say nothing. An author, as a mere author, is outside all that. He is not even an uncle. He is a freeman and an equal, like the postman, the butcher, and the dog next door.

The Bible exhorts parents and caregivers to provide love and instruction for little ones (Deuteronomy 4:6–9, Matthew 19:13–14). Certainly this is not a place for "baby talk" but showing respect to their hearts and minds as little people who can understand important concepts.

*Look for opportunities to listen to what children say,
and treat them with the respect they deserve.*

***

FOR FURTHER READING: *Of This and Other Worlds* by C. S. Lewis,
"On Three Ways of Writing for Children"

READ: Acts 2:40–47

Mere Christianity?

And they continued steadfastly in the apostles' doctrine and fellowship, in the breaking of bread, and in prayers.   —Acts 2:42

It is a common mistake for people to assume that C. S. Lewis' classic apologetic work *Mere Christianity* is designed to have readers take Christianity seriously. Often the term *mere* refers to something that has scant sufficiency. For example, "Do you think you can redo the landscaping with just a mere shovel and hoe?"

But Lewis had a different meaning in mind. He got the phrase "Mere Christianity" from the seventh-century English Puritan church leader Richard Baxter. In his book *Church-History of the Government of Bishops*, Baxter wrote: "I am . . . a MEER [sic] CHRISTIAN, of no other Religion . . . . I am against all Sects and dividing Parties."

Lewis also clarified that he used the word *mere* as a gateway to choosing a home church: "I hope no reader will suppose that 'mere' Christianity is here put forward as an alternative to the creeds of the existing communions. . . . It is more like a hall out of which doors open into several rooms. If I can bring anyone into that hall I shall have done what I attempted. But it is in the rooms, not in the hall, that there are fires and chairs and meals."

The central teachings of "mere" Christianity have broadened the appeal of Lewis across many denominations.

FOR FURTHER READING: Preface to *Mere Christianity* by C. S. Lewis, page xv

READ: 1 Corinthians 2:14–16; 3:1–15

Party Spirit

For when one says, "I am of Paul," and another, "I am of Apollos,"
are you not carnal?   —1 Corinthians 3:4

In *The Last Battle,* the devious ape Shift presents a false Aslan. However, he is eventually shown to be nothing but a donkey dressed up in a lion's skin. When this occurs, a recommitment to the true Aslan is called for. But the dwarfs won't be taken in. They consistently assert loyalty to their own group by chanting, "The Dwarfs are for the Dwarfs!"

Lewis' illustration of doubt and party spirit has strong parallels in Scripture. In his book *He That Is Spiritual,* Lewis Sperry Chafer describes the terrible party spirit and split loyalties of the congregation in Corinth (1 Corinthians 3:1–3). He writes, "For a Christian to glory in sectarianism is 'baby talk' at best, and reveals the more serious lack of true Christian love which should flow out to all."

The solution to such divisive behavior is for believers to confess their sin, be filled with the Spirit, and concentrate on being of the same mind in Christ. This can only occur through following Christ's own example of humble servanthood and focusing on the needs of others (Philippians 2:1–11).

We are not to rally around our favorite Christian leader in
factious groups but to join in unity around the one true Christ.

For Further Reading: *The Last Battle* by C. S. Lewis, chapter 11

READ: Leviticus 23

Cycles of Celebration

One person esteems one day above another; another esteems every day alike. Let each be fully convinced in his own mind.
—Romans 14:5

In *The Screwtape Letters,* C. S. Lewis comments on the value of fasts and feasts in the church calendar: "[God] gives them in His Church a spiritual year; they change from a fast to a feast, but it is the same feast as before."

As a medieval scholar, Lewis recognized the cycles of fast days and feast days built into the calendar of the Middle Ages. Where Christmas and Easter come to mind in the Christian celebrations, the medieval person was reminded every month of something to celebrate. Here is a look at medieval reminders: January, celebration of the wise men visiting the baby Jesus; February, St. Valentine's romantic love; March, Easter celebration of Christ's resurrection; April, All Fool's Day with jokes and jests; May, celebration of spring with dancing around the maypole; June held a Midsummer Eve bonfire, speaking of St. George slaying the dragon; July observed St. Swithin's Day—patron saint connected with the need for rain; August saw Lamas (Loaf) Day, a harvest festival; September honored Michael the Archangel with Michaelmas; October saw the Feast of St. Crispin; November reflected on past believers on All Saint's Day; and December looked to Christmas and celebrating Christ's birth.

Let's look for ways to celebrate what Jesus has done for us.

*Every month holds a reason to celebrate what
God has done for us through Christ.*

FOR FURTHER READING: *The Screwtape Letters* by C. S. Lewis, letter 25

READ: Isaiah 40:1–31

Out of Date

*The grass withers, the flower fades, but the word of our God stands
forever.* —Isaiah 40:8

Pop artist Andy Warhol is credited with coining the phrase: "fifteen
minutes of fame." These words reflect the times. Rather than looking
to great people and lasting works of creativity or industry, we spread
newsworthiness around to everyone with little attention to what is truly
exceptional.

World events, celebrity status, trends in fashion all carry their own
particular shelf life. Like a can of soup in the cupboard, all will eventually go out of date. But there are truths that have withstood the test
of time. They have an inherent quality, which instructs the mind and
challenges the heart in subsequent generations.

Among those enduring works, one book stands alone. It is the Word
of God. Having been given to us by the very breath of God, inspired
Scripture has a unique staying power (Isaiah 40:8). Because the Bible
reveals God's nature and purposes for us, it uniquely challenges each
new generation. It is timeless because it speaks of eternal realities. C. S.
Lewis wisely observed: "All that is not eternal is eternally out of date."

*Celebrities and trends come and go, but
the eternal Word is here to stay.*

FOR FURTHER READING: *The Four Loves* by C. S. Lewis, Introduction

Teachable Toddler

From childhood you have known the Holy Scriptures, which are able to make you wise for salvation through faith which is in Christ Jesus. —2 Timothy 3:15

Authors Leland Ryken and Marjorie Lamp Mead tell the story of three-year-old Ryan, who asked his mother to read to him *The Lion, the Witch and the Wardrobe.* "Finding it easier to comply than to dissuade him from his choice, and assuming that the toddler would quickly grow bored with the advanced story, his mother began to read aloud from the book. So it was that without context or discussion, the story was gradually read, chapter by chapter, to the captivated young listener. This reading pattern continued until one evening . . . Ryan sidled up to a dinner guest . . . and in a whisper confided: 'Have you heard? Aslan is on the move!'"

Little children are emotional and informational sponges. They often pick up more than we realize. When Paul wrote to young Pastor Timothy, he grounded his exhortation in the wonderful Bible training he had received as a child from his grandmother and mother. Although Timothy had sat under Paul's inspired teaching, the foundation upon which his spiritual understanding was constructed began when he was a small child (2 Timothy 3:15).

Do you know a child who might benefit from your spiritual insights?

For Further Reading: *A Reader's Guide Through the Wardrobe* by Leland Ryken and Marjorie Lamp Mead

READ: Genesis 2:8–25

Devotions in a Garden

And they heard the sound of the LORD God walking in the garden in the cool of the day. —Genesis 3:8

Have you ever wondered how beautiful the first garden must have been? Think of the fresh breeze blowing through the trees and the fragrant aroma of the flowers. Listen to the chirping, the baying, and the cries of completely domesticated animals at peace with the world, each other, and man. Look at the lush rolling hills of grass and diverse colors of flora. It is here in the Garden of God that man and woman communed in awe of the Creator who loved them (Ezekiel 28:13). With Eve as his helpmeet, Adam tended the garden with joy. As they worked, they offered up sacrifices of praise (Hebrews 13:15).

It has been many long centuries since the dreadful day when the first man and woman chose to act independently from God (Genesis 3). Sin entered into the world and with it suffering, pain, and death (Romans 5:12–21). But for the redeemed in Christ, nature can still provide a wonderful environment for worship. C. S. Lewis wrote: "Say your prayers in a garden early, ignoring steadfastly the dew, the birds and the flowers, and you will come away overwhelmed by its freshness and joy."

As in Eden, the beauty of nature can still serve as a joyous environment for worshipping God.

FOR FURTHER READING: *The Four Loves* by C. S. Lewis, chapter 2

READ: 2 Timothy 2:1–15

A Craftsman's Care

Be diligent to present yourself approved to God, a worker who does not need to be ashamed, rightly dividing the word of truth.
—2 Timothy 2:15

Many have benefited from the clarity of C. S. Lewis as a writer. In fact the British Broadcasting Corporation (BBC) actively recruited Lewis for his radio talks during World War II because he could make the profound simple to understand. Lewis had a lifelong love affair with words. Shunning the vague and speculative discourses that others gave, he expressed himself in carefully chosen words. In many respects he might be compared to a skilled craftsman in his attention to detail and design. In his book *Studies in Words*, Lewis wrote: "Language which can with the greatest ease make the finest and most numerous distinctions of meaning is best."

The apostle Paul exhorted young Timothy to pursue a craftsman's care when interpreting and teaching the Word of God. In fact, he uses the term "rightly dividing" to convey the idea of "cut straight." This most likely refers to trying to accurately represent what the author intended and conveying it to those who would learn from it. When we read, study, and teach the Word of God, we would do well to respect what it says instead of what we wish it had said.

Only when we honor the intent of a Bible passage can we rightly apply it to our lives.

For Further Reading: *Studies in Words* by C. S. Lewis, chapter 1

The Gaze and Touch of God

O LORD, You have searched me and known me. —Psalm 139:1

In his book *Companion to Narnia*, Paul L. Ford shows a special ability in distilling Lewis' thoughts. Here is one of Ford's short summaries on how Lewis viewed prayer:

> In prayer we allow ourselves to be known as persons before God. In prayer we unveil before God. We learn, first, to tolerate and then to welcome God's loving gaze and touch. Prayer is then personal contact between incomplete persons and God; in this contact he shows himself to us and, un-self-aware, we become persons. This process begins when we show God who we are now and what we honestly want. Whatever desires we have must be subject to our prayers. Petition, penitence, thanksgiving, and adoration are the traditional four forms in which this growth as persons through personal contact with God takes place. *Prayer is the beginning of heaven* (*Companion to Narnia* by Paul L. Ford, p. 350).

Certainly David felt a heavenly connection through prayer when he wrote: "Surely goodness and mercy shall follow me all the days of my life; and I will dwell in the house of the LORD Forever" (Psalm 23:6).

*It is in God's gaze and touch that
we find our true personhood.*

FOR FURTHER READING: *Companion to Narnia* by Paul L. Ford, "Prayers"

READ: 2 Peter 3:1–11

The Deplorable Word

The heavens will pass away with a great noise, and the elements will melt with fervent heat; both the earth and the works that are in it will be burned up. —2 Peter 3:10

In *The Magician's Nephew*, Queen Jadis of the dying world called Charn is brought back to life when a visiting boy, Digory, rings an enchanted bell. Jadis tells him that as she tried to defeat her rival sister she had used "the deplorable word." Jadis' enchanted pronouncement killed the entire populous by turning them into statues. Later in the story Aslan tells the children that someone in their world may discover a terrible means of destroying all life. Some have seen this as a veiled reference to the atomic bomb.

For those of us who grew up under the shadow of the threat of nuclear war in the 1960s, anxiety about the world's end was widespread. Yet the Bible tells us that the end of the world is not under the control of evil beings or "deplorable words." Instead, our material universe will go through a transformation in the capable hands of a providential God. It is He who guides the course of history. In its place, God will create a new heaven and a new earth for us in which we will share a glorious future with Him (Revelation 21:1).

The future of our fallen world is in the capable hands of a providential God who will redeem heaven and earth for His glory.

FOR FURTHER READING: *The Magician's Nephew* by C. S. Lewis, chapter 5

READ: Psalm 116; Romans 8:38–39; Revelation 14:13

Facing Death

Precious in the sight of the LORD is the death of His saints.
—Psalm 116:15

As mentioned on February 5, Dr. Armand Nicholi has been teaching a course for years on "The Question of God." In it he compares and contrasts the lives and worldviews of Sigmund Freud and C. S. Lewis. Although Freud and Lewis had many things in common in their background, a huge contrast between the two developed once Lewis came to faith in Christ.

Not only did a spiritual perspective permeate Lewis' life experience, but it also informed his attitude toward death. Indeed, how people view the conclusion of their life on earth tells us much about how they view life. While Freud was morbidly preoccupied with his own extinction, Lewis exuded an almost joyous contemplation of the afterlife. Lewis said, "If we really believe what we say we believe—if we really think that home is elsewhere and that this life is a 'wandering to find home,' why should we not look forward to the arrival?" Lewis saw death as a gateway to glory: "Blessed are the dead who die in the Lord" (Revelation 14:13; cf. Psalm 116:15). Isn't that a better attitude toward facing death?

*Our view of life after death will
alter how we view life on earth.*

FOR FURTHER READING: *The Question of God*
by Armand Nicholi, chapter 9

READ: John 15:1–8

Heaven on Earth

He who has My commandments and keeps them, it is he who loves Me. And he who loves Me will be loved by My Father, and I will love him and manifest Myself to him. —John 14:21

In a letter to a friend, C. S. Lewis wrote: "Heaven enters wherever Christ enters, even in this life." Although this declaration is very heartwarming, how can this really be true? After all, isn't heaven in a different place from our world?

From the eternal perspective, heaven is found primarily in our relationship with God—not in a place. The idyllic setting of the garden of Eden was in a sense heaven on earth. It was not characterized by billowy clouds and angels playing harps. Instead, it was a fruitful place of vegetable and animal life where harmonious fellowship with God was experienced in the cool of the day (Genesis 1–2).

To restore our relationship with God, Christ went to great lengths. Becoming a human in the virgin's womb, He grew to manhood, taught us of His Father's kingdom, and then died paying the penalty for our sin and rising from the dead (Romans 3:23; 6:23). Now fellowship with God has been restored for all who believe in Him (John 1:12). Union with Christ is the foundation for experiencing heaven on earth (John 15:1–8).

To fellowship with Christ throughout the day is to begin to experience heaven.

━━━━━━━━━━━━━━━━━━━━━━━━━━━━━━━━━━━━━━━

FOR FURTHER READING: *The Letters of C. S. Lewis to Arthur Greeves,* edited by Walter Hooper

READ: Revelation 20:1–15

Frightening Fairy Tales

The devil, who deceived them, was cast into the lake of fire and brimstone where the beast and the false prophet are. And they will be tormented day and night forever and ever. —Revelation 20:10

Sometimes the Narnia Chronicles come under fire for their portrayal of witches, sea serpents, and other scary beings. Some would remove all such threats from reading material for children. But is this really a good idea? G. K. Chesterton, who had a profound effect on C. S. Lewis' thinking, had this to say about the subject: "Fairy tales are not responsible for producing fear in children . . . Fairy tales do not give the child the idea of the evil or the ugly; that is in the child already, because it is in the world already. . . . The baby has known the dragon intimately ever since he had an imagination. What the fairy tale provides for him is a St. George to kill the dragon."

Both Chesterton and Lewis believed that seeing how good defeats evil in a fantasy world helps prepare the child for moral conflict in the real world. The inspired viewpoint of Scripture does not censor out the struggle with evil; in fact, in its often vivid portrayal of struggle, Scripture points to God's ultimate victory over evil through the Lord Jesus Christ (Revelation 20:10).

Children can learn moral teaching and personal resilience through fairy tales.

FOR FURTHER READING: *Into the Wardrobe: C. S. Lewis and the Narnia Chronicles* by David C. Downing, chapter 7

READ: 1 Corinthians 11:23–26

In Remembrance

For as often as you eat this bread and drink this cup, you proclaim the Lord's death till He comes. —1 Corinthians 11:26

On November 22, 2013, a memorial honoring C. S. Lewis was placed in Westminster Abbey in London. At the ceremony, Dr. John Hall, the Dean of Westminster, said, "Fifty years after the death of C. S. Lewis, we assemble to give thanks for his life and work. We celebrate his work as a scholar, as one of the most significant Christian apologists of the twentieth century, and as the author of stories that have inspired the imagination and faith of countless readers and filmgoers. . . . As we celebrate C. S. Lewis, so we shall pray that scholars, writers, and apologists may be inspired by his example, and that his work will continue to exercise an influence for good on young and old alike."

Meriting a plaque at Westminster Abbey is a great honor. But there is another memorial that is of infinitely greater significance. It is our Lord's Memorial Feast, or communion. The taking of the bread and the cup at the Lord's Supper is a reminder of His sacrificial death given for the remission of sins. It was this central theme of redemption that drove Lewis to creatively present the good news to all who would hear.

Jesus Christ's death, burial, and resurrection:
The most memorable series of events in history.

FOR FURTHER READING: *Mere Christianity* by C. S. Lewis, book 4, chapter 4

READ: 1 Peter 1:5–15

Memory's Warehouse

For this reason I will not be negligent to remind you always of these things, though you know and are established in the present truth. —2 Peter 1:12

In reflecting on the power of memory, C. S. Lewis wrote: "Each great experience is 'a whisper which memory will warehouse as a shout.'"

The United States has its own warehouse. The Smithsonian Institution has been called "the nation's attic." It holds more than 137 million items, and that number grows every year. The variety of objects in the museum range from an Apollo lunar landing module to Dorothy's ruby slippers from the film *The Wizard of Oz*. Less than two percent of the items are on display at any given time. The rest are kept in warehouses.

All believers have certain Bible truths and spiritual experiences stored in their memory. But only a fraction is forefront in the mind at any given time. That is why it is good for us to be reminded of truths we already know. Recalling the past provisions of God can also give us encouragement in the present. Whether the memory seems like a whisper or a shout, it is good to reacquaint ourselves with God's truth and faithfulness by calling these memories to mind (2 Peter 1:12).

We need to be reminded of spiritual truths we already know.

FOR FURTHER READING: *Present Concerns: Essays by C. S. Lewis,* "Talking About Bicycles"

READ: Matthew 6:28–30

Glories of the Garden

The wilderness and the wasteland shall be glad for them, and the desert shall rejoice and blossom as the rose. —Isaiah 35:1

What is your favorite kind of flower? Would it be roses, day lilies, daffodils, or something else? In the dead of winter, nothing arouses more anticipation of spring than the hope of seeing and smelling God's bouquet when it arrives.

C. S. Lewis, who loved nature, said this about the glories of the garden: "A garden . . . teems with life. It glows with colour and smells like heaven and puts forward at every hour of a summer day beauties which man could never have created and could not even, on his own resources, have imagined."

We are told in Scripture that God has revealed "His eternal power and Godhead" through the things that are made (Romans 1:20). Every spring God trumpets His reality through the vibrant colors and fragrant perfumes of a variety of lovely flora. In our Lord's Sermon on the Mount, He looked upon the lilies of the field rightly and said, "even Solomon in all his glory was not arrayed like one of these" (Matthew 6:28–29). This spring, why not find ways of making the beauty and fragrance of flowers part of the celebration?

The amazing variety of colors, shapes, and fragrances of flowers glorifies their Creator.

FOR FURTHER READING: *The Four Loves* by C. S. Lewis, chapter 6

READ: Luke 22:1–42

Prayer Formula?

Father, if it is Your will, take this cup away from Me; nevertheless not My will, but Yours, be done. —Luke 22:42

When as a child Jack Lewis learned that his mother had cancer, he prayed to "the magician" god to heal his mother and restore her to full health. However, months later little Jack was ushered in to see the dead body of his beloved mother before her burial. His hopes were dashed.

Later on, after his conversion to Christianity, Lewis did recover his belief that God does answer prayer. But he also saw that prayer was not a magic formula that would grant whatever we asked. Instead, he realized that answers to prayer were guided by God's sovereignty: "In Gethsemane the holiest of all petitioners prayed three times that a certain cup might pass from Him. It did not. After that the idea that prayer is recommended to us as a sort of infallible gimmick may be dismissed."

As our Lord prayed, so should we. Sometimes God may surprise us in the way He says "yes" to a particular prayer. But if the answer is "no," then we must echo our Lord's words of submission: "Nevertheless not My will, but Yours, be done" (Luke 22:42).

> *God's sovereignty guides His answers to our prayers—not our prayer formulas.*

FOR FURTHER READING: *The World's Last Night and Other Essays* by C. S. Lewis, "The Efficacy of Prayer"

READ: Hebrews 11:1–40

Feeding on Feelings

He did not waver at the promise of God through unbelief, but was strengthened in faith, giving glory to God, and being fully convinced that what He had promised He was also able to perform.
                                                             —Romans 4:20–21

In his essay "The World's Last Night," C. S. Lewis wrote, "Feelings come and go, and when they come a good use can be made of them: they cannot be our regular spiritual diet." Each of us has a different temperament. Some endure great highs and deep lows while others experience a more steady emotional state. Nonetheless, feelings are an important aspect of the Christian journey.

As Lewis pointed out, however, we cannot make emotions our "regular diet." A popular evangelistic booklet has included a helpful way of thinking about feelings and the walk of faith. "The Train Illustration" shows an engine (Fact), a coal car (Faith), and a caboose (Feeling). The facts about Christ make the Christian life go. Faith is the fuel that unites trust with God's promise in His Word. And feeling comes along for the ride. When a person puts his or her trust in the changeableness of feelings, that person is at the mercy of fluctuating moods. Therefore, it is essential that the Christian walk by faith in Scripture—realizing that feelings will vary depending upon spiritual disciplines, circumstances, sleep, diet, and physical health.

*Faith accesses the fact of God's Word, and
feelings come along for the ride.*

For Further Reading: *The World's Last Night and Other Essays*
by C. S. Lewis, "On Obstinacy of Belief"

READ: 2 Corinthians 3:1–18

Compelling Characters

But we all, with unveiled face, beholding as in a mirror the glory of the Lord, are being transformed into the same image from glory to glory, just as by the Spirit of the Lord. —2 Corinthians 3:18

Sometimes while reading a novel or watching a movie we encounter characters that we find compelling. We may even discover from what they say and do a helpful narrative to guide us on life's sometimes puzzling path. Yet in doing so we may forget that the author breathed the words into the characters' mouths. These characters, though compelling, do not inhabit our real world. Concerning this important distinction C. S. Lewis wrote: "It is only in Shakespeare's play that we call the characters, as well as the author, poets . . . Shakespeare makes you believe that Othello and Macbeth really spoke as we hear them."

Fictional characters can entertain and instruct all of us. But in the Christian life there is one ultimate compelling character. It is the Lord Jesus Christ, who is the source of all reality. He not only inhabits our real world but He is also Lord of heaven and earth. The life He led is the ultimate drama. And as we read what the Lord Jesus Christ said and did during His time on Earth, we can become gradually more like Him (2 Corinthians 3:18).

We can be inspired and instructed by fictional characters, but the ultimate source of authentic life transformation is Jesus Christ.

FOR FURTHER READING: *Selected Literary Essays* by C. S. Lewis, "Variations in Shakespeare and Others"

READ: Isaiah 50:4–10

A Word to the Weary

The Lord GOD has given Me the tongue of the learned, that I should know how to speak a word in season to him who is weary.
—Isaiah 50:4

Our Lord seemed to give C. S. Lewis sensitivity for bringing the truth to hurting people at their point of need. Often this happened through letter writing—of which he once told a friend: "My correspondence involves a great number of theological letters already which *can't* be neglected because they are answers to people in great need of help and often in great misery."

During the Babylonian captivity, Israel was in great misery. But the prophet Isaiah comforted them by speaking of the future Messiah who would give consolation and listen to heart concerns: "The Lord GOD has given Me the tongue of the learned, that I should know how to speak a word in season to him who is weary" (Isaiah 50:4).

Jesus Christ has fulfilled that messianic prophecy. He said, "Come to Me, all you who labor and are heavy laden, and I will give you rest" (Matthew 11:28). And unlike the Pharisee legalists of His day, Jesus *listened* to the heart concerns of those who desperately needed the grace of God (John 4:1–42).

Today, why not bring a word to the weary through what you say or write?

FOR FURTHER READING: *The Letters of C. S. Lewis to Arthur Greeves*, edited by Walter Hooper

READ: Ecclesiastes 4:9–12

The Same Language

Two are better than one . . . . For if they fall, one will lift up his companion. —Ecclesiastes 4:9–10

Interests and thought processes differ from person to person. Is it any wonder that there are personality conflicts from time to time? But occasionally we encounter someone who thinks very much like we do. We feel as if we speak the same language.

When C. S. Lewis read a book by Charles Williams, the connection was instantaneous. To Williams, Lewis wrote, "A book sometimes crosses one's path which is so like the sound of one's native language in a strange country that it feels almost uncivil not to wave some kind of flag in answer. I have just read your *Place of the Lion* and it is to me one of the major literary events of my life—comparable to my first discovery of George MacDonald [and] G. K. Chesterton." When Lewis and Williams met, they knew they had connected as lifelong friends.

The Bible tells us of the multiple benefits of friendship—not only in appreciating life but also as a united front in facing life's threats: "Though one may be overpowered by another, two can withstand him. And a threefold cord is not quickly broken" (Ecclesiastes 4:12).

Friends can help each other grow—and ward off enemies.

READ: Revelation 21

Will All Be Saved?

Do not fear those who kill the body but cannot kill the soul. But rather fear Him who is able to destroy both soul and body in hell.
—Matthew 10:28

C. S. Lewis considered pastor and author George MacDonald to be his spiritual mentor. MacDonald, however, differed with Lewis on one key doctrine. MacDonald was convinced that the love and grace of God was so great that all people would eventually be saved. Although Lewis hoped that this might be the case, he never could accept "universalism" as scriptural. In *The Problem of Pain*, Lewis wrote, "Some will not be redeemed. There is no doctrine which I would more willingly remove from Christianity than this, if it lay in my power. But it has the full support of Scripture and, specially, of our Lord's own words; it has always been held by Christendom; and it has the support of reason."

Central in Lewis' reasoning is the issue of free will. We have met those who show nothing but contempt for God. Being masters of their own fate repels any consideration of someone else as their master and lord. It is this stubborn independence that will have eternal consequences. Most certainly God loves the human race, but He will never violate the free will He has given to members of the human race.

God appeals to the human will but does not violate it.

FOR FURTHER READING: *The Problem of Pain* by C. S. Lewis, chapter 8

READ: John 14:1–15

Custom Made

In My Father's house are many mansions; if it were not so, I would have told you. I go to prepare a place for you. —John 14:2

If you go online, you can find many links to custom-made homes. Special materials and craftsmanship go into these houses to match the occupant with the dwelling place.

In reflecting on the heavenly home awaiting each believer, C. S. Lewis said, "Your soul has a curious shape . . . a key to unlock one of the doors in the house with many mansions. For it is not humanity in the abstract that is to be saved, but you—you, the individual reader. . . . Blessed and fortunate creature, your eyes shall behold Him and not another's. All that you are, sins apart, is destined, if you will let God have His good way, to utter satisfaction. . . . Your place in heaven will seem to be made for you and you alone, because you were made for it."

When our Lord told His disciples He was going to prepare a place for them (and us), He had each unique believer in mind. If you have ever felt that you didn't fit in this world, it is most likely that you are being custom-made to occupy a heavenly dwelling where you will enjoy a perfect fit.

Each believer is being custom-made to perfectly fit in a uniquely designed eternal home.

For Further Reading: *The Problem of Pain,* by C. S. Lewis, chapter 10

READ: 1 Samuel 18:1–3; Ecclesiastes 4:9–10; John 15:12–15

Lifelong Friends

*Two are better than one, because they have a good reward for
their labor.* —Ecclesiastes 4:9

Jack Lewis and his brother Warnie were lifelong friends. During their
childhood, they invented an imaginary world named Boxen that was
filled with imaginative talking animals. Here is an excerpt of a letter
from nine-year-old Jack to his brother Warnie:

> *My dear Warnie,*
>
> *At present Boxen is slightly convulsed. The news has just reached her that
> King Bunny is a prisoner. . . . such were the state of affairs recently: but
> the able general Quicksteppe is taking steps for the rescue of King Bunny.*
>
> *Your Loving Brother,*
> *Jacks*

The brothers' friendship endured two major wars, different career
tracks, and the loss of Jack's wife to cancer. Jack and Warnie realized
that: "Two are better than one, because they have a good reward for
their labor" (Ecclesiastes 4:9). In middle age, Warnie assisted Jack in
answering his heavy load of readers' correspondence. But their friendship was not exclusive. Indeed, their shared imaginative lives expanded
into the Inklings study group. So a friendship that had begun in
childhood between two brothers would continue on. It blessed others
through meaningful correspondence and spilled over into shared learning and writing on the journey of faith.

> *Lifelong friendships are hard to come by and
> take care and nurture to endure.*

FOR FURTHER READING: *The Collected Letters of C. S. Lewis,* volume 1

READ: 1 Thessalonians 5:9–11; Hebrews 2:14–18

Fear of Death

Through death He might destroy him who had the power of death,
that is, the devil, and release those who through fear of death were
all their lifetime subject to bondage. —Hebrews 2:14–15

In *Out of the Silent Planet*, Oyarsa the guardian angel of the planet Malacandra talks of life and death issues with Dr. Weston, who wants to exploit his world: "The weakest of my people does not fear death. It is the Bent One [Satan], the lord of your world, who wastes your lives and befouls them with flying from what you know will overtake you in the end. If you were subjects of Maledil [God] you would have peace."

Both J. R. R. Tolkien and C. S. Lewis believed that fantasy can provide a unique viewpoint by looking through a Christian lens into an imaginary world. In Oyarsa's statement we see that the fear of death is a result of the activities of the devil on the human race in our real world. It is the devil that first misled the human race into sin with its consequence of spiritual and physical death. The Scriptures tell us, however, that Jesus Christ defeated the devil by dying for our sins and then rising victoriously from the dead. Death has been "swallowed up in victory" (1 Corinthians 15:54).

The believer does not need to fear death because Christ's
resurrection promises our own glorified future with Him.

For Further Reading: *Out of the Silent Planet* by C. S. Lewis, chapter 20

What Are We Becoming?

Bear one another's burdens, and so fulfill the law of Christ.
—Galatians 6:2

In C. S. Lewis' essay "The Weight of Glory," he writes about growing in Christlikeness: "It is a serious thing to live in a society of possible gods and goddesses, to remember that the dullest and most uninteresting person you talk to may one day be a creature which, if you saw it now, you would strongly be tempted to worship, or else a horror and a corruption such as you now meet, if at all, only in a nightmare. . . . All day long we are, in some degree, helping each other to one or other of these destinations. . . . There are no ordinary people. You have never talked to a mere mortal."

The power of becoming like Christ is found in the Holy Spirit. But God has chosen for us to access this life transformation through dependence on Him and interaction with other believers. The "one another" passages of the Bible show how we receive mutual help from each other: love (Romans 13:8), prayer (James 5:16), service (Galatians 5:13), exhortation (Hebrews 10:24), and submission (Ephesians 5:21). We need each other to grow in Christlikeness.

*In what ways can you cultivate Christlikeness
in yourself and encourage it in others?*

FOR FURTHER READING: *The Weight of Glory*
by C. S. Lewis, "Transposition"

READ: Luke 24:1–35; John 20:11–23; 21:1–14

Comings and Goings

Now it came to pass, as He sat at the table with them, that He took bread, blessed and broke it, and gave it to them. Then their eyes were opened and they knew Him; and He vanished from their sight. —Luke 24:30–31

In each of the Chronicles of Narnia, Aslan comes and goes in seemingly unpredictable ways. In *The Magician's Nephew*, he is first seen singing a new world into existence. In *The Lion, the Witch and the Wardrobe*, Aslan has been seen "on the move" by some Narnians. In *Prince Caspian*, he is seen initially only by Lucy. In *The Horse and His Boy*, he changes form to aid Shasta. In *The Silver Chair*, Aslan draws the children to his country to send them on a mission. In *The Voyage of the Dawn Treader*, Aslan shows up to save Lucy from the sin of vanity. And in *The Last Battle* he intervenes only after a great deception has been foisted on faithful Narnians.

In our real world, the surprise appearance of God as a baby is followed later by His surprising ministry of authoritative teachings with signs and wonders. But after our Lord's resurrection, His appearances and exits are even more unexpected (Mark 16:9-14; Luke 24:15, 36; John 20:14, 19, 26; 21:4). Similarly, in our own lives Jesus Christ's interaction is sometimes unexpected because He meets us at our point of need.

We are never alone, for Jesus Christ is always near and ready to come to our aid.

FOR FURTHER READING: *A Family Guide to Narnia*
by Christin Ditchfield, foreword

READ: John 1:1–14; Philippians 2:5–11

Our Common Lord

For in Him dwells all the fullness of the Godhead bodily.
—Colossians 2:9

C. S. Lewis corresponded with a distinguished Roman Catholic priest, Don Giovanni Calabria (1873–1954). Calabria was known for his deep spiritual walk. Although Lewis never chose to become a Catholic himself, he did recognize "mere Christianity," in other words, agreed upon Christian beliefs that he shared with devout Catholics. To Fr. Calabria, he wrote: "Cease not to make mention of me before our common Lord (true God and the only true Man—for all we others, since the Fall of Adam are but half men)."

Lewis does not mean to say that we are half human because of our sin. What he means is that fallen humans are not what God intended. To see what a fully human looks like, we need to behold the speech, thoughts, and behavior of Jesus Christ. The apostle John beheld Christ's glory as God dwelled among us through the incarnation (John 1:1, 14). As we read the inspired text that records His divine life, we can become transformed into the same image (2 Corinthians 3:16–18). To know Him is to love Him, and to love Him is to become like Him (1 John 3:2–3).

The ancient creeds tell us that Jesus Christ is God being of one substance with the Father.

FOR FURTHER READING: *The Latin Letters of C. S. Lewis*

READ: 1 Kings 21:27–29; 2 Chronicles 20:1–4;
Nehemiah 1:4–6; Matthew 4:1–3; Acts 13:1–3

Fasting or Dieting?

*I have treasured the words of His mouth more than my necessary
food.* —Job 23:12

C. S. Lewis loved to eat, and he also enjoyed going on long walks.
When health issues prevented him from his long excursions on foot, he
recognized that he was gaining weight and needed to go on a diet. In
a letter he lamented: "Perhaps if we had done more voluntary fasting
before, God would not now have put us on these darn diets!"

What does the Bible say about fasting? Here are just a few observations about the rationale of going without food for our spiritual benefit: To limit physical longings and feed spiritual ones (Job 23:12); to
humble ourselves before God in yieldedness (Psalm 35:13; 1 Kings
21:27–29); to strengthen our focus on God in prayer (Daniel 9:1–3); to
pray through a time of repentance (Nehemiah 1:4–6); to seek direction
and wisdom from God (Acts 13:1–3; 14:23); to increase our faith as we
face threatening opposition (2 Chronicles 20:1–4); and to prepare for
spiritual warfare (Matthew 4:1–3).

After consulting with a physician about our health, some of us might
want to consider periodic fasting for spiritual benefit. It can help us take
our eyes off the things of this world and focus more completely on God.

*A discipline of fasting can have both
spiritual and health benefits.*

For Further Reading: *Fasting for Spiritual Breakthrough*
by Elmer L. Towns

God, Change Him!

O Jerusalem, Jerusalem, the one who kills the prophets and stones those who are sent to her! How often I wanted to gather your children together, as a hen gathers her chicks under her wings, but you were not willing! —Matthew 23:37

Do you have a troubling person in your life? If so, you most likely have beseeched God to "change him or her." Yet when the person's negative behavior persists, you may wonder if God is listening. C. S. Lewis comes to our aid on this question: "God has made it a rule for Himself that He won't alter people's character by force. He can and will alter them—but only if the people will let Him."

For thousands of years, national Israel was promised a Messiah who would come and redeem them and the world. Yet when Christ arrived testifying to them with signs and wonders, the nation rejected Him (John 1:1–13). In spite of this free-will choice, the Bible tells us that a remnant will be saved. When people reject the light of God, they do so with divine permission. God will not violate their free wills. Lewis understood that a universe filled with "automaton" creatures would never produce loving *and* obedient persons. The offer for salvation is open to all. But only those who chose can receive it.

God wants willing subjects to follow Him,
not robots that follow a prescribed program.

―――――――――――――――――――――――

For Further Reading: *God in the Dock*
by C. S. Lewis, "The Trouble with 'X'"

Wise Friends

He who walks with wise men will be wise, but the companion of fools will be destroyed. — Proverbs 13:20

From the early 1930s until the late 1940s, a group of scholars met in various English pubs to compare notes on different writing projects. The informal group was called the Inklings. From this gathering of friends came the classic trilogy *Lord of the Rings* and other great works.

But this informal association of scholars also had an impact on the individual lives of its participants. It was through friendship and dialogue with one of these Inklings members, J. R. R. Tolkien, that C. S. Lewis had come to faith in Christ years earlier. And throughout Lewis' life these friendships stimulated his mind, conscience, and heart. Lewis said of the intelligence boost one receives from the right kind of friends: "The next best thing to being wise oneself is to live in a circle of those who are."

Much of life is a challenge in problem solving. And getting input from wise friends can be a great help along the way. "Without counsel, plans go awry, but in the multitude of counselors they are established" (Proverbs 15:22).

Wise friends provide helpful advice in facing life's challenges

FOR FURTHER READING: *C. S. Lewis: Apologist, Philosopher, & Theologian,* edited by Bruce L. Edwards

Time and Eternity

He has made everything beautiful in its time. Also He has put eternity in their hearts, except that no one can find out the work that God does from beginning to end. —Ecclesiastes 3:11

When King Solomon spent time and resources seeking a productive life, he often ended each task with a sense of futility (Ecclesiastes 1:2). But there were exceptions along the way, especially when his heart was made full by what he saw.

Today's Scripture reading is one of those positive moments. The passage seems to almost overreach in its celebration of the goodness of life. But in context it makes sense. During the cycles of life, beautiful experiences come our way. A newborn baby or a couple exchanging wedding vows are part of life's experiences and in different ways are beautiful.

But we also have the sense of the infinite beyond time. There seems to be something more behind what we see and hear. The big picture of how God works cannot be envisioned in the human mind because it is finite. How should this affect the way we live? C. S. Lewis wisely believed that our highest calling is to be "found at one's post as a child of God, living each day as though it were our last, but planning as though our world might last for a hundred years."

We should celebrate the blessing of today but anchor our viewpoint in God's eternity.

FOR FURTHER READING: *God in the Dock*
by C. S. Lewis, "Cross Examination"

READ: Mark 4:22; Luke 12:3; 2 Corinthians 5:10

Secret Sins

He who covers his sins will not prosper, but whoever confesses and forsakes them will have mercy. —Proverbs 28:13

Some people almost make it their career to ignore God. They think that if they deny His existence or take great care in hiding their sin all will be well. Yet the Bible tells us that our best efforts cannot hide us from the holy eyes of God.

When Adam chose to act independently from God, his best effort was to hide his nakedness with fig leaves and take cover in the forest. God found him anyway (Genesis 3:7-11). Later, Achan took forbidden booty after a military victory and hid it in his tent. This was discovered, and he was punished (Joshua 7:1-25).

C. S. Lewis warned us about this fallacy of hiding from God: "No possible complexity which we can give to our picture of the universe can hide us from God: there is . . . no forest, no jungle thick enough to provide cover."

To be fallen human beings means that we will sin. But the solution to the problem is not hiding. The solution is to receive God's gift of salvation (John 3:16). And once we have experienced new birth, we should keep short accounts with God through confession, repentance, and obedience (Proverbs 28:13).

> *We should grow in a transparent relationship*
> *with God so He can transform us.*

FOR FURTHER READING: *God in the Dock* by C. S. Lewis,
"Dogma and the Universe"

READ: 1 Corinthians 1:18–25

Fools for Christ

For the message of the cross is foolishness to those who are perishing, but to us who are being saved it is the power of God.
—1 Corinthians 1:18

It is one of the great paradoxes of the career track of C. S. Lewis that his popular appeal as a Christian writer progressively made him an outcast with the Oxford intellectually elite. Becoming a recognizable voice on the BBC during World War II and being put on the cover of *Time* magazine seemed to cheapen the currency of Oxford.

But this kind of reproach also extends to any of us who publically confess the name of Jesus Christ. The apostle Paul was highly educated, having studied under Gamaliel—one of the top scholars of his day. Yet Paul understood, as he proclaimed the gospel to kings, peasants, artisans, and rabbinic teachers, that those who would not receive this divine message thought him foolish (1 Corinthians 2:14–16). Only through the illuminating work of the indwelling Holy Spirit can a person see the value of Christ's redemption. Both the apostle Paul and C. S. Lewis shared the status of fools in the eyes of the unredeemed—as do all of us who profess Christ's name. Here's the good news: In Christ we have a divine wisdom others cannot know.

The foolishness of God is wiser than men, and the weakness of God is stronger than men. —1 Corinthians 1:25

FOR FURTHER READING: *Surprised by Joy* by C. S. Lewis, chapter 15

Extraordinary Grace

God is love. —1 John 4:8

The human instinct to get right with God usually falls into the mode of trying to do more good works than bad. But a stark contrast to this view is seen in the biblical concept of salvation. Scripture tells us that we are weak and powerless to save ourselves. Into this dilemma is introduced a divine solution made possible by someone else: "For when we were still without strength, in due time Christ died for the ungodly. For scarcely for a righteous man will one die; yet perhaps for a good man someone would even dare to die. But God demonstrates His own love toward us, in that while we were still sinners, Christ died for us" (Romans 5:6–8).

C. S. Lewis reflected on the motive behind this extraordinary act of grace: "God did not die for man because of some value He perceived in him. . . . As St. Paul writes, to have died for valuable men would have been not divine but merely heroic; but God died for sinners. He loved us not because we were lovable, but because He is Love."

The starting point for getting right with God
is realizing that we are sinners and that God
has provided salvation through His Son.

FOR FURTHER READING: *The Weight of Glory*
by C. S. Lewis, "Membership"

READ: Job 40:1–14; 42:1–6

God in the Dock

Shall the one who contends with the Almighty correct Him? He who rebukes God, let him answer it.   —Job 40:2

Some who read the title of Lewis' essay "God in the Dock" might mistakenly think it refers to God being placed in a dock by the sea. But Lewis was actually thinking of an English courtroom in which the "dock" was where one accused of a crime sat as his case was tried.

Lewis observed that in the ancient world human beings felt guilty before their Creator. But the modern man accuses God for creating such an imperfect world. Of this, Lewis comments: "[Modern man] is quite a kindly judge: if God should have a reasonable defence for being the god who permits war, poverty and disease, he is ready to listen to it."

The idea of God being on trial is pervasive today, but it's not anything new. This theme has been part of the human experience from ancient times. Job shows us how accusing God will be reversed when we stand before Him (Job 40:1–14). It is all right to bring our questions to God, but we must always remember that He is the righteous judge (Revelation 20:11–15).

> *We may ask questions about God's ways, but we must always revere His sovereignty and justice.*

FOR FURTHER READING: *God in the Dock*
by C. S. Lewis, "God in the Dock"

READ: Revelation 21:1–8

Gloriously New

Now I saw a new heaven and a new earth, for the first heaven and the first earth had passed away. Also there was no more sea.
—Revelation 21:1

The new heaven and the new earth represent a startling mode of existence. So many attempts to portray what our future home will be like fail because it has not been created yet. But there is an interesting use of the Greek word for *new* that gives us a hint of what we will find there. The actual word, *kainos*, connotes something that is a fresh creation but is built on an earlier original design.

Why are the new heaven and the new earth described in this way? It most likely means a redeemed universe will follow a pattern of existence already familiar to us. When we walk through a mountain valley and see a fresh stream and the blue sky above, it may very well be this pattern that will be made afresh and indestructible for us to enjoy in eternity. The beauties of the heavens and the earth we now enjoy will be magnified in our glorious future home. Lewis anticipated that joy when he wrote: "Pitch your demands heaven-high and they'll be met. Ask for the Morning Star and take (thrown in) your earthly love."

We will be surprised in the new heaven and the new earth to see the familiar within the gloriously new.

FOR FURTHER READING: *Poems* by C. S. Lewis, "Five Sonnets"

READ: Psalm 14:1–7; Romans 1:18–25

Where Is God?

The fool has said in his heart, "There is no God." —Psalm 14:1

On April 12, 1961, Yuri Gagarin became the first human to orbit the earth. He has been credited with saying of his space flight: "I looked and looked, but I didn't see God." Later Gagarin and others denied he made this controversial statement. Some believe the attributed quote was invented and circulated by those who were of an atheist persuasion and had access to the press. In any event, atheists today still push the idea of the impossibility of finding God, whom they say does not exist.

The apostle Paul believed differently. In his letter to the Romans, he proclaims, "[God's] invisible attributes are clearly seen, being understood by the things that are made" (1:20). Because God is an invisible Spirit, we should look for the evidence of His existence in creation. C. S. Lewis said, "Looking for God . . . by exploring space is like reading or seeing all Shakespeare's plays in hope that you will find Shakespeare as one the characters . . . Shakespeare is in one sense present at every moment in every play. But he is never present in the same way as Falstaff or Lady Macbeth."

The beauties of nature bear witness to a mighty, creative Artist.

FOR FURTHER READING: *Christian Reflections*
by C. S. Lewis, "The Seeing Eye"

READ: Psalm 63:1–8; Mark 1:21–35

Early Morning Hours

Now in the morning, having risen a long while before daylight, [Jesus] went out and departed to a solitary place; and there He prayed. —Mark 1:35

Mark records an incredible, exhausting evening when our Lord healed many sick and cast out demons. The drama and demands of such an extended ministry would tire even those who simply observed. The next morning the disciples were fast asleep catching up on their rest, which had been depleted by their shared ministry, when Jesus Christ did something unexpected. Long before the sun had even begun to rise, He quietly went out into the country, found a solitary place, and began to pray. In the stillness of the morning, the Son of God sought fellowship with His Father and asked for direction.

Not all of us are morning people. But there is something about the stillness of the early morning hours that can help steady our hearts before our heavenly Father. C. S. Lewis had discovered early morning as a great time to rejuvenate. In one of his letters he commented: "I am a barbarously early riser. . . . I love the empty, silent, dewy, cobwebby hours." And in that same early morning freshness David sought spiritual communion: "O God, You are my God; early will I seek You" (Psalm 63:1).

Before our day begins, the early morning hours can be a haven to fellowship with God and seek His direction.

FOR FURTHER READING: *Letters to an American Lady* by C. S. Lewis

READ: 2 Corinthians 5:1–17

Still Under Construction

Therefore, if anyone is in Christ, he is a new creation; old things have passed away; behold, all things have become new.
—2 Corinthians 5:17

Have you ever lived in a house that was being remodeled? Furniture has to be moved and placed under protective tarps. The loud hammering of nails and the buzz of saws cutting pieces of wood interrupt your thoughts as workers apply their skills. When you leave to go on an errand, you return to a house that does not feel familiar to you. The design may have been agreed upon, but in its unfinished state the house looks disfigured and maybe even odd.

As born-again believers in Jesus Christ, we have a new nature that has been designed for heaven. And yet now as we make choices, think thoughts, and interact with others, we are painfully aware that we are bound by the imperfections of our old life. The oft-used motto "Be patient with me, I am still under construction" really seems to fit our lives. Of this C. S. Lewis wrote, "A new Nature is being not merely made but made out of an old one. We live amid all the anomalies, inconveniences, hopes and excitements of a house that is being rebuilt."

*Our lives are being rebuilt to make us
ready for a new dwelling place.*

FOR FURTHER READING: *Miracles* by C. S. Lewis, chapter 16

READ: Genesis 12:4; Exodus 7:7; Deuteronomy 34:1–7

Too Old to Be Productive?

Moses was one hundred and twenty years old when he died. His eyes were not dim nor his natural vigor diminished.
—Deuteronomy 34:7

In 1949 C. S. Lewis wrote in a letter to a friend: "I am now in my fiftieth year. I feel my zeal for writing, and whatever talent I originally possessed, to be decreasing; nor (I believe) do I please my readers as I used to. . . . Perhaps it will be the most wholesome thing for my soul that I lose both fame and skill lest I were to fall into that evil disease, vain glory." The irony is that after this perceived "dry spell" in writing, Lewis went on to write *The Narnia Chronicles, Reflections on the Psalms, The Four Loves, Studies in Words, A Grief Observed,* and other books and essays.

Some middle-aged people may wonder about their future productivity. But the Bible speaks of many seniors who began vital ministries. Abram was 75 when he was called to the Promised Land (Genesis 12:4). And Moses was 80 years old when God called him to deliver Israel from bondage (Exodus 7:7). He was given 40 years of further ministry before his death at age 120 (Deuteronomy 34:7). By the grace of God some of our most productive years begin at middle age.

God has called each of us to be productive no matter our age.

For Further Reading: *Letters: C. S. Lewis, Don Giovanni Calabria*

READ: John 10:1–18; Matthew 4:1–11

Right Deed—Wrong Motive

*When you ask, you do not receive, because you ask with wrong
motives, that you may spend what you get on your pleasures.*
—James 4:3 (NIV)

In *The Magician's Nephew*, Aslan sends Digory on a mission to obtain
an enchanted fruit to be planted in Narnia for its protection from the
wicked witch.

When Digory finds his way to the magical tree, he encounters
Queen Jadis, who tempts him to take one of the fruit and deliver it to
his dying mother in his world. Digory resists this temptation and follows Aslan's instructions perfectly. As a reward for his obedience, Aslan
himself gives Digory a fruit to take home to his ailing mother to affect
her cure.

Many biblical themes can be seen in this subplot. The witch climbed
over a gated wall where the enchanted tree grew (see John 10:1). The
witch and the boy meet in a garden similar to the garden of Eden
account (Genesis 3). And Digory is tempted to do a right deed (healing his mother) the wrong way (by disobeying Aslan). Similarly, Satan
offered the kingdoms of the world to Christ but with the corrupt motive
of having the Son of God worship him (Matthew 4). The Scriptures
demand not only right choices but also correct motives.

*The decisions we make should be matched by
righteous acts linked with godly motives.*

FOR FURTHER READING: *A Family Guide to Narnia*
by Christin Ditchfield, Introduction to the Magician's Nephew

READ: Acts 8:5–40

Gifted to Witness

Do the work of an evangelist. —2 Timothy 4:5

In the first years of the Christian church, apostles, prophets, pastors, and teachers played a vital role in winning people to faith in Christ and grounding them in the Word (Ephesians 4:11). Those with a special gift for fruitful witness were called "evangelists." Their title came from *euangelion* or "good news." Philip is designated as one of these gifted individuals who used Bible teaching and dialogue with the Ethiopian eunuch to win him to Christ (Acts 8:5–40).

In 2 Timothy 4:5 we see an interesting application of the role of evangelist to someone without the actual gift of evangelist. Paul exhorted Pastor Timothy to "do the work of an evangelist." Each believer is to be a fruitful witness even when not possessing the gift of evangelist.

Evangelism can be carried out no matter the gifts a Christian possesses. If you were asked what C. S. Lewis' gifts were, you might say, "teacher," "writer," "imaginative thinker," or "spiritual counselor." Yet when Lewis was asked about his writing contribution he said, "Most of my books are evangelistic." We should follow his example and in our own gift mix "do the work of an evangelist."

Not every Christian will have the gift of evangelist,
but every Christian should be a fruitful witness.

FOR FURTHER READING: *God in the Dock* by C. S. Lewis, "Rejoinder to Dr. Pittenger"

READ: Psalm 119:9–16

Percolating Life

All Scripture is given by inspiration of God, and is profitable for doctrine, for reproof, for correction, for instruction in righteousness.
—2 Timothy 3:16

In *Hamlet*, Shakespeare gives us a unique vision of a play within a play. Angry that his uncle murdered his father, Hamlet decides to have some dramatists put on a play that will expose the crime. As Hamlet coaches the actors, he explains that a good play will "hold, as 'twere, the mirror up to nature; to show virtue her own feature, scorn her own image." In other words, good drama, like all good literature, will give us a reflection of real life from which we can learn.

The Word of God is fully inspired by God, but it is also considered to be great literature (2 Timothy 3:15–16). Written in narrative, poetic, wisdom, and epistle forms, it dramatizes the relentless wooing of a gracious God to a fallen race made in His image. The Bible has been given to us to engage our hearts and minds through different literary expressions that touch our lives.

In *The Allegory of Love*, C. S. Lewis wrote, "There is nothing in literature which does not, in some degree, percolate into life." The truths we learn from great writing passed through the filter of Scripture should percolate in our lives.

We should grow in our appreciation of the different ways we can see God in literature.

FOR FURTHER READING: *The Allegory of Love* by C. S. Lewis, chapter 3

READ: 2 Timothy 4:1–10

Keep the Faith!

Demas has forsaken me, having loved this present world, and has departed for Thessalonica.   —2 Timothy 4:9–10

In 1542 the College of St. Mary Magdalene at Cambridge University was established on a site previously occupied by Benedictine monks. It adopted as its motto *Garde Ta Foy,* which is French for "Keep Your Faith." In the 1950s, C. S. Lewis accepted the call to serve there as Chair of Medieval and Renaissance Literature.

Magdalene's motto to "Keep Your Faith" is an echo from its earlier Christian roots. When Paul was awaiting certain execution at the hands of Rome, he wrote his final letter to young Pastor Timothy. In reflecting on his long service for Christ, Paul wrote: "I have fought the good fight, I have finished the race, I have kept the faith" (2 Timothy 4:7).

Paul then goes on to express his deep concern that Demas, his former colleague in ministry, had abandoned him. The reason he gives is that Demas had "loved this present world." What a study in contrasts we see with Paul "keeping the faith" and Demas abandoning it. The committed believer must cultivate a love for God, others, and the kingdom yet to come.

Keeping the faith for a lifetime does not happen automatically but requires perseverance in cultivating love for the things God loves.

FOR FURTHER READING: *Jack* by George Sayer, chapter 22

READ: Ecclesiastes 3:1–8; Ephesians 5:15–16

Redeeming the Time

To everything there is a season, a time for every purpose under heaven. —Ecclesiastes 3:1

In his book *C. S. Lewis: A Biography*, Roger Lancelyn Green describes Lewis' sensitivity to his use of time as a professor: "If he was at all late in arriving at the lecture, he would begin it even before he entered the hall: several times the great voice came booming up the steps outside the hall door and Lewis would enter in haste, lecturing vigorously." One can't help but chuckle thinking of the professor's voice heard at a distance and getting louder until he finally entered the classroom with the lecture uninterrupted. But Lewis' behavior did send a message to the students that he cared about his use of time on their behalf.

Paul tells us, "See then that you walk circumspectly, not as fools but as wise, redeeming the time, because the days are evil" (Ephesians 5:15–16). The meaning of the phrase "redeeming the time" connotes looking for opportunities to do good and buying them up by spending time on them. As you look at your calendar today, what opportunity to serve others might be yours to redeem?

God wants us to take the time to find opportunities to benefit others.

FOR FURTHER READING: *C. S. Lewis: A Companion & Guide* by Walter Hooper, "The Life of C. S. Lewis"

READ: John 15:7; James 4:3; 1 John 5:14–15

Prayers Granted or Denied?

And whatever you ask in My name, that I will do, that the Father may be glorified in the Son. —John 14:13

Have you ever seen permissive parents who give their children anything they want? Deserts and candies are gobbled down while healthy vegetables are bypassed. Sticking to assignments at school is not monitored; so bad grades are dismissed as the teacher's fault. Soon disturbing behavioral patterns begin to form—along with bad character qualities. But the root of these maladies is the parental "yes" to all requests.

Perhaps this can help explain why God does not answer every prayer request in the affirmative. He is interested in making us into children of God that display the work of divine grace to His glory. A "yes" to every prayer request will not achieve this result. C. S. Lewis wrote, "Prayer is request. The essence of request, as distinct from compulsion, is that it may or may not be granted. And if an infinitely wise Being listens to the requests of finite and foolish creatures, of course He will sometimes grant and sometimes refuse them." The purpose of prayer is not to see that all our needs are met but that we give God greater freedom to transform us into the image of His Son (Romans 8:28–29).

Because we are being made into the image of Christ,
God does not answer every prayer request with a "yes."

FOR FURTHER READING: *The World's Last Night and Other Essays* by C. S. Lewis, "The Efficacy of Prayer"

READ: Genesis 3:1–7

Questioning Scripture

Now the serpent was more cunning than any beast of the field which the LORD God had made. And he said to the woman, "Has God indeed said, 'You shall not eat of every tree of the garden'?"
—Genesis 3:1

C. S. Lewis admired and often quoted Pascal, the great physicist and Christian writer. But in one of his letters Lewis rejected Pascal's disagreement with parts of the Bible: "Yes, Pascal does contradict several passages in Scripture and must be wrong."

In Genesis 3 we see a disturbing scene in which deceit is used to undermine the Word of God. A serpent indwelt by a mighty fallen angel questions the one prohibition given the newly created human couple to not eat of the Tree of the Knowledge of Good and Evil. The devil's first step is to encourage Eve to question the Word of God (Genesis 3:1). He then denies that the two humans will die if they eat it by saying that God does not want them to become like Him— knowing good and evil (vv. 2–5). The appeal of the forbidden fruit is so great that Eve eats it—as does her husband Adam (vv. 6–7). Tragically, the fall of the human race followed—with all of its terrible consequences. The Christian should be ever vigilant to detect deceptive strategies people use to question the Word of God. Our best defense is to affirm, as Jesus did, "It is written!"

Jesus Christ had absolute trust in Scripture, and we should emulate that same confidence.

READ: Job 3:1–26; Psalm 30:1–12

Life Turned Upside Down

You have turned for me my mourning into dancing; you have put off my sackcloth and clothed me with gladness. —Psalm 30:11

About Shakespeare's play *Hamlet*, C. S. Lewis said, "Its true hero is man—haunted man—man with his mind on the frontier of two worlds, man unable either quite to reject or quite to admit the supernatural, man struggling to get something done as man has struggled from the beginning, yet incapable of achievement because of his ability to understand either himself or his fellows or the real quality of the universe which has produced him." Because Hamlet's uncle had murdered his father, Hamlet's life had been turned upside down.

In the Old Testament, we read of another man who experienced calamitous circumstances. His name was Job, and the long book that bears his name reflects his struggles with trying to understand relationships, tragic loss, the universe, and the God who seems so silent through it all. Few of us will get through this life without having to face despair. But in Christ there is always hope despite life's tragedies (Psalm 30:1–12). It was Jesus who promised us peace and joy in tribulation (John 16).

Though our world may be turned upside down, the firm foundation of Christ through His Word can bring stability.

FOR FURTHER READING: *Selected Literary Essays* by C. S. Lewis, "Hamlet: The Prince or the Poem?"

READ: John 21:1–22

Your Own Story

Jesus said to [Peter], "If I will that he remain till I come, what is that to you? You follow Me." —John 21:22

In *The Horse and His Boy*, Aslan reviews part of the life story of an arrogant princess named Aravis. When Aravis is told of wounds she has inflicted on one of her slaves, the princess asks if any more harm will come to her servant. Aslan then replies, "Child, I am telling you your story, not hers. No one is told any story but their own." It is a central theme in the Narnia Chronicles that Aslan deals with each of the characters on a one-to-one basis.

When Jesus Christ appeared to the fishermen who had been His disciples for more than three years, He initially soothed their concerns by making them a fish breakfast. But before long Peter was confronted about his love for the Savior. Jesus then predicted that Peter would die a martyr's death. Peter looked over at John and questioned what his future might hold. Our Lord responded, "If I will that he remain till I come, what is that to you? You follow Me" (John 21:22). Jesus Christ deals with each of us on a one-to-one basis of love and accountability.

*Each of us is living out our own story under
the loving guidance of Jesus Christ.*

FOR FURTHER READING: *The Horse and His Boy*
by C. S. Lewis, chapter 14

READ: 1 Samuel 16:1–13

The Person Inside

For the LORD does not see as man sees; for man looks at the outward appearance, but the LORD looks at the heart." —1 Samuel 16:7

The two most famous members of the Inklings were J. R. R. Tolkien and C. S. Lewis. But there were other interesting authors who participated in this dynamic small group. One such person, Charles Williams, relocated from London to Oxford because of the air raids. After reading each other's works, Lewis and Williams became fast friends. Yet in a surprising letter to another friend, Lewis used frank language to contrast Williams' physical appearance with the person inside: "[Charles Williams] is an ugly man with rather a cockney voice. But no one ever thinks of this for five minutes after he has begun speaking. His face becomes almost angelic. Both in public and private he is of nearly all the men I have met, the one whose address most overflows with love."

Looks can be deceiving. When the Lord led Samuel to anoint a new king to replace the wayward King Saul, the prophet fell into the error of letting physical appearance cloud his judgment. When the youngest and shortest of Jesse's sons turned out to be David, it was he who was the chosen king of Israel based on his heart, not on his height (1 Samuel 16:7).

In our working relationships with others, we should strive not to focus on the outward appearance, but on the positive qualities within.

FOR FURTHER READING: *The Collected Letters of C. S. Lewis,* volume 2

READ: Revelation 21:1–13

Eastern Sea

And he . . . showed me the great city, the holy Jerusalem, descending out of heaven from God, having the glory of God. Her light was like a most precious stone, like a jasper stone, clear as crystal.
—Revelation 21:10–11

The eastern border of Narnia is a body of water known as the Eastern Sea. Eventually this waterway leads to the Last Sea, which actually borders Aslan's Country. Here the water is fresh, not salty. Passengers who drink from it find they need less sleep and food. The sun appears three times its normal size, and the sky and sea are flooded with light.

C. S. Lewis used these metaphors to give us a sense of the vivid beauty of heaven. Yet he also understood how our emotional experiences might fluctuate. But for believers in Christ, a "mountaintop experience" certainly may come our way during our spiritual journey. Sometimes it is a deep sense of the overwhelming love God has for us. At other times, it's a powerful sense of overflowing joy when our besetting sins seem to evaporate since glory feels so near. These sneak previews of our heavenly home may not last, but they help reinforce our true spiritual destination and give us encouragement along the way: "For our citizenship is in heaven, from which we also eagerly wait for the Savior, the Lord Jesus Christ" (Philippians 3:20).

Mountaintop experiences encourage faith, but faithfulness in the valley is what really counts.

FOR FURTHER READING: *Companion to Narnia* by Paul F. Ford, "Aslan's Country"

Friends Not Servants

No longer do I call you servants, for a servant does not know what his master is doing; but I have called you friends, for all things that I heard from My Father I have made known to you.

—John 15:15

One of the great delights of C. S. Lewis' life was the making and sustaining of friendships. In one of his letters, he discussed this dynamic in working with students: "Indeed this is the best part of my job. Every given year the pupils I really like are in a minority; but there is hardly a year in which I do not make some real friend. I am glad that people become more and more one of the sources of pleasure as I grow older."

The Lord Jesus also valued the intimacy of friendship. As He neared the end of His sojourn in this world, He drew close to His disciples and told them they were not considered slaves but friends. The basis for this friendship was the disclosure of truths the Father had given to His Son Jesus—truths He had shared with His disciples. Now the disciples were being brought into the divine inner circle.

Abraham's walk of faith resulted in a friendship with God (James 2:23). That same offer of friendship is open to us today through the work of the incarnate Son of God. That friendship is not just lifelong—it extends into eternity!

The believer will always serve his Master, but the relationship is also one of friendship.

FOR FURTHER READING: *The Letters of C. S. Lewis to Arthur Greeves,* edited by Walter Hooper

READ: Psalm 1:1–6; 1 Corinthians 2:10–16

Redeemed Imagination

Let the words of my mouth and the meditation of my heart be acceptable in Your sight, O LORD, my strength and my Redeemer.
—Psalm 19:14

C. S. Lewis illustrates how a godly imagination might actually be used in God's service. In the essay "It All Began with a Picture," Lewis explains how the stories of Narnia began when at age 16 he saw "a picture of a Faun carrying an umbrella and parcels in a snowy wood." Years later he tried to write a story about it. At first there was no reference to the great lion, but once Aslan was introduced, he "pulled the whole story together, and soon He pulled the six other Narnian stories in after Him." Imagination can be redeemed for God's service as we bring "every thought into captivity to the obedience of Christ" (2 Corinthians 10:5).

Our imaginations can cultivate good or evil thoughts. After the fall of Adam and Eve, a generation arose that grieved the heart of God: "The LORD saw that the wickedness of man was great in the earth, and that every intent of the thoughts of his heart was only evil continually" (Genesis 6:5). But as is always the case in redemption, there is hope of restoring our thought life by the grace of God (Romans 12:1–2; 1 Corinthians 2:10–16).

> *Our imagination can be renewed by the Spirit and the Word and used in service for God.*

FOR FURTHER READING: *Of This and Other Worlds* by C. S. Lewis, "It All Began with a Picture"

READ: Deuteronomy 16:13–17

Gracious Memories

You shall observe the Feast of Tabernacles seven days, when you have gathered from your threshing floor and from your winepress. And you shall rejoice in your feast. —Deuteronomy 16:13–14

Out of the Silent Planet is the first in a trilogy of science fiction novels by C. S. Lewis. The hero, Professor Ransom, is kidnapped and taken to the planet Malacandra. There he meets an intelligent race of beings called "hrossa," who look like otters. In one discussion with a befriended hrossa, Ransom hears their philosophy of pleasure and memories: "A pleasure is full grown only when it is remembered. You are speaking, Hmân, as if the pleasure were one thing and the memory another. It is all one thing."

Lewis loved to highlight spiritual truths in the context of story. God exhibited this approach by preserving not only the story of His redemptive works but also the memorial feasts to remind His people of major events in it: "You shall observe the Feast of Tabernacles seven days, when you have gathered from your threshing floor and from your winepress. And you shall rejoice in your feast" (Deuteronomy 16:13–14).

So many blessings from God can be forgotten if we don't recall them and give thanks for them. What thanksgiving traditions can you introduce in your family to keep gracious memories of God's provision alive?

Recall a provision God has given you, and rejoice in it through prayer and praise.

FOR FURTHER READING: *Out of the Silent Planet* by C. S. Lewis, chapters 11–12

READ: 2 Thessalonians 2:1–12

Self-Deception

And [the angel] cast [Satan] into the bottomless pit, and shut him up, and set a seal on him, so that he should deceive the nations no more till the thousand years were finished. —Revelation 20:3

In *An Experiment in Criticism*, C. S. Lewis wisely observed: "Nothing can deceive unless it bears a plausible resemblance to reality." It is certainly the devil's strategy to mix truth with lies. He used this technique successfully with Eve in the garden of Eden (Genesis 3) and with our Lord unsuccessfully in the wilderness (Matthew 4). And even today "plausible truths" have a way of making their way into our thoughts and often our decisions.

How do we know that half-truths have led us into self-deception? Here is a short list of possible scenarios, taken from the Word of God, to help us diagnosis this malady: When we neglect to confess our sin to God (1 John 1:8); when our self-esteem is not grounded in humility (Galatians 6:3–5); when we let our tongues say things that harm others (James 1:26); when we deny that sin has consequences (Galatians 6:7); when we have an inflated view of our own wisdom (1 Corinthians 3:18); when we accept that an ungodly lifestyle has a place in the kingdom of God (6:9); and when we choose questionable friends (15:33).

The cure to self-deception is to welcome the light of God's Word and the honest feedback of godly friends.

FOR FURTHER READING: *An Experiment in Criticism* by C. S. Lewis, chapter 6

READ: Matthew 4:1–11, 17; Romans 1:18–25

Rebels to the Last

Who exchanged the truth of God for the lie, and worshiped and served the creature rather than the Creator, who is blessed forever.
—Romans 1:25

In exploring the psychology of Lucifer the fallen archangel, John Milton described his primary motivation: "Better to reign in Hell, than serve in Heaven." The scriptural accounts indicate Satan above all desires to "be as the Most High" (Isaiah 14:12–14; Ezekiel 28). It is this urge to be the master of one's own fate and not yield to the Creator that drives the evil heart. This kind of spiritual infection has spread to the human race through the fall of Adam and Eve (Genesis 3).

But why would unrepentant sinners apparently share the same destiny as fallen angels in hell? C. S. Lewis reflected: "I willingly believe that the damned are, in one sense, successful, rebels to the end; that the doors to hell are locked on the *inside*." When people obstinately refuse the rule of God in their hearts, they are choosing a life of self-isolation from the source of spiritual life. This is why Jesus' central message was "Repent, for the kingdom of heaven is at hand!" (Matthew 4:17). Jesus Christ is the King of heaven and earth. To submit to Him leads to heaven, but to resist Him leads to eternal separation (Revelation 20:15).

Resisting the kingdom of heaven will have lasting consequences for all spiritual rebels.

FOR FURTHER READING: *The Problem of Pain* by C. S. Lewis, chapter 8

READ: Job 4:1–21

Night Terrors

In disquieting thoughts from the visions of the night, when deep sleep falls on men, fear came upon me, and trembling, which made all my bones shake. —Job 4:13–14

One of the scariest scenes in the *Voyage of the Dawn Treader* is when the Narnian sea vessel enters the Dark Islands. As the people of that ship rescue the lost Lord Rhoop, he tells them that this is the place where all their worst fears can come true. Fortunately, Aslan sends an albatross to lead the ship back into the light of the outside world.

As a child, C. S. Lewis was no stranger to night terrors. Yet this did not dissuade him from writing fairy tales with scary scenes. He explained, "For in the fairy tales, side by side with the terrible figures, we find the immemorial comforters and protectors, the radiant ones. . . . It would be nice if no little boy in bed . . . thinking he hears a sound, were ever at all frightened. But if he is going to be frightened, I think that he should think of giants and dragons than merely burglars. And I think St. George, or any bright champion in armour, is a better comfort than the idea of the police." C. S. Lewis believed that reading about good overcoming evil gave a child resilience in facing real threats.

Reading fantasy can help give us courage in facing struggle in the real world.

FOR FURTHER READING: *Of This and Other Worlds* by C. S. Lewis, "On Three Ways of Writing for Children"

READ: 1 Corinthians 12:1–31

Cookie Cutter Christians

There are diversities of gifts, but the same Spirit. There are differences of ministries, but the same Lord. —1 Corinthians 12:4–5

What marvelous diversity we find in the body of Christ! No two conversions are alike nor are two spiritual walks. Saul of Tarsus became Paul the theologian and church planter. Simon the fisherman became Peter, apostolic witness to the Jews. James, the skeptical half-brother of Jesus, became a major leader in the Council of Jerusalem.

In our zeal to see others come to Christ, however, we can sometimes make the mistake of thinking that the new believer's spiritual walk should identically mirror our own. This is a serious error. Cookie cutters might be the best way to ensure cookies turn out the same, but God wants diversity among His followers. C. S. Lewis advised that although we may be eager to see our loved ones converted to faith in Christ, we must not expect this process to "conform to some ready-made pattern of our own."

As we see seekers become believers, we should patiently watch the activity of God in their lives. At the same time, we learn to recognize characteristics that are different from ours and celebrate those differences.

*Jesus Christ is the ultimate disciple maker of new believers—
not us. He delights in His followers' individuality.*

READ: Revelation 20:1–6

The Golden Age

[The redeemed] shall be priests of God and of Christ, and shall reign with Him a thousand years. —Revelation 20:6

The Golden Age of Greece took place when Pericles (495–429 BC) sat on the throne. The Elizabethan Age (1558–1603) has been called England's Golden Age. In both cases political stability and economic growth helped these nations to flourish intellectually and in the arts. Interestingly, Narnia is also said to have a Golden Age. This is the time when the four Pevensie children—Peter, Edmund, Susan, and Lucy— sat upon the four thrones at Cair Paravel. In each of these cases the effective leadership of kings and queens helped set the stage for such times of flourishing.

The apostle John tells us there is coming a time when the Son of God will sit on the throne in Jerusalem, and the redeemed will reign with Him for a thousand years (Revelation 20:1–6). Because Jesus Christ is perfect humanity and undiminished deity, He will rule like none other before Him. It will be the great privilege of the redeemed to serve the King of Kings and Lord of Lords. All other Golden Ages will then seem to be only a dim shadow of that glorious time with the Savior!

We can look forward to a time when we will reign with Jesus Christ for a thousand years.

FOR FURTHER READING: *The Horse and His Boy* by C. S. Lewis, chapter 15

Church Unity

That they all may be one, as You, Father, are in Me, and I in You;
that they also may be one in Us, that the world may believe that
You sent Me. —John 17:21

When answering a series of impromptu questions delivered in a business setting, C. S. Lewis was asked if the time was ripe for Christians to reunite in a common faith. His response: "Divisions between Christians are a sin and a scandal, and Christians ought at all times to be making contributions toward re-union, if it is only by their prayers."

It would be easy for one to conclude that Lewis thought visible unity between churches was more important than doctrinal truth. But this was not the case. He sent an early draft of *Mere Christianity* to an Anglican, a Methodist, a Presbyterian, and a Roman Catholic for suggestions on any rewrites. He did this because they believed in the core doctrines of the faith. Lewis, however, carried on a lifetime battle with clergy who accommodated an anti-supernatural Christian faith. In fact, in his book *The Great Divorce*, Lewis describes an apostate Anglican priest whose heresies have made saving faith in the gospel impossible. For Lewis, core beliefs are the basis for any legitimate unity among Christians.

Sound doctrine on the essentials is the only source
of legitimate unity among Christians.

FOR FURTHER READING: *God in the Dock* by C. S. Lewis,
"Answers to Questions on Christianity"

READ: Hebrews 13:1–21

A Temporary Place

For here we have no continuing city, but we seek the one to come.
—Hebrews 13:14

C. S. Lewis said, "Our Father refreshes us on the journey with some pleasant inns, but will not encourage us to mistake them for home." His point of an earthly home being at best a temporary dwelling placing is insightful.

The book of Hebrews was written to Jewish Christians who were experiencing persecution. Having been raised in Judaism, they were tempted to go back into it. Central to the Jews' traditional faith were the ceremonies that took place in the temple in Jerusalem. Ironically, several years after the book of Hebrews was written, the Romans destroyed the temple. The Jews were sent to wander the world and long for their homeland.

Other inspired epistles speak of the transitory nature of this world and the believers' ultimate destination of heaven as their eternal home (Philippians 3:20; 1 Peter 2:11). All of us are tempted to make a temporal place or earthly relationships the focus of our lives. But this is a mistake. Our homes, which warm our hearts, are at best "pleasant inns." We must refocus on the eternal home that awaits us. It will never fade away.

Although we may enjoy temporary inns on our journey
here, our true home is in another world.

For Further Reading: *The Problem of Pain* by C. S. Lewis, chapter 7

READ: 1 Kings 18:20–40; 19:1–18

Mountaintop Experiences

[God] also brought me up out of a horrible pit, out of the miry clay, and set my feet upon a rock, and established my steps. He has put a new song in my mouth. —Psalm 40:2–3

In responding to a letter from a recent convert, C. S. Lewis addressed the emotional high the new believer was experiencing. Like getting a big push when we first start riding a bike, the rush of excitement will not last with the same intensity. As we continue riding the bike, we need to use our legs to move us along and our hands and arms to steer. But Lewis did not leave the subject without a word of celebration for the joys of new conversion: "So enjoy the push while it lasts, but enjoy it as a treat, not as something normal."

The highs and lows of the walk of faith require personal adjustment. When Elijah stood alone competing with pagan priests about who was the real God of Israel, joy must have overwhelmed him when fire fell from heaven demonstrating that Yahweh was the undisputed Lord (1 Kings 18). But when the wicked Queen Jezebel hunted him to take his life, Elijah fell into depression and did not want to go on living (ch. 19). Only the tender care of an angel and the revelation of God could restore him. Enjoy the mountains, but remember there are valleys ahead!

We learn from God both in the mountains and the valleys of our emotional experience.

FOR FURTHER READING: *Collected Letters of C. S. Lewis,* volume 3

READ: Proverbs 22:6; Ephesians 4:11–16

Needing to Be Needed

*But we were gentle among you, just as a nursing mother cherishes
her own children.* —1 Thessalonians 2:7

The right kind of parenting works itself out of a job. The dependence
of a baby will change as the child grows up. Finally, the day will come
when as a young adult the person will seek life on his or her own. But
sometimes the parenting process can get stuck. In *The Four Loves*, C. S.
Lewis observed that even a mother's love can become misdirected: "The
maternal instinct . . . is a gift-love, but one that needs to give; therefore
needs to be needed. But the proper aim of giving is to put the recipient
in a state where he no longer needs our gift."

Interestingly, Paul used the illustration of a nursing mother to
describe his own care for the Christians in Thessalonica (1 Thessalonians 2:7). This care was needed when they were new believers in
Christ. But Paul never intended believers to remain spiritual babies
(1 Corinthians 3:1–3). Instead he cultivated dependence upon the Lord
Jesus and not himself. Indeed, his ultimate goal was to encourage their
spiritual growth so they could become self-sustaining and mature in
Christ (Ephesians 4:13). Christians, like children, need to grow up.

*Our love for others should not make them dependent on
us but should help them grow in maturity in Christ.*

READ: Job 41:1–34

Sea Serpent!

Can you draw out Leviathan with a hook, or snare his tongue with a line which you lower? — Job 41:1

In *The Voyage of the Dawn Treader*, a terrifying sea serpent attack is repulsed by a young boy named Eustace Scrubb. Not only is this encounter with a monster deeply dramatic, but it also evokes a remarkable change in the character of Eustace. Aslan has turned him from a whining brat into a boy of courage.

Sightings of sea serpents have been recorded in the logs of ships for centuries. What are we to think of these reports? On October 13, 2013, a group of people found an eighteen-foot-long oarfish off the coast of Southern California's Catalina Island. This may well have been the kind of fish mariners spotted.

The Bible uses the word "Leviathan" to describe something like a sea serpent (Job 41:1). The Hebrew word could be literally translated "twisting monster." Many have wondered about the meaning of the word with speculations ranging from whales to pythons to crocodiles. But the point of this Bible verse is to emphasize man's powerlessness against even the beasts and fish of nature. The mystery and power of God's great creatures make His mighty works evident to all.

The mysterious creatures that walk the earth
and swim in the deep should remind us of
our smallness before a mighty Creator.

For Further Reading: *The Voyage of the Dawn Treader*
by C. S. Lewis, chapter 8

READ: 2 Timothy 2:1–10

A Fellow Patient

Imitate me, just as I also imitate Christ.   —1 Corinthians 11:1

When C. S. Lewis learned that a young man had been converted after reading his writings, Lewis said, "My feeling about people in whose conversion I have been allowed to play a part is always mixed with awe and even fear. . . . By writing the things I write, you see, one especially qualifies for being hereafter 'condemned out of one's own mouth.' Think of me as a fellow-patient in the same hospital who, having been admitted a little earlier, could give some advice."

Despite being aware of our imperfections, the Bible writers exhort us to set a pattern for others to follow (1 Corinthians 11:1). Paul tells others to "imitate" him using the Greek word *mimic*. It was used of a child following the behavior of an adult. Applying this idea to spiritual character transformation, he wrote: "Therefore be imitators of God as dear children" (Ephesians 5:1). Also, when Paul developed leaders to share the work, he exhorted them to serve as models of ministry as he had tried to do: "In all things [show] yourself to be a pattern of good works" (Titus 2:7).

> *We should set a good example for others*
> *but realize we are all imperfect.*

FOR FURTHER READING: *A Severe Mercy* by Sheldon Vanauken

READ: Psalm 127:3–5; Ephesians 6:1–4

Disappointment with Dad

But if anyone does not provide for his own, and especially for those of his household, he has denied the faith and is worse than an unbeliever. —1 Timothy 5:8

Fighting in the trenches during World War I, Jack Lewis was wounded and lay in a hospital bed far from home. Lewis wrote to his father, Albert, to ask him to come and see him with all haste: "Wherever I am I know that you will come and see me. . . . I was never before so eager to cling to every bit of our old home life and to see you. . . . Come and see me, I am homesick, that is the long and short of it." Sadly, despite this earnest plea, Lewis' father never came to visit.

Jack must have been devastated by this instance of emotional neglect. But we must not generalize on this sad picture. Certainly, Albert was a complex man who had a strained relationship with both his sons. But Albert did generously provide financial support for Jack's Oxford education—including advanced degrees. After his father had passed on, Jack Lewis began to find ways of telling others of his father's positive qualities.

Although we may have been disappointed by a parent, it is important to find ways to honor our father and mother (Ephesians 6:2).

Parents may fail us, but Scripture tells us we should still honor them.

READ: John 1:35–42

Mentoring Others to Faith

He first found his own brother Simon, and said to him, "We have found the Messiah" (which is translated, the Christ). And he brought him to Jesus. —John 1:41–42

The Bible is filled with mentor relationships: Moses and Joshua; Elijah and Elisha; Jesus and Peter; Paul and Timothy are just a few. Although mentoring in Scripture usually takes place between believers, some mentoring actually can bring an unbeliever to faith.

One evening J. R. R. Tolkien, Lewis, and another colleague took an after-dinner walk where their conversation turned to mythology. Lewis dismissed both Christianity and pagan myths as being invented by human imagination. But Tolkien, who was a Christian, pushed back. Tolkien argued that pagan myths only foreshadowed what God really did in the first century through His Son Jesus Christ. This spiritual mentoring set C. S. Lewis on a journey that would ultimately lead to his conversion to Christianity.

In the New Testament we see how another brought someone to the Savior. Andrew had grown up in a fishing family where undoubtedly he had seen Peter his older brother take the lead. But one day Andrew met Jesus of Nazareth and became convinced that He was the Messiah. Andrew ran to Peter and then brought him to the Savior.

*Relationship is at the heart of mentoring,
and this can be a stepping stone to faith.*

FOR FURTHER READING: *Surprised by Joy* by C. S. Lewis, chapters 14–15

READ: Psalm 16:11; Acts 4:31; Romans 5:5; 15:13

Filling an Empty Vessel

And do not be drunk with wine, in which is dissipation; but be filled with the Spirit. —Ephesians 5:18

C. S. Lewis has wisely observed: "God gives His gifts where He finds the vessel empty enough to receive them." In Paul's day, people filled themselves up with all kinds of substitutes. Devotees of the god Dionysus gave themselves over to alcohol and promiscuity. Stoics filled their minds with a strict philosophy of self-denial. Still others devoted themselves to helping the Romans build an empire. But in each case they were not filled with the power of the living God. Each had filled themselves with God substitutes, so God could not fill them with himself.

Today, even believers in Christ can be tempted to "fill up" on all kinds of substitutes for God. Materialism, workaholism, and busyness often can fill a believer's life to the gills. The problem is not the activity itself but the fact that it crowds out God.

The Scriptures do not demand that we forsake all activity. But they do require that Christ be number one and that our hearts and minds be sufficiently open to receive God's blessing and direction. Do you have any activities or relationships that should be curtailed so they don't crowd out God?

God wants to fill us with joy and peace
so we may abound in joy.

FOR FURTHER READING: *Letters to Malcolm: Chiefly on Prayer* by C. S. Lewis, chapter 17

READ: 1 Samuel 1:1–2:21

Childhood Backgrounds

But Samuel ministered before the LORD, even as a child, wearing a linen ephod. —1 Samuel 2:18

Because God answered Hannah's prayer to have a child, she took her son Samuel to the temple for a lifetime of service. The child wore an ephod, which was a shoulder garment used by those who served in the temple. Although the boy Samuel was not of the tribe of Levi, he was given a role in the temple because he had been dedicated to the Lord. Even while Samuel was still a child, the Lord audibly called him to serve as one of the great prophets of ancient Israel. Through him would come the anointing of the first king, Saul, and then the great King David.

As a child, C. S. Lewis was free to explore and to learn from books at home. Lewis later used those ideas to witness to his generation and beyond: "I am a product of long corridors, empty sunlit rooms, upstairs indoor silences, attics explored in solitude, distant noises of gurgling cisterns and pipes, and the noise of wind under the tiles. Also, of endless books." Even though Lewis' background was nothing like Samuel's, God used them both for His service. What is your background?

God uses different backgrounds to mold His servants for their future call.

FOR FURTHER READING: *Surprised by Joy* by C. S. Lewis, chapter 1

READ: Psalm 139:1–24

My Own Person

He who finds his life will lose it, and he who loses his life for My sake will find it. —Matthew 10:39

Today a growing number of people feel self-actualization is more important than social responsibility to others. When conflicts arise between personal needs and obligations to family, coworkers, or neighbors, many decide in favor of self interests.

A self-centered life orientation is not a modern development. Indeed, a wealthy elite has often surfaced in many societies. When this occurs, the idle rich look for endless diversions for entertainment. But despite one's socioeconomic resources, the desire to be one's own person is part of human nature.

As a young man, C. S. Lewis was not only intellectually arrogant but also self-absorbed. When he encountered Jesus Christ, however, friends observed that he became focused on meeting the needs of others. In a letter, Lewis commented on how faith in Christ affects one's self-esteem: "I became my own only when I gave myself to Another." Jesus Christ claimed that only through relationship with Him could a person really find true identity: "For whoever desires to save his life will lose it, but whoever loses his life for My sake will find it" (Matthew 16:25). Are you your own person—or is your identity in Jesus?

Only in yielding to Christ can we find our true selves.

READ: Romans 8:18–28

Cosmic Consequences

For the earnest expectation of the creation eagerly waits for the revealing of the sons of God. —Romans 8:19

Perelandra is the second book in C. S. Lewis' space trilogy. The storyline tells of Dr. Elwin Ransom, who was called to Perelandra to keep the Eve of that world from falling into sin through the demonic influence of a physicist named Dr. Weston. By far the most poetic of Lewis' science fiction works, *Perelandra* often shows how the redemption provided on earth will someday affect the whole universe. We see this in Ransom's reflection: "Every minute it became clearer to him that the parallel he had tried to draw between Eden and Perelandra was crude and imperfect. What had happened on Earth, when Maleldil [God] was born a man at Bethlehem, had altered the universe forever."

In Paul's inspired letter written to the church at Rome, we are told that all of creation now groans under the curse resulting from man's fall into sin (Romans 8:22). But through Christ's redemption a restoration will occur in which all of nature will be transformed. The birth of Christ on that first Christmas day will someday have an impact on even the most distant galaxy.

What happened at Bethlehem so many years ago has cosmic consequences.

FOR FURTHER READING: *Perelandra* by C. S. Lewis, chapter 11

Fundamentalist

This beginning of signs Jesus did in Cana of Galilee, and manifested His glory; and His disciples believed in Him. —John 2:11

Around the time of World War I, doctrinal disagreements between Protestant modernists and Protestant conservatives began to intensify. A publication called *The Fundamentals*, which spelled out the basics of the Christian faith, was circulated through many Protestant churches. Near the top of the list of important doctrines were miraculous claims of Scripture such as the virgin birth.

The labels of "liberal" and "fundamentalist" were used in doctrinal wars. Liberals were accused of denying the cardinal doctrines of the Christian faith and replacing them with a social gospel. Fundamentalists were viewed as being anti-intellectual, legalistic in lifestyle, and self-righteous.

Interestingly, C. S. Lewis did not fit the stereotype of a fundamentalist yet was sometimes called one. He drank beer and smoked with his friends down at the pub. Yet his defense of the miraculous witness of Christian claims won him a hearing by many. In his book *Reflections on the Psalms*, Lewis said, "I have been suspected of being what is called a Fundamentalist. That is because I never regard any narrative as unhistorical simply on the ground that it includes the miraculous." Certainly, C. S. Lewis believed in the fundamentals of the faith.

The fundamentals of the faith include the inspiration of Scripture, the virgin birth, the deity of Christ, and His resurrection.

FOR FURTHER READING: *Reflections on the Psalms* by C. S. Lewis, chapter 11

READ: 1 Peter 2:1–9

Nobleman or Commoner?

But you are a chosen generation, a royal priesthood, a holy nation, His own special people, that you may proclaim the praises of Him who called you out of darkness into His marvelous light.
—1 Peter 2:9

The three great class divisions of medieval England were nobleman, commoner, and clergy. Each had a specific calling before God and fit into a carefully constructed network of obligations and provisions under law. Narnia has some of these elements in its story line.

In *The Magician's Nephew*, we see a remarkable process by which a commoner is transformed into a king. Frank, a London cab driver, has been taken to the newly created world of Narnia. As the plot develops, he exhibits noble character qualities of kindness and courage. Recognizing the measure of the man, Aslan asks Frank if he would consider becoming Narnia's first monarch. Trusting the lion's assessment of his own abilities, Frank humbly agrees.

Later, in *The Last Battle*, we see the newly created Narnia. There King Frank and Queen Helen are seated in the garden of the West. They show us that character and heart are rewarded with lasting positions of power. In 1 Peter 2:9, the apostle tells us that the faithful in Christ will be given positions of royal power in a new world of praise and joyous service. Although we now seem like common people, then we will be transformed into glorious royalty.

The greatest king and the most humble servant is Christ. In heaven we will follow that example.

FOR FURTHER READING: *The Last Battle* by C. S. Lewis, chapter 16

READ: Psalm 16:1–11

Echoes of Heaven

You will show me the path of life; in Your presence is fullness of joy;
at Your right hand are pleasures forevermore. —Psalm 16:11

Early in the morning of each new day, even before the light of dawn appears, the sound of bird songs can be heard. C. S. Lewis found an echo of heaven in the sounds nature provides for us. To him they spoke of another world: "I can't hear the song of a bird simply as a sound. Its meaning or message . . . comes with it inevitably. . . . This heavenly fruit is instantly redolent of the orchard where it grew. This sweet air whispers of the country from whence it blows. It is a message. We know we are being touched by a finger of that right hand at which there are pleasures for evermore."

For the Christian, the ultimate new day was inaugurated on that first Easter morning. Undoubtedly, in the garden where Jesus' tomb was located a symphony of birds joined in celebrating the sun soon to rise. But the Son of God—when He exited the tomb and stood clothed in a glorified body—proclaimed the redemption of all things in heaven and earth (Psalm 16:8–11; Acts 2:25–31). As you go through your daily routine today, be alert for any echoes of heaven that nature might provide for you.

Sounds and sights of nature can be echoes from heaven
pointing to the One who is the source of lasting joy.

FOR FURTHER READING: *Letters to Malcolm: Chiefly on Prayer*
by C. S. Lewis, chapter 17

READ: Luke 5:1–10

Nature Obeys

"Master, we have toiled all night and caught nothing; nevertheless at Your word I will let down the net." And when they had done this, they caught a great number of fish, and their net was breaking.
—Luke 5:5–6

In today's reading we see disappointed fishermen. Peter and his brother had fished all night long and caught nothing. Yet when the young rabbi from Nazareth told Peter to lower his nets, the fisherman complied. Right away, the swirling and wiggling of scores of fish threatened to break the nets. When Peter called for assistance from his fishing partners in another boat, the catch was so great the two boats nearly sank. Peter rightly viewed this as a miracle and felt unworthy to be in Christ's presence. But Jesus calmed him and predicted that he would become a fisher of men.

How could waters that seemed to have no fish suddenly teem with an abundance of them? The answer is that the King of heaven and earth was there, and those fish responded to His sovereign call. C. S. Lewis said, "The fitness of the Christian miracles and their difference from these mythological miracles lies in the fact that they show invasion by a Power which is not alien . . . They proclaim that He who has come is not merely a king, but *the* King, [nature's] king and ours."

Jesus Christ is the Creator, so nature responds to Him as an obedient subject to the King.

For Further Reading: *Miracles* by C. S. Lewis, chapter 15

READ: Luke 3:1–23; John 20:1–31

Your Age in Heaven

Now Jesus Himself began His ministry at about thirty years of age.
—Luke 3:23

How old will we be in heaven? Will believers who died when they were in their nineties look that age in the new heaven and new earth? What about children who have died in the Lord? Will they be perpetually children in heaven?

The Bible does not give us precise answers to those questions. But we can speculate. When Jesus began His ministry on earth, He was about thirty years of age. His ministry lasted for three and a half years. So although His glorified body was different in many ways from ours, it was built upon the model of a body of someone who was thirty-three years old. Some scholars think that believers may be given bodies of young adults like Jesus' resurrection body. Of this, Lewis wrote: "One gets glimpses, even in our country, of that which is ageless—heavy thought in the face of an infant, and frolic childhood in that of a very old man." It may be that we find in heaven something like Lewis' view of Aslan's country: "People [have] no particular ages in Aslan's country."

The glorified body that is promised to all who believe is ageless.

For Further Reading: *The Silver Chair* by C. S. Lewis, chapter 16

READ: Matthew 28:1–20

The Angel Sat Down

And behold, there was a great earthquake; for an angel of the
Lord descended from heaven, and came and rolled back the stone
from the door, and sat on it. —Matthew 28:2

The Bible teaches us of a race of super spirit beings called angels. Apparently their creation preceded ours. They belong to one of two groups: fallen angels, who opposed the will of God, and good angels, who remained loyal to Him. The infection of sin that started in the heart of an archangel named Lucifer then spread to the human race through Adam and Eve. The story of the Bible tells how Jesus came into our world to redeem fallen humanity. It is a drama that angels long to look into (1 Peter 1:12).

Although angels possess personalities as we do, they do not have bodies. They are pure spirit. Nevertheless, they accommodate us by appearing as shining creatures, which can appear in a form similar to ours. In the Preface to *The Screwtape Letters*, C. S. Lewis observed that "[Angels] are given human form because man is the only rational creature we know." On resurrection morning when Jesus was raised from the dead, an angel was sent to move the stone away and then sit down on it. We are not sure why, but this story seems to suggest that the angel understood that the work of redemption through Christ was finished and that we could rest in it (Hebrews 10:12).

> *The resurrection of Christ is a landmark of the*
> *complete work of salvation on our behalf.*

FOR FURTHER READING: *The Screwtape Letters* by C. S. Lewis, Preface

READ: Psalm 39:1–5

Chatterbox

Be still, and know that I am God. —Psalm 46:10

In the Narnia Chronicles we meet Pattertwig, a remarkable talking red squirrel. He is almost the size of a terrier and is by his very nature a chatterer. When he attends Prince Caspian's war council, however, the squirrel frantically rushes about calling for silence before the meeting gets under way.

How many times do we find ourselves chattering about life's ups and downs? Concern over threatening circumstances, frustrations with relationships, and even unexpected blessings can set the stage for our becoming a real chatterbox.

Commenting on life's experience is not necessarily a bad thing. When it gets our focus off God, though, we can become obsessed with our circumstances. We would do well to learn from Pattertwig. He may have been a chatterer, but he knew there are times that call for silence.

The psalmist has wisely reflected on a similar theme: "I was mute with silence" (Psalm 39:2). In the psalmist's prayers, his inner quiet provided the atmosphere to learn about God and to assess his soul in His holy presence: "LORD, make me to know my end, and what is the measure of my days" (v. 4).

*Dear God, help me to still my heart in Your
presence and to listen in silence to Your voice.*

FOR FURTHER READING: *Prince Caspian* by C. S. Lewis, chapter 7

READ: Matthew 13:1–58

Called to Tell Stories

On the same day Jesus went out of the house and sat by the sea.
And great multitudes were gathered together to Him, so that He
got into a boat and sat; and the whole multitude stood on the
shore. Then He spoke many things to them in parables.

—Matthew 13:1–3

The history of human culture has had "story" at its center. Around the fire at night, ancient man told stories of the hunt and of victory between warring tribes. At the amphitheater in classical Greece, the traveling bard told of Ulysses in the great seafaring saga. In Rome, Virgil wrote the classic story *Aeneid*, which gave the mythical history of that great city. And then when God in human form stepped into history, Jesus Christ told stories to explain God's redemption.

Story has the unique capability of encapsulating and applying truth. This is one major reason C. S. Lewis became a champion of story. Concerning this, Lewis wrote: "I should like to be able to believe that I am here in a very small way contributing . . . to the encouragement . . . of story that can mediate imaginative life to the masses while not being contemptible to the few."

When sharing spiritual truths—ranging from evangelistic witness to giving hope in times of despair—telling stories can uplift, instruct, and help others understand "The Greatest Story Ever Told."

The Bible is filled with stories that can fire the imagination,
inspire the heart, and transform the soul.

FOR FURTHER READING: *Of Other Worlds: Essays and Stories*
by C. S. Lewis, "On Stories"

READ: Philippians 1:1–17

Defending the Gospel

Knowing that I am set for the defense of the gospel.
—Philippians 1:17 (KJV)

Many sincere believers have adopted a conversational style of witnessing. In fact, some would go so far as to try to agree with unbelievers about almost anything. In doing so, it is hoped they can get a hearing for the gospel. But keeping the faith also includes taking a stand to defend it. C. S. Lewis wrote, "As Christians we are tempted to make unnecessary concessions to those outside the Faith. We give in too much. . . . We must show our Christian colours, if we are to be true to Jesus Christ."

Paul was an ardent defender of the faith. Despite the joyful themes of Paul's letter to the Philippians, it reveals struggles with those who opposed his ministry. Nonetheless, the apostle tells us that he was committed to defending the gospel come what may. Often he would find common ground, and he was also a master of dialogue (Acts 17:22–31). We should agree with unbelievers whenever possible and especially be good listeners. But when the supernatural gospel is proclaimed, it should be kept intact just as Paul proclaimed it.

When we witness, we must defend the gospel—
not apologize for it.

FOR FURTHER READING: *God in the Dock*
by C. S. Lewis, "Cross Examination"

READ: Luke 15:11–32

Hope for Post-Christians

Although they knew God, they did not glorify Him as God, nor were thankful, but became futile in their thoughts, and their foolish hearts were darkened. —Romans 1:21

Have you ever run into someone who comes from a Christian background but denies the faith? Ironically, he might be more difficult to win to Christ than a spiritual seeker. Why? Well, the post-Christian thinks he already knows what Christians believe, and he doesn't want it. In a letter to his friend Don Giovanni Calabria, C. S. Lewis made this observation: " 'Post-Christian man' is not the same as 'pre-Christian man.' He is as far removed as virgin is from widow: there is nothing in common except want of a spouse: but there is a great difference between a spouse-to-come and a spouse lost."

Yet there is hope for the "post-Christian." Lewis himself was raised by believing parents, but as a young man he lost his faith and embraced atheism. It was through a slow process of books and friends, both of which challenged his heart and mind, that the prodigal would eventually come home. Jesus told the parable of a wayward son who was drawn back to his father's embrace (Luke 15:11–32). Even a generation of "post-Christians" can be brought back into the fold.

God can use patient friends to help post-Christians return to faith in Christ.

FOR FURTHER READING: *The Latin Letters of C. S. Lewis*

READ: Exodus 25:1–40

Let Me Draw You a Picture

*Three bowls shall be made like almond blossoms on one branch,
with an ornamental knob and a flower, and three bowls made
like almond blossoms on the other branch, with an ornamental
knob and a flower—and so for the six branches that come out of
the lampstand.* —Exodus 25:33

In *The Collected Letters of C. S. Lewis*, we get a glimpse into the world of
Jack Lewis the sketch artist. In a letter to his godson Laurence Harwood,
Lewis used a variety of drawings to punctuate his correspondence. A
picture of a castle is used to refer to Jack's college. Lewis comments on
the many rabbits on the grounds and draws an example. Jack talks of
how much he loves the frost of winter and sketches an angel ornament
for a Christmas tree in celebration of Christ's birth soon to come. Playful
images add to the joy of show-and-tell between different generations.

Pictures, like anything, can be used for good or ill. In the pagan
world, false gods were represented by idols, which misled entire people
groups away from the living God. This is why the first commandment
prohibits making graven images for worship. But despite this commandment, God gave Israel the freedom to artistically create symbols of spiritual truth in the tabernacle (Exodus 25:1-40). It was here in the context
of worshipping the one true living God in Spirit and in truth that illustrations were permitted. Here God drew a picture of His redemptive
grace.

*Using art to communicate personal experience and
Christian faith can be a means of growth for others.*

FOR FURTHER READING: *The Collected Letters of C. S. Lewis,* volume 2

READ: Psalm 143:1–12

Hard to Get to Know

Cause me to know the way in which I should walk, for I lift up my soul to You.   —Psalm 143:8

In Lyle Dorsett's book *Seeking the Secret Place: The Spiritual Formation of C. S. Lewis,* the author observes how Lewis was a little hard to get to know: "Owen Barfield confessed that despite their close and long standing relationship, 'He stood before me as a mystery as solidly as he stood beside me as a friend.' Perhaps C. S. Lewis' most enduring legacy will be that in the final analysis we do not see him clearly at all, because he stands in the shadows, as it were, like a soldier at a fork in the road on the edge of a combat zone. He briskly motions the troops on toward the proper direction. No one really see or pays close attention to the one directing the troops. They are too preoccupied with the action that lies ahead."

Yet Lewis was remarkably self-revealing in his own awareness of the reality of the living Christ, the experience of redemption, and a gratefulness for heaven. His Englishness may have played into some inhibitions in working with others. But his Christian faith and writing gifts provided an avenue for self-disclosure so powerful that many of us feel close to him without ever having met him.

No matter our personalities, each of us can find ways to reach out to others.

FOR FURTHER READING: *Seeking the Secret Place: The Spiritual Formation of C. S. Lewis* by Lyle Dorsett, Introduction

The Gethsemane Prayer

And [Jesus] said, "Abba, Father, all things are possible for You. Take this cup away from Me; nevertheless, not what I will, but what You will."　　　　　　　　　—Mark 14:36

What did Jesus mean by the following promise? "For assuredly, I say to you, whoever says to this mountain, 'Be removed and be cast into the sea,' and does not doubt in his heart, but believes that those things he says will be done, he will have whatever he says" (Mark 11:23). Most likely our Lord was using hyperbole to illustrate how the prayer of faith can overcome insurmountable obstacles. However, just having enough faith is not the only factor that enters in. There is also the issue of God's will concerning the granting of a prayer request.

We should ask ourselves why Christ himself couldn't remove the obstacle of the cross in Mark 14. The answer lies in our Lord's own prayer: "Abba, Father, all things are possible for You. Take this cup away from Me; nevertheless, not what I will, but what You will" (v. 36).

Clearly, a prayer will receive a "yes" response only when it conforms to the Father's will. Of this C. S Lewis wrote in *Letters to Malcolm: Chiefly on Prayer*: "For most of us the prayer in Gethsemane is the only model. Removing mountains can wait." It's God's will, not the mountain, that makes the difference.

As we deeply implore God for something in prayer, our attitude needs to be "not my will, but Your will be done."

For Further Reading: *Letters to Malcolm: Chiefly on Prayer*
by C. S. Lewis, chapter 7

READ: Proverbs 28:15; 29:2; John 20:19–29

The Righteous in Hiding

When the wicked rise to power, people go into hiding; but when the wicked perish, the righteous thrive. —Proverbs 28:28 (NIV)

Near the beginning of *Prince Caspian*, we see a young prince being told of the golden age of Narnia when talking animals abounded and a mysterious lion named Aslan ruled. But Prince Caspian is told by his wicked uncle, who rules the land, that these stories are only make-believe. Later as the story develops, the young prince discovers that talking animals who are loyal subjects of the old Narnia have gone into hiding. Through his leadership and the help of the Pevensie children, the oppressor is overthrown and loyal Narnians come out into the open to thrive in a happy land once again.

The Proverbs often observe the impact of oppressive regimes over their people. "When the wicked rise to power, people go into hiding; but when the wicked perish, the righteous thrive" (28:28 NIV). When corrupt and self-centered dictators come to power, the righteous who fear their persecution may take cover. When the wicked perish, however, a sense of freedom brings the righteous back into the open. In this new environment the righteous can flourish.

Godly leadership protects the rights and promotes the responsibilities of the righteous.

FOR FURTHER READING: *A Family Guide to Narnia* by Christin Ditchfield, Introduction to Prince Caspian, chapter 6

READ: Job 29:1–6

The Good Old Days

Just as I was in the days of my prime, when the friendly counsel of God was over my tent. — Job 29:4

You'll notice that in today's key verse Job speaks of the days of his youth. The term *prime* literally means "autumn." This was when the crops had been harvested and prosperity was measured. In that vision of the past Job saw his children gathered around him in happy family repose. In a land where sheep, goats, and cows were central to the economy, Job uses "thick cream" or "butter" to describe how prosperity flowed over his path (v. 6). Likewise, the imagery of olive oil used for cooking, light, and medicine illustrates this time of plenty. Now Job was destitute, in ill health, and grieving the death of his children. One solace for him was to live in the past.

Sometimes when we are facing hard times, we find our thoughts moving back to a happier time. C. S. Lewis periodically experienced this longing himself. In a letter, Lewis wrote: "Why is it that one can never think of the past without wanting to go back?" Yet God is vitally interested in our engagement with the present He has provided. We may appreciate the past, but we must intentionally live in the present.

Memories of past happiness are a comfort, but we need to draw on God's grace for today's challenges.

FOR FURTHER READING: *The Letters of C. S. Lewis to Arthur Greeves,* edited by Walter Hooper

READ: Mark 5:1–20

"My Name Is Legion"

Then [Jesus] asked [the man with an unclean spirit], "What is your name?" And he answered, saying, "My name is Legion; for we are many."
—Mark 5:9

The book that brought C. S. Lewis international fame was *The Screwtape Letters*. His renown was so great that he appeared on the cover of *Time* magazine in 1947. His cover painting depicted him flanked by an angel's wing and a demonic figure. The title read: "Oxford's C. S. Lewis: His heresy: Christianity." Lewis proclaimed that the war in heaven had come to earth and only through Christ could we have the victory.

In our reading today we see a dramatic scene of deliverance from demon possession. The legion of demons inside the possessed man fear immediate judgment. Because of this, they beg Jesus to cast them into the many swine nearby. The Lord agrees to this arrangement, and hundreds of demon-possessed pigs run down the hill and drown in the sea.

When the man has been delivered from demonic control, he wants nothing more than to be with Jesus. But the Lord tells him: "Go home to your friends, and tell them what great things the Lord has done for you, and how He has had compassion on you" (Mark 5:19). Deliverance is a testimony to the power and grace of God.

Under Christ's authority we need not fear the fallen angels He defeated at the cross.

FOR FURTHER READING: *The Screwtape Letters* by C. S. Lewis, Introduction

READ: Psalm 127:3; Mark 10:13–16

Relating to Children

Take heed that you do not despise one of these little ones, for I say to you that in heaven their angels always see the face of My Father who is in heaven.   —Matthew 18:10

Although C. S. Lewis took children into his home for protection during the bombing raids of World War II, he did not especially feel comfortable with them. In *The Abolition of Man*, he wrote: "I myself do not enjoy the society of small children . . . I recognize this is a defect in myself." Despite this natural predisposition, Lewis worked hard at relating to children. For him it took the form of kindness in response to their letters. Shortly before his death, the last letter C. S. Lewis wrote was to a boy named Philip. Lewis compliments the boy's writing and expresses appreciation that he likes the Narnia Chronicles.

The Lord Jesus placed a high value on children. In today's Bible quote we have a remarkable reason given for this esteem (Matthew 18:10). He tells us to treat children with value because angelic beings oversee their lives and have direct access to God. The Bible does indeed bear witness to the reality of guardian angels (Daniel 10:10–14; Acts 12:15; Hebrews 1:14; Revelation 1:20). If God places such value on little ones, so should we.

Not all of us may appreciate small children, but we should all work at showing them respect and kindness.

For Further Reading: *C. S. Lewis: Letters to Children,*
edited by Lyle W. Dorsett and Marjorie Lamp Mead

READ: Romans 10:1–21

Misguided Zeal

For I bear them witness that they have a zeal for God, but not according to knowledge. —Romans 10:2

Saul of Tarsus was culturally, religiously, and theologically "a Hebrew of the Hebrews" (Philippians 3:3–6). Then he met the risen Christ on the road to Damascus (Acts 9), and his life trajectory changed forever. He became Paul the evangelist, who proclaimed the faith he once persecuted. But as Paul evangelized his fellow Jews, it was heartbreaking to see that many rejected his message. Yet Paul realized there would be a remnant of Israel who would one day trust in Jesus as Messiah (Romans 9:27–29).

In Romans 10:2, we see that Paul commended the Jews for their zeal for God. But he also said that this was "not according to knowledge." The righteousness they were seeking to establish for themselves was futile. Instead, the true source of righteousness comes through faith in Christ's atoning work on Calvary.

As Christians, we too should be discerning about what drives our spiritual zeal. Sometimes it can be something that excites us and not something that has been put in our hearts by God. C. S. Lewis said, "The danger of mistaking our merely natural, though perhaps legitimate, enthusiasm for holy zeal, is always great." Let's be wary of misguided zeal.

*We must not mistake human enthusiasm
for holy zeal given to us by God.*

FOR FURTHER READING: *God in the Dock* by C. S. Lewis,
"Meditation on the Third Commandment"

READ: Philippians 3:7–14

Maintaining Focus

One thing I do, forgetting those things which are behind and reaching forward to those things which are ahead.

—Philippians 3:13

In 1963 a representative from the Billy Graham Evangelistic Association interviewed C. S. Lewis at Cambridge. The questions spanned a variety of topics, but evangelism and writing were two of the major themes. When asked about a writer developing a personal writing style, Lewis encouraged clarity of expression. Then he added a few words about not losing one's audience: "I sometimes think that writing is like driving sheep down a road. If there is any gate open to the left or the right the readers will most certainly go into it."

Lewis, who was a logical and clear writer, saw the dangers of going off on tangents. In many ways the apostle Paul held similar values. He was a single-minded man. The thing foremost on his mind was the upward call of God (Philippians 3:13–14). Like Lewis and Paul, we too should be clear about what we're saying, particularly regarding spiritual matters. Both for ourselves and for those who look to us for spiritual direction, keeping our priorities straight and our message clear is essential.

Keeping ourselves and others on track should be the priority of our Christian walk.

FOR FURTHER READING: *God in the Dock* by
C. S. Lewis, "Cross-Examination"

READ: Genesis 3:1–7

The Apologist's Doubts

[The serpent] said to [Eve], "Has God indeed said, 'You shall not eat of every tree of the garden'?" —Genesis 3:1

During C. S. Lewis' life, he was considered a brilliant defender of the faith. Indeed as bombs were being dropped on London by Nazi Germany, many of the English were glued to the wireless to hear his radio addresses. Lewis' easy, conversational style and brilliant, logical arguments brought people to the truth of redemption through Christ. He introduced to the skeptic compelling reasons to believe and to the believer arguments to strengthen their faith.

Ironically, Lewis would sometimes experience a spell of doubt about what he had just said: "Apologetic work is so dangerous to one's own faith. A doctrine never seems dimmer to me than when I have just successfully defended it."

From the beginning of the human race, planting doubts has been the work of the devil (Genesis 3:1–7). Today our spiritual adversary continues to use questions, half-truths, and denial to undermine the faith of the believer. Our response should be to submit to God, resist the devil, and keep our spiritual armor intact (Ephesians 6:10–18; James 4:7). The doubts will eventually lift, and the truth of Christ will prevail.

Faith in God's truth can ultimately conquer any doubts that might arise.

FOR FURTHER READING: *The Collected Letters of C. S. Lewis*, volume 2

READ: John 1:1–14

The Word of God

And the Word became flesh and dwelt among us, and we beheld His glory, the glory as of the only begotten of the Father, full of grace and truth. —John 1:14

C. S. Lewis wrote, "It is Christ Himself . . . who is the true word of God. The Bible, read in the right spirit and with the guidance of good teachers, will bring us to Him." But in what sense is our Lord the Word?

The renowned Bible teacher Warren Wiersbe answered this question in three helpful points. *Jesus Christ is the eternal Word* (John 1:1–2). Christ is eternal, preexisting Abraham (8:58); the Alpha and Omega (Revelation 1:8); and God's final revelation (Hebrews 1:1–3). *Jesus Christ is the creative Word* (John 1:3). Genesis 1:1 and John 1:1 show Christ as the agent of creation. Through Him all things visible and invisible in heaven and on earth were made (Colossians 1:16). The new heaven and new earth likewise will be created by Him (John 14:1–5). *Jesus Christ is the incarnate Word* (John 1:14). The Divine Spirit who is Creator and Lord took on human form in the virgin's womb (Luke 1:29–38). As a man, He would experience hunger, thirst, and fatigue. Yet as God, He would demonstrate miraculous powers to heal and even raise the dead (Mark 1:32–34; John 11:1–44).

Jesus Christ is the Word of God—full of grace and truth.

READ: Leviticus 23:1–44

The Christian Year

For indeed Christ, our Passover, was sacrificed for us.
—1 Corinthians 5:7

For those who have "high church" affiliations, the richness of the Christian calendar can be quite compelling. Based on the ancient Jewish calendar, the early church recognized Epiphany, Lent, Holy Week, Easter, Pentecost, and Advent. As a member of the Church of England, C. S. Lewis availed himself of the spiritual prompts throughout the year. Of the Christian year he told a confidant: "The complexity—the close texture—of all the great events in the Christian year impresses me more and more. Each is a window opening on the total mystery."

Central to all Jewish Feasts was the Passover. In preparation for this feast was the Festival of Unleavened Bread (Exodus 12:15–20; 13:1–10) in which all leaven (a symbol of sin) was removed from each home in preparation for the Passover Lamb. Christians understand that Jesus Christ is "the Lamb of God who takes away the sins of the world!" (John 1:29; Hebrews 10:10, 14). Even when we celebrate communion we acknowledge part of the Christian year that observes various aspects of the ministry of Christ.

The Christian calendar can be a means
of reminding us—throughout the seasons—
of Christ's ministry for each of us.

FOR FURTHER READING: *The Collected Letters of C. S. Lewis*, volume 3

READ: John 8:31–47

Propaganda

*You are of your father the devil, and the desires of your father
you want to do. He was a murderer from the beginning, and does
not stand in the truth, because there is no truth in him. When he
speaks a lie, he speaks from his own resources, for he is a liar and
the father of it.*   —John 8:44

Propaganda is false or exaggerated ideas that are circulated in order to
help a cause or political leader. During World War II, Joseph Goebbels
was the propaganda minister of the Nazi party in Germany. He said,
"If you tell a lie big enough and keep repeating it, people will eventually
come to believe it."

In C. S. Lewis' book *That Hideous Strength,* we learn of the National
Institute for Co-ordinated Experiments (N.I.C.E.), a sinister organization
using the news media for evil purposes. One of their propagandists explains
which group to target: "Why you fool, it's the educated reader who *can*
be gulled. All our difficulty comes with the others. When did you meet a
workman who believes the papers? He takes it for granted that they're all
propaganda . . . . He is our problem. We have to recondition him. But the
educated public, the people who read the highbrow weeklies, don't need
reconditioning. They're all right already. They'll believe anything."

In our reading today, we see how the devil can influence groups to
oppose Christ and His followers (John 8:31–47). Our wisest response is
to immerse ourselves in the Word and use spiritual discernment so we
don't believe the same lies (Ephesians 6:17).

*Let's meditate on God's Word to avoid being
poured into the world's mold.*

FOR FURTHER READING: *That Hideous Strength* by C. S. Lewis, chapter 3

Grief's Merry-Go-Round

For my sighing comes before I eat, and my groanings pour out like water. —Job 3:24

When C. S. Lewis lost his wife, Joy, to cancer, he felt a terrible rhythm of loss: "In grief nothing stays put. One keeps on emerging from a phase, but it always recurs. Round and round. Everything repeats. Am I going in circles, or dare I hope I am on a spiral?"

Have you ever watched small children on a merry-go-round? Around and around and up and down they go. In a darker way, deep grief can seem like a merry-go-round of sadness. Thoughts of painful loss and longing come and go in repetitive cycle. The ups and downs of depression carry a familiar pattern from which one feels there is no escape.

The Bible is filled with saints who experienced the joys of gains and the agonies of losses. Yet the God of grace was with them in each life experience. When on the merry-go-round of grief, we should seek Him out during the ups and downs of our emotions. The God of all comfort will give grace to endure until we make our way through (Psalm 30:5).

The God of all comfort is with us in the inevitable cycles of gain and loss.

FOR FURTHER READING: *A Grief Observed,* by C. S. Lewis, chapter 3

READ: 1 Thessalonians 4:13–18

Rapture Medicine

Men of Galilee, why do you stand gazing up into heaven? This same Jesus, who was taken up from you into heaven, will so come in like manner as you saw Him go into heaven. —Acts 1:11

Do Christians look for the return of Christ only as an escape? C. S. Lewis did not feel that way. His tremendous writing and teaching productivity was joyfully driven by the return of Christ. Of this he wrote: "It [the second coming of Christ] is the medicine our condition especially needs."

But in what respect is the coming rapture medicine for the soul? A brief review of valuable Bible verses can help us answer that question. First, it gives us hope for a better world to be ushered in by the glorified Christ (Titus 2:13). Second, the believer who sets his focus on Christ tends to experience purifying (1 John 3:2–3). Third, the awareness that this world will end motivates us to live more circumspect lives (2 Peter 3:10–11). Fourth, the unknown time of Christ's return prompts us to live responsibly (Matthew 24:44). And fifth, we are assured that death and decay will be swallowed up in a new and glorious future (1 Corinthians 15:51–52). The return of Christ brings hope, purity, godliness, productivity, and anticipation. What could be better medicine for the soul?

The blessed hope of Christ's return should motivate us to productivity and godliness.

FOR FURTHER READING: *The World's Last Night and Other Essays* by C. S. Lewis, "The World's Last Night"

READ: Luke 2:1–20

Wonder of Bethlehem

And without controversy great is the mystery of godliness: God was manifested in the flesh, justified in the Spirit, seen by angels, preached among the Gentiles, believed on in the world, received up in glory. —1 Timothy 3:16

In C. S. Lewis' science fiction work *Perelandra*, the Adam of that world expresses praise for God becoming man on Earth in order to redeem the universe. Prayerfully reflect upon this poem about the wonder of Bethlehem and God's act of redemption.

Ode to Perelandra
by Dennis Fisher

The cosmic dance of love in God
Began before our world was trod.
But humans fell in sin and shame,
Alas the dance was harmed by pain.
Then came the tale of Christ's
    own birth,
A human baby born on earth,
To know the joys and hurts of life,
To show us love in God's delight.
Then other worlds would come to see
That God the Man nailed to a tree
Would die for sin in pain and stress,
Redeeming worlds with all to bless.

The cosmic dance restored by grace,
A song of joy from every race,
Children of God in glory clothed,
Eternal tale sung by this ode.

The morning star before the sun,
An open tomb, glory begun,
Galaxy, stars, and planets all,
Will be made new by His own call.

What happened in Bethlehem impacted the entire universe.

READ: 1 John 1:1–10

Artificial Light

But if we walk in the light as He is in the light, we have fellowship with one another, and the blood of Jesus Christ His Son cleanses us from all sin. —1 John 1:7

Did you know that C. S. Lewis gave fashion advice? In his book of essays *The World's Last Night*, he observed: "Women sometimes have the problem of trying to judge by artificial light how a dress will look by daylight. That is very like the problem of all of us: to dress our souls not for the electric lights of the present world but for the daylight of the next. The good dress is the one that will face that light. For that light will last longer."

Sometimes we can fall into the error of evaluating our moral and spiritual life by what the world currently says is good and true. The follower of Christ, however, is not a true citizen of this world but of the one yet to come. We need to place ourselves under the holy light of that future world.

Our reading today tells us how to walk in God's light. The way to the well-lit path is to confess and forsake sin so we can be cleansed by the blood of Christ. This restores fellowship with the Source of true light and enables us to walk aright by the guidance of His Word.

The light of the next world guides our lives—
not the artificial light of this present age.

FOR FURTHER READING: *The World's Last Night and Other Essays*
by C. S. Lewis, chapter 7

READ: Matthew 6:24; Luke 12:15; 1 Timothy 6:6–10

A Dragon's Greed

One person gives freely, yet gains even more; another withholds unduly, but comes to poverty. —Proverbs 11:24 (NIV)

In *The Voyage of the Dawn Treader*, we meet Eustace Scrubb, a spoiled cousin of the Pevensie children. Always looking out for himself, Eustace finds a dragon's lair filled with gold. Falling asleep, the greedy boy goes through an unexpected transformation: "Sleeping on a dragon's hoard with greedy, dragonish thoughts in his heart, he had become a dragon himself." Only through the painful experience of becoming a dragon and then enduring Aslan's help in transforming him back into a boy does Eustace become a kinder and more generous soul.

The Bible warns us against the soul-destroying influence of greed. A person consumed with avarice is headed down the destructive road of placing far more value on things than on people (1 Timothy 6:6–10). Conversely, the generous person who gives freely will also receive back (Acts 20:35), while the stingy person will find his resources diminished (Proverbs 11:24). Paul tells us "godliness with contentment is great gain" (1 Timothy 6:6). It makes sense. We came into this world with nothing, and we can't take anything with us when we depart.

Contentment and generosity are the antidotes for a greedy heart.

FOR FURTHER READING: *Voyage of the Dawn Treader*
by C. S. Lewis, chapter 6

Growing Up in Christ

Till we all come to the unity of the faith and the knowledge of the Son of God, to a perfect man, to the measure of the stature of the fullness of Christ. —Ephesians 4:13

When we visit a young couple with a newborn baby, we are emotionally moved by the tender scene. What lies ahead for the child's parents will be a demanding but rewarding labor of love. Helping the child learn to sleep through the night and weaning the child from milk so she can start eating solid food will only be the start of parental goals. The basic education of an elementary-aged child will eventually be followed by the challenges of rearing a teenager. But even after the child has become a young adult and leaves the nest, the parents will have a vested interest in their child continuing to become a responsible and mature person.

In his book *The Four Loves*, C. S. Lewis reflected on God's parenting process for each of us with these words: "God, who needs nothing, loves into existence wholly superfluous creatures in order that He may love and perfect them." God loves us too much to leave us as spiritual infants. He wants us to grow into mature followers of His beloved Son (Ephesians 4:13). Maturing in Christ will have its growing pains, but our heavenly Father delights in even our baby steps of obedience.

New birth brings spiritual infants into the world so they can grow up in the likeness of Christ.

FOR FURTHER READING: *The Four Loves* by C. S. Lewis, chapter 6

READ: Acts 13:1–12

Fellow Travelers

The Holy Spirit said, "Set apart for me Barnabas and Saul for the work to which I have called them." —Acts 13:2 (NIV)

Who among us does not benefit from walking and talking with those who have gone on before? In a letter to a friend, C. S. Lewis wrote about this. He said, "Luckily the world is full of books [from other times] . . . one finds oneself on the main road with all humanity, and can compare notes with an endless succession of previous travelers."

In God's good providence, the Bible contains many wonderful stories of companions on faith's journey. Tracing Paul's life, for instance, impresses us with the necessity of travel companions. Barnabas extended the right hand of fellowship to a newly converted Paul (Galatians 2:9). Soon Paul and Barnabas were sent out on an extensive mission trip (Acts 13). Eventually, Mark was added to the team—although he quit when the going got tough (Acts 15:36–41). And despite Paul's split with Barnabas, Paul acquired another travel companion in Silas (v. 40). Like Paul, we should not make life's trek alone. Christian friends and biblical characters can be rich resources as we learn how they traveled the pathway. They are ideal fellow travel companions on the journey of faith.

Through good books we can compare notes with others who have gone before us in our spiritual journey.

FOR FURTHER READING: *The Letters of C. S. Lewis to Arthur Greeves,* edited by Walter Hooper

READ: Hebrews 4:14–16; 5:5–8

Christ's Empathy

For we do not have a High Priest who cannot sympathize with our weaknesses, but was in all points tempted as we are, yet without sin.
—Hebrews 4:15

To have someone empathize with our situation has a way of lightening our load. But here's something even better: In our relationship with God, we have an additional source of kind understanding. It is the Lord Jesus himself, who experienced suffering like us while still maintaining God's unique viewpoint on the problem. In addition, Christ gave us His own Spirit not only to comfort but also to sustain us through temptations and trials. Of this, C. S. Lewis wrote, "God, who foresaw your tribulation, has specially armed you to go through it, not without pain but without stain."

In ancient Israel, God's people came to the high priest who represented them before a holy God through sacrifice and prayers. In so doing, they repeatedly brought the awareness of their own unworthiness to mind. But the book of Hebrews shows that God has provided a better way. Jesus Christ is the ultimate Great High Priest, who provides both atonement and empathetic understanding. It is His compassion that connects and fills us with the power to go on.

Christ understands your struggles right now and will give you the grace to see you through.

READ: John 14:15–24

Reciprocal Love

Jesus answered and said to [Judas], "If anyone loves Me, he will keep My word; and My Father will love him, and We will come to him and make Our home with him." —John 14:23

In *The Four Loves*, C. S. Lewis' book that explores the nature of love, the author reflects on the reciprocal love exchanged by the different members of the Trinity: "The Father gives all He is and has to the Son. The Son gives Himself back to the Father, and gives Himself to the world, and for the world to the Father, and gives the world (in Himself) back to the Father too."

Theologians have long observed that the sense of community shared by humanity in the institutions of marriage and neighborhoods has been shared by the triune God from all eternity. There within the Godhead we see a reciprocal love, which the three persons of the Trinity have invited redeemed humanity to share.

On the night before going to the cross, Christ told His disciples that they would experience a new kind of fellowship with Him. Instead of being in physical proximity to Him, He and the Father would come to dwell within them through the Holy Spirit (John 14:19–20). This spilling of divine love into our lives should move us to let it flow to others. In turn, we will experience it flowing back to us from other believers. That's the joy of reciprocal love.

Christians are to model the giving and receiving love of the triune God.

FOR FURTHER READING: *The Four Loves* by C. S. Lewis, chapter 1

READ: Romans 5:12–21

Choices Have Consequences

For as by the one man's disobedience the many were made sinners,
so by the one man's obedience the many will be made righteous.
—Romans 5:19 (ESV)

In C. S. Lewis' science fiction novel *Perelandra*, Professor Elwin Ransom has been sent to another planet to prevent the inhabitants from falling into sin. Although he tries to talk himself out of his duty, he finally realizes the weighty consequences of his choice: "Either something or nothing must depend on individual choices. And if something, who could set bounds to it? A stone may determine the course of a river. He was that stone at this horrible moment which had become the centre of the whole universe. The eldila [angels] of all worlds, the sinless organisms of everlasting light, were silent in Deep Heaven to see what Elwin Ransom of Cambridge would do."

In today's passage, we read Paul's treatment of the far-reaching choices of the two Adams (Romans 5:12–21). The first Adam partook of the forbidden fruit—resulting in sin passing to himself and his descendants. The second Adam, Jesus Christ, freely chose to become our sin bearer on the cross—making peace with God possible. The choices of the two Adams show how powerful our decisions can be. In our walk with God today, we need to be prayerfully aware that our choices have consequences.

The second Adam is our model for prayerful and godly decisions.

FOR FURTHER READING: *Perelandra* by C. S. Lewis, chapter 11

READ: Acts 17:22–31

The One True God

Paul . . . said, "Men of Athens, I perceive that in all things you are very religious; for as I was passing through and considering the objects of your worship, I even found an altar with this inscription: TO THE UNKNOWN GOD. Therefore, the One whom you worship without knowing, Him I proclaim to you." —Acts 17:22–23

"We trust not because *'a* God' exists, but because *'this* God' exists," wrote C. S. Lewis. Why would he make this kind of statement? Then, as now, some people view God as an energy force that animates all living things while others bow before idols who represent an invisible divine being. Why would it make any difference about the kind of God we trust?

In Lewis' search for a spiritual reality beyond our visible world, he found that Jesus of Nazareth stood in a unique place as the real God only foreshadowed by ancient gods. Lewis would also come to see that the miracles Jesus Christ performed had the mark—the style—of those done by the Creator of our world. It was this God who had come to us in human form and in history who was the One who could be trusted for both daily life and life after death. He is the one true God.

God became a man and dwelt among us full of grace and truth.

FOR FURTHER READING: *The World's Last Night and Other Essays* by C. S. Lewis, "On Christianity in Belief"

READ: Mark 5:21–43

"Talitha, Cumi"

Then [Jesus] took the child by the hand, and said to her, "Talitha, cumi," which is translated, "Little girl, I say to you, arise."
—Mark 5:41

In Mark 5:41 we see the dramatic story of a dead child being brought back to life. Jesus led the mother and father of the dead girl into the room where her body lay. As He took her lifeless hand into His own, Christ was violating the Jewish prohibition against touching a dead body (Leviticus 21:1; Numbers 5:2–4). Yet as the Lord of life, Jesus would not be dissuaded from this act of compassion. Mark then gives us the actual Aramaic words Jesus spoke: "Talitha, cumi," which means, "Little girl, arise!" The child came back to life and even walked around the room. The parents were overwhelmed with amazement and joy. Then Christ told them not to share the miracle with others outside and to give the child something to eat.

Some people try to emphasize the compassion of Jesus while attempting to explain away the miracle. But raising the girl back to life also functioned as an unmistakable indication through this "sign and wonder" to her Jewish parents that the prophet from Nazareth was their Messiah. C. S. Lewis said, "A naturalistic Christianity leaves out all that is specifically Christian." The miracle of "Talitha, cumi" is Jesus' indication of who He really is.

*Miracles of compassion attested to the
Messianic nature of Jesus of Nazareth.*

FOR FURTHER READING: *Miracles* by C. S. Lewis, chapter 16

READ: 2 Timothy 1:3–12

Our Past and Present

When I call to remembrance the genuine faith that is in you, which dwelt first in your grandmother Lois and your mother Eunice, and I am persuaded is in you also.   —2 Timothy 1:5

In the book *The Allegory of Love*, C. S. Lewis observed: "Humanity does not pass through phases as a train passes through stations: being alive, it has the privilege of always moving yet never leaving anything behind. Whatever we have been, in some sort we are still." What we are now is part of what we have been in the past.

This can be seen in the life of Paul's disciple Timothy. As a child, Timothy's spiritual life had been molded by his grandmother Lois and his mother, Eunice. These women helped ground the faith of the boy Timothy in the Scriptures (2 Timothy 3:15). Timothy the man had been molded earlier as Timothy the child. What he had been as a child was still part of what he became as an adult (1:5).

It is good to realize that what we are now is part of a growing process from our past. In this way we can gain stability from what has grounded us, and we also take care to compensate for struggles from our earlier life. In the trajectory of our lives, the grace of God is always there to help us as we grow.

Understanding our past can help us grow in the present.

FOR FURTHER READING: *The Allegory of Love* by C. S. Lewis, chapter 11

READ: 1 Timothy 5:1–8

Charity Begins at Home

But if anyone does not provide for his own, and especially for those of his household, he has denied the faith and is worse than an unbeliever. —1 Timothy 5:8

Throughout the life of C. S. Lewis, family challenges were clearly evident. Whether it was responding to Mrs. Moore's many domestic demands or covering for his brother's alcoholism, Lewis often had his hands full. Yet he also realized that home is where the true test of charity lies. Of this Lewis wrote: "It is terrible to find how little progress one's philosophy and charity have made when they are brought to the test of domestic life."

In the Christian life, we can adopt a variety of well-intentioned ministry orientations. For the evangelist at heart, spreading the gospel can reign supreme. Likewise, the altruistic believer might focus on random acts of kindness. All these orientations are good, but none should supersede our domestic priority.

Life is comprised of competing responsibilities. That is why when ministry to others and needs at home come into competition, the family must always win out. Paul tells us that providing for one's own home is so essential that to not do so is equivalent to denying the Christian faith. The one who neglects the needs of family is worse than an unbeliever because even they recognize this priority (1 Timothy 5:8).

When ministry to others and needs at home come into competition, the family must win out.

For Further Reading: *The Letters of C. S. Lewis to Arthur Greeves,* edited by Walter Hooper

READ: Exodus 38:1–15

Different Kind of Mirrors

[Bezalel] made the basin of bronze and its stand of bronze, from the mirrors of the ministering women who ministered in the entrance of the tent of meeting. —Exodus 38:8 (ESV)

In the ancient Middle East, people used polished brass metal for mirrors instead of glass. When bronze metal was needed to construct the hand basin in the tabernacle, the women of Israel donated their polished bronze mirrors. It has been wisely observed: "That which once reflected their natural faces was now to be used to remind men of their need of spiritual cleansing that they might reflect the glory of God."

Often we look to other sources for a reflection of ourselves. What our friends say or the recognition we receive at work may be the reflection we use to measure ourselves by. But seeking a flattering image from the wrong source can be misleading. In *The Voyage of the Dawn Treader*, Lucy discovers a magical book with a spell to make her beautiful. Aslan helps her see that this kind of uncontrolled desire will lead down a path of destruction.

The Christian's true mirror is the Word of God. James tells us it shows what we look like on the inside (James 1:23–24). The Bible offers the most reliable reflection we have, and we can depend on God to make the changes that really count.

The reflection we see in the Bible helps us work on who we are on the inside.

FOR FURTHER READING: *The Voyage of the Dawn Treader*
by C. S. Lewis, chapter 10

READ: Matthew 25:31–45

Seeing the Needy as Christ

The King will answer and say to them, "Assuredly, I say to you, inasmuch as you did it to one of the least of these My brethren, you did it to Me." —Matthew 25:40

In a letter to his friend Don Giovanni Calabria, C. S. Lewis talked about his view of people who are in need: "In the poor man, who knocks at my door, in my ailing mother, in the young man who seeks my advice, the Lord Himself is present: therefore let us wash His feet."

In Christ's prediction of His return, He commends those who demonstrated a heart of compassion: "Then the King will say to those on His right hand, 'Come, you blessed of My Father, inherit the kingdom prepared for you from the foundation of the world: for I was hungry and you gave Me food; I was thirsty and you gave Me drink; I was a stranger and you took Me in; I was naked and you clothed Me; I was sick and you visited Me; I was in prison and you came to Me.' . . . 'Assuredly, I say to you, inasmuch as you did it to one of the least of these My brethren, you did it to Me'" (Matthew 25:34–36, 40). The key to helping the needy is to see them as Christ does.

We should ask God to help us see those in need as Christ himself does—and then respond with Christlike compassion.

FOR FURTHER READING: *The Latin Letters of C. S. Lewis*

READ: Isaiah 14:12–15; Ezekiel 28:11–19

Evil Imitation

I will make myself like the Most High. —Isaiah 14:14 (ESV)

In C. S. Lewis' fantasy novel *The Last Battle,* the evil ape Shift dupes Narnia's inhabitants into thinking he is the spokesman for Aslan. Actually, Shift has put a lion skin around a donkey named Puzzle. When Narnia's enemies, the Calormenes, become part of the scheme, Shift decides to combine the identity of their vulture-headed god Tash with the fake Aslan. He tells all who will listen that both are the same god, Tashlan. In this way the crafty ape wishes to consolidate his power.

Lewis' retelling of the story of Antichrist in Narnian terms is insightful. He understood that evil imitates. This is clear from the early records of the Bible concerning the origin of evil. In Isaiah 14 we read of how the archangel Lucifer fell into sin through pronouncement: "I will make myself *like* the Most High" (Isaiah 14:14 ESV).

False doctrine has a way of borrowing biblical truths and then recombining them into falsehood. Even in the garden of Eden, we see the devil citing God's Word out of context in order to deceive Adam and Eve (Genesis 3:1–6). The discerning Christian must remember that evil imitates.

*Just because someone claims the Word of God
as his authority does not mean that what he
says accurately represents God's truth.*

FOR FURTHER READING: *The Last Battle*
by C. S. Lewis, chapter 9

READ: Psalm 119:1–18

Why and How?

Open my eyes, that I may see wondrous things from Your law.
—Psalm 119:18

On the subject of literary criticism, C. S. Lewis wrote: "The genuine critical question [is] 'Why, and how, should we read this?'"

This is an important question to bring to personal Bible study. Any passage we read belongs to a book within the inspired collection of Scripture. The Pentateuch gives us an overview of the origin of all life and the beginning of God's chosen people. The historical books show the Jews occupying the Promised Land, the rise of the royal throne, and the deportation of the Hebrew people to a foreign country. The wisdom literature gives us insight into the human experience of testing and praise. Prophetic books speak words of exhortation to Israel and promises for God's future kingdom. The Gospels record Christ's life, teaching, death, resurrection, and ascension. The book of Acts tells us of the expansion of the early church. And the Epistles record correspondence from the apostles with practical and doctrinal content. Finally, the book of Revelation tells us of the end times and of God's future kingdom.

When we study a Bible passage, we should first ask where it fits into God's redemptive story. Then we should ask, "How can it change my life?"

*Each book of the Bible represents a different
chapter in God's redemptive story.*

FOR FURTHER READING: *What the Bible Is All About*
by Henrietta Mears

READ: Psalm 45:1–17

The Writer's Heart

My heart is composing a goodly matter; I speak of the verses which I have made concerning the King; my tongue is the pen of a ready writer. —Psalm 45:1 (KJ21)

Do you have the passion to write? C. S. Lewis seems to have had it. He said, "I am sure that some are born to write as trees are born to bear leaves." And in today's Scripture reading we read words written by "a ready writer."

Recording a wedding between the house of David and a princess bride, the author of Psalm 45 reveals a heartfelt conviction to put down on paper the vivid life experiences he sees and feels. "My tongue is the pen" refers to an instrument ready to be used by God (v. 1). The words flow fast because their inspiration has brought a fluency of expression. The writer's heart helps capture and convey to others the events of life.

Not all of us will become published writers. But there are advantages to writing down our experiences for personal growth and encouragement to others. Some have taken up the discipline of writing their personal experiences in a journal. The person they were years ago can give insight on how to face current issues. Others take pen (or smartphone) in hand to compose words of encouragement to those in need. You don't have to be C. S. Lewis to be a "ready writer."

All of us can exhibit a writer's heart by encouraging others with our words.

FOR FURTHER READING: *The Letters of C. S. Lewis to Arthur Greeves,* edited by Walter Hooper

READ: Psalm 61:1–8

A Place of Shelter

For You have been a shelter for me, a strong tower from the enemy.
—Psalm 61:3

In the beautiful pictorial book *The Inklings of Oxford* by Harry Lee Poe and James Ray Veneman, beautiful images of an ancient university city are exhibited. But the book also contains unexpected photos such as that of the concrete bomb shelter Jack Lewis built during World War II. Realizing that aerial bombardment by German planes was a real possibility, Jack began to pour the cement to create this underground structure to keep his family safe during an air raid.

Life is often filled with conflict. When we feel vulnerable, a place of shelter is what we need. In Psalm 61, we read that David experienced great comfort from the protection God provided him. The Hebrew word *mahseh* gives the idea of "shelter from danger" (v. 3). The high ground of protection can also be seen in the tower imagery attributed to God (v. 3). But most importantly, David, a man after God's own heart, wanted to draw his strength from being in God's holy and loving presence (v. 4). Only there can peace and joy be experienced in relationship with the Creator, Redeemer, and Friend. That is our real place of shelter.

For the believer, God alone is the ultimate shelter.

FOR FURTHER READING: *The Inklings of Oxford*
by Harry Lee Poe and James Ray Veneman

READ: 1 Corinthians 13:8–12

Only a Sketch

Now we see in a mirror, dimly, but then face to face. Now I know in part, but then I shall know just as I also am known.
—1 Corinthians 13:12

In *The Weight of Glory*, C. S. Lewis tells the story of a woman who gave birth to a son while confined as a prisoner in a dungeon. Since the boy had never seen the outside world, his mother tried to describe it by making pencil drawings. Later, when he and his mother were released from prison, the simple pencil sketches were replaced by the actual images of our beautiful world.

In a similar way, the inspired picture the Bible gives us of heaven will someday be replaced by joyful, direct experience. Of this, Paul wrote, "Now we see in a mirror, dimly, but then face to face. Now I know in part, but then I shall know just as I also am known" (1 Corinthians 13:12). Yet Paul's confidence in future glory gave him strength in the midst of trial (Romans 8:18).

Our current idea of the glories of heaven is only a simple sketch. But we can be completely confident in Jesus' claim that He has gone to prepare a place for us (John 14:1–3). The best is yet to come!

One day our current idea of heaven will be replaced by the glory of its reality.

FOR FURTHER READING: *The Weight of Glory*
by C. S. Lewis, "Transposition"

READ: 1 Corinthians 13:1–13

Childish Things

When I was a child, I spoke as a child, I understood as a child, I thought as a child; but when I became a man, I put away childish things. —1 Corinthians 13:11

The serious work of a scholar and an appreciation for fairy tales would appear to be mutually exclusive concepts. C. S. Lewis, however, was a remarkable example of someone who excelled at both. At Oxford he wrote works on literary criticism that are still highly valued today. In addition, Lewis spent considerable time writing in the genre of fairy tale through the Narnia Chronicles. Of fairy tales, Lewis wrote: "When I was ten, I read fairy tales in secret and would have been ashamed if I had been found doing so. Now that I am fifty I read them openly. When I became a man *I put away childish things*, including the fear of childishness and the desire to be very grown up."

Why did Lewis cling to fairy tales long into his mature years? Perhaps part of the answer lies in what he said in *Mere Christianity* about heart and mind: "[God] wants a child's heart, but a grown-up's head. He wants us to be simple, single-minded, affectionate, and teachable, as good children are; but He also wants every bit of intelligence we have to be alert at its job, and in first-class fighting trim." In our maturity, may we also cherish things that keep our hearts as soft as a child's.

> *God wants the heart of a child but also all the intelligence we have for His use.*

FOR FURTHER READING: *Of Other Worlds: Essays and Stories* by C. S. Lewis, "On Three Ways of Writing for Children"

READ: Ephesians 1:3–14; 3:1–9

An Exciting Mystery

Having made known to us the mystery of [God's] will, according to His good pleasure which He purposed in Himself.
—Ephesians 1:9

In C. S. Lewis' science fiction work *Out of the Silent Planet*, Dr. Elwin Ransom reflects on the excitement of seeing a mystery open up before him on another world: "To every man, in his acquaintance with a new art, there comes a moment when that which before was meaningless first lifts, as it were, one corner of the curtain that hides its mystery, and reveals, in a burst of delight which later and fuller understanding can hardly ever equal, one glimpse of the indefinite possibilities within."

After Saul of Tarsus encountered the risen Christ, he was transformed into the apostle Paul. As a child he had been schooled in the separation between Jews and Gentiles. God had a special relationship with the Hebrews that pagans would never know. But when Paul came to Christ, God showed him an exciting mystery. He revealed how Christ's atoning work would be extended to all who believe. And He proclaimed this message: "The Gentiles should be fellow heirs, of the same body, and partakers of His promise in Christ through the gospel" (Ephesians 3:6). The exciting mystery had been revealed!

God wants us to explore the exciting mystery that we are blessed in the heavenly places in Christ.

FOR FURTHER READING: *Out of the Silent Planet* by C. S. Lewis, chapter 19

READ: Romans 16:1–27

Ministry Bond

I thank my God upon every remembrance of you, always in every prayer of mine making request for you all with joy, for your fellowship in the gospel from the first day until now.

—Philippians 1:3–5

In his essay "Kipling's World," C. S. Lewis sees how common work can lead to a common bond: "What Kipling chiefly communicates—and it is, for good and for ill, one of the strongest things in the world—is the peculiar relation which men who do the same work have to that work and to one another . . . We who are of one trade (whether journalists, soldiers . . . or what you will) know so many things that the outsider will never, never understand . . . We belong. It is a bond which in real life sometimes proves stronger than any other."

Certainly, the bond of ministry shares that same kind of connection. Paul told the church at Philippi of his appreciation for them in the "fellowship in the gospel" (Philippians 1:5). Likewise, in the final chapter of Paul's letter to the church at Rome, we see a long list of people and relationships in ministry. These greetings and commendations include no less than twenty-seven people. Reciprocally, Paul sends other greetings from the colleagues who are with him. To serve Christ together is to experience a valuable ministry bond.

*The camaraderie of the gospel binds active
Christians in a shared sense of mission.*

FOR FURTHER READING: *Selected Literary Essays*
by C. S. Lewis, "Kipling's World"

READ: 1 John 5:1–21

Avoiding Idols

Little children, keep yourselves from idols. —1 John 5:21

In *The Great Divorce*, we read how legitimate affections can make themselves into false gods:

"Human beings can't make one another really happy for long . . . You cannot love a fellow-creature fully till you love God . . . No natural feelings are high or low, holy or unholy, in themselves. They are all holy when God's hand is on the reigns. They all go bad when they set up on their own and make themselves into false gods."

The love for a child, romantic feelings between a man and a woman, and other affections are all gifts from God. But if these emotional connections replace our love for our Creator, they can become a form of idolatry. The last verse of John's first epistle ends with a startling statement: "Little children, keep yourselves from idols" (1 John 5:21). Because this verse does not really fit the content that has preceded it, one might conclude that it is as a startling "PS" put there for emphasis. In the apostle's day, temples to Artemis, Aphrodite, Apollo, and other pagan gods abounded. But most likely in writing to a Christian audience, John was thinking of any attachment that would rival the love of God. Listen to John—and Lewis—and avoid the idols of our world.

Only when we submit our affections to God's
guidance can they be effectively expressed.

FOR FURTHER READING: *The Great Divorce* by C. S. Lewis, chapter 11

READ: Psalm 121:1–8

Pilgrimage

I will lift up my eyes to the hills—from whence comes my help? My help comes from the LORD, who made heaven and earth.
—Psalm 121:1–2

C. S. Lewis revered Chaucer's *Canterbury Tales*: "For many historians of literature, and for all general readers, the great mass of Chaucer's work is simply a background to the *Canterbury Tales*, and the whole output of the fourteenth century is simply a background to Chaucer."

In high school, many of us read Chaucer's *Canterbury Tales* because it gave us a window into the lives of different kinds of customs, vocations, and attitudes that were part of the medieval world. It tells the story of various people going on a spiritual pilgrimage to the English city of Canterbury.

Those from Roman Catholic and Eastern Orthodox traditions see the value of making one's way to a holy site for spiritual inspiration. Even some Protestants will make their way to the Holy Land to see the places where our Lord ministered, taught, died, and rose from the dead.

Psalm 121 is about spiritual pilgrimage. It is called a "Song of Ascents." During the annual festivals, the Hebrew people made pilgrimages to the temple at Jerusalem, which was built on a hilly region. As the faithful approached their spiritual destination, they ascended singing this psalm in worship. What joy we experience when we praise God while going to our place of worship!

Going to a place of spiritual inspiration can encourage us in our day-to-day journey to our eternal home.

FOR FURTHER READING: *The Allegory of Love* by C. S. Lewis, chapter 4

READ: Mark 7:1–37

Ephphatha

Then, looking up to heaven, [Jesus] sighed, and said to [the deaf man], "Ephphatha," that is, "Be opened." —Mark 7:34

Sometimes we are given front row seats to watch the miracles of our Lord. In today's reading we watched Jesus Christ place His fingers in a deaf man's ears. Christ looked up to His Father and sighed in empathy for the man's long struggle with deafness and muteness. Jesus then said, "Ephphatha"—which is Aramaic for "be opened." This man's ears were opened, and his tongue was loosed immediately.

In his book *Miracles*, C. S. Lewis tells us that God always is behind the everyday healing process we experience. Whether it is a cut finger or surgical wounds, God has designed the body to heal itself. Indeed, without this provision of healing, none of us would have survived childhood. Yet Lewis wisely observes the reality of divine supernatural healing, which took place through Christ's ministry: "But once God did [healing] visibly to the sick in Palestine, a Man meeting with men. . . . The Power that always was behind all healings puts on a face and hands." Those deformities and severe illnesses that could not be restored by natural process were remedied through the supernatural touch of the Son of Man.

Jesus Christ could speak a word and nature was obligated to respond: "Ephphatha: Be opened."

FOR FURTHER READING: *Miracles* by C. S. Lewis, chapter 15

READ: Hebrews 11:1–10

Hope

Having been justified by His grace we should become heirs according to the hope of eternal life. —Titus 3:7

James Stuart Bell's book *From the Library of C. S. Lewis* contains many key sources that informed the thinking of C. S. Lewis. One citing in the book is from Martin Luther's *Table Talk*. It sets forth the great reformer's views on the human need for hope: "Everything that is done in the world is done by hope. No husbandman would sow one grain of corn, if he hoped not it would grow up and become seed; no bachelor would marry a wife, if he hoped not to have children; no merchant or tradesman would set himself to work, if he did not hope to reap benefit thereby. How much more, then, does hope urge us on to everlasting life and salvation?"

Luther understood that expecting a positive outcome in the walk of faith is grounded in the character of the God of grace. Hebrews tells us, "Now faith is the substance of things hoped for, the evidence of things not seen" (Hebrews 11:1). What follows in Hebrews 11 is a fascinating list of Old Testament believers whose lives were changed by hoping in the faithfulness of God. Do we share this hope?

God has built the need for hope into every aspect of life.
Let's have hope as we face each problem today.

For Further Reading: *From the Library of C. S. Lewis*
by James Stuart Bell, Introduction

READ: Deuteronomy 6:4–9

Spiritual Influence

And these words which I command you today shall be in your heart. You shall teach them diligently to your children, and shall talk of them when you sit in your house, when you walk by the way, when you lie down, and when you rise up.

—Deuteronomy 6:6–7

C. S. Lewis answered a letter from a little girl named Sarah. In his correspondence Lewis shared about a new acquaintance he had made at the college: "I am getting to be quite friends with an old Rabbit who lives in the Wood at Magdalen [College]. I pick leaves off the trees for him because he can't reach up to the branches and he eats them out of my hand. One day he stood up on his hind legs and put his front paws against me, he was so greedy. I wrote this about it: 'A funny old man had a habit of giving a leaf to a rabbit. At first it was shy. But then, by and by, it got rude and would stand up to grab it.'"

We can learn from Lewis' correspondence with children. Sometimes in our zeal to nurture the spiritual lives of children we try to focus as often as possible on Bible verses. But as we see in this letter to a child, Lewis took time to share a fun interaction with a member of God's creation. Is there any better way to celebrate God's creation than with a greedy rabbit?

Children can be spiritually influenced by enjoying life experiences with us.

For Further Reading: *C. S. Lewis: Letters to Children* by Lyle W. Dorsett and Marjorie Lamp Mead

READ: Acts 14:8–18

Leveraging Legends

Now when the people saw what Paul had done, they raised their voices, saying in the Lycaonian language, "The gods have come down to us in the likeness of men!"　　　—Acts 14:11

In *That Hideous Strength,* C. S. Lewis explores spiritual warfare between a Christian community and evil leaders at a university. Although Ransom is the spiritual director of a Christian fellowship, he also enlists help from Merlyn from the time of King Arthur. In this way Lewis is able to retain Christian beliefs while still using medieval ideas to illustrate the war against scientific evil. At one point Ransom tells his colleagues, "We in this house are all that is left of Logres [King Arthur's kingdom often also called Camelot]." He is able to say this because of the deeply Christian underpinnings of that legendary kingdom.

The apostle Paul was no stranger to encountering legend and myth and turning it to his advantage in explaining the gospel. On Mars Hill, as he preached on "the unknown God," he cited a pagan poet who had described God's nature in a way compatible with Scripture (Acts 17:22–34). And when the pagans mistook him for a pagan god after seeing the miracle he had performed, he pointed to the living God of Scripture in Christ (Acts 14).

Even legend, myth, and pagan ideas can be taken captive and repurposed in Christ's service.

FOR FURTHER READING: *That Hideous Strength* by C. S. Lewis, chapter 10

READ: 2 Timothy 3:16–17; 2 Peter 1:16–21

Bible Translations

And the common people heard Him gladly. —Mark 12:37

Many of us love the familiar eloquence of the King James Version of the Bible. Psalm 23 and other wonderful passages of Scripture just don't touch the heart as does the 1611 translation.

However, in the early seventeenth century when it was translated, the KJV was not considered eloquent. It was thought of as an easy-to-read edition designed for the general population. In fact, the three committees in London, Oxford, and Cambridge that translated the Greek and Hebrew biblical texts were commissioned to make it understandable to the average person of their day. It is only the passage of time and the changes in our language along the way that make it sound so lofty and eloquent to our modern ears.

In the introduction to J. B. Phillips' *Letters to Young Churches,* C. S. Lewis writes: "The same divine humility which decreed that God should become a baby at a peasant-woman's breast . . . decreed also that He should be preached in a vulgar, prosaic and unliterary language." In response to Jesus' preaching, we are told, "the common people heard Him gladly" (Mark 12:37). Whatever translation we choose, we should keep in mind that the message of the Bible is meant to be accessible to all.

The Bible's message should be clear and understandable.

For Further Reading: *God in the Dock* by C. S. Lewis, "Of Modern Translations of the Bible"

READ: Acts 20:1–27

An Education in Itself

For I have not shunned to declare to you the whole counsel of God.
—Acts 20:27

C. S. Lewis has an explanation for the success of John Bunyan's *Pilgrim's Progress*. In *Mere Christianity*, Lewis wrote: "One of the reasons why it needs no special education to be a Christian is that Christianity is an education itself. That is why an uneducated believer like Bunyan was able to write a book that has astonished the whole world."

John Bunyan had little formal education and had the modest occupation of tinker, an itinerant tinsmith who mended household utensils. Because he would not become a member of the Church of England, he was forbidden to preach. When he would not obey this prohibition, Bunyan was put in prison. Astonishingly, his sentence turned out to be twelve long years. During that time Bunyan devoted himself to writing *Pilgrim's Progress* and other theological works.

When God got ahold of the apostle Paul's life, He revealed His redemptive plan of grace that was anticipated in the Old Testament. Because of his preaching, the apostle Paul, like Bunyan, was no stranger to imprisonment, and while there he wrote several letters that would become for millions of believers an education in itself.

In our study of Scripture, we come to understand
that "Christianity is an education itself."

For Further Reading: *Mere Christianity* by C. S. Lewis, Book 3

READ: Colossians 3:2; 2 Timothy 2:4; Titus 2:11–14; 1 John 2:15–17

Creature Comforts

The cares of this world, the deceitfulness of riches, and the desires for other things entering in choke the word, and it becomes unfruitful.   —Mark 4:19

In *The Silver Chair,* the fourth of C. S. Lewis' seven Chronicles of Narnia books, Eustace and Jill, along with their companion Puddleglum, have been sent on a mission to rescue Prince Rilian. Because their arduous trek includes long marches, hunger, and cold, Jill is tempted to listen more to the lure of promised comforts than to remember their mission of rescue. She has been told of "gentle giants" in Harfang who will give them food, warmth, and shelter. The giants invite them to celebrate the autumn feast with them. What Jill doesn't understand is that she and Eustace are to be eaten by the giants. Fortunately, the children escape and eventually rescue Prince Rilian.

The seductive allure of the world can be a threat to the believer as he fulfills his mission on earth. Yet God can strengthen us to resist creature comforts. Moses illustrates this: "By faith Moses, when he became of age, refused to be called the son of Pharaoh's daughter, choosing rather to suffer affliction with the people of God than to enjoy the passing pleasures of sin" (Hebrews 11:24–25). A life of royal comforts was abandoned in order to follow the call of God.

> *When creature comforts compete with our call, we can ask the Lord for a heart of obedience.*

FOR FURTHER READING: *The Silver Chair* by C. S. Lewis, chapter 8

READ: Genesis 1:1–5, 26–29; John 1:1; Colossians 1:16

Dream of the Rood

And God said, "See, I have given you every herb that yields seed which is on the face of all the earth, and every tree whose fruit yields seed; to you it shall be for food. —Genesis 1:29

J. R. R. Tolkien was a lifelong friend of C. S. Lewis, and the two critiqued each other's writings in a group they called the Inklings. Tolkien was a renowned scholar of Anglo-Saxon literature, and this provided a resource out of which the marvelous world of *The Lord of the Rings* came.

Much Anglo-Saxon literature was influenced by the Christian faith. *The Dream of the Rood* tells the story of the crucifixion and resurrection of Christ from the viewpoint of the tree that supplied the wood for the cross. The tree does not want to participate in the torture and murder of its Creator. However, it is commanded to do so in order that Christ might provide redemption for all who believe.

Sometimes God is criticized for standing aloof from a world He created—a world filled with pain. But this Anglo-Saxon story and the witness of Scripture showcase a remarkable insight. Jesus Christ created our world, allowed free will that produced sin, and then entered history to suffer for our redemption. Jesus did indeed create the tree that would become the cross on which He died for you and me.

In order to redeem us, and all of creation, Christ died on a cross.

For Further Reading: *The Dream of the Rood: An Old English Poem Attributed to Cynewulf*

READ: Psalm 27:1–14

Poet as Storyteller

Though an army may encamp against me, my heart shall not fear;
though war may rise against me, in this I will be confident.
—Psalm 27:3

In his book *English Literature in the Sixteenth Century: Excluding Drama*, C. S. Lewis writes of his favorite poet Edmund Spenser. "Spenser is an essentially narrative poet. No one loves him who does not love his story; outside the poems to the books and cantos he scarcely writes a line that is not for the story's sake. His style is to be judged as the style of a storyteller."

Spenser himself tells us what he writes of: "Fierce warres and faithfull loves shall moralize my song." The life story of King David would seem to be one of those kinds of stories. It is replete with its own tales of war and love contained within the music of the Psalms. In Psalm 27 we read of the comfort and confidence the great king experiences in the context of war. David tells us that even in combat his deepest desire is to spend time adoring his Creator and Redeemer in the sanctuary: "One thing I have desired of the LORD, that will I seek: That I may dwell in the house of the LORD all the days of my life, to behold the beauty of the LORD" (v. 4). God's presence can sustain us even in life's most challenging conflicts.

In the midst of conflict, great comfort and confidence can
be found in trusting and adoring the living God.

FOR FURTHER READING: *English Literature in the Sixteenth Century: Excluding Drama* by C. S. Lewis, Book 3

READ: Hebrews 11:1–16

Homesick

But now they desire a better, that is, a heavenly country. There-
fore God is not ashamed to be called their God, for He has pre-
pared a city for them. —Hebrews 11:16

In C. S. Lewis' science fiction work *Out of the Silent Planet*, Elwin
Ransom and two other companions are in a race against time to make
it back to Earth from Mars before their oxygen runs out. Ransom's
longing for home intensifies as he takes his turn in steering the space-
craft toward his home planet: "Now that he was navigating, his celestial
mood was shattered. Wild, animal thirst for life, mixed with homesick
longing for the free airs and the sights and smells of earth—for grass
and meat and beer and tea and the human voice—awoke in him."

In a different culture far away from home, we often are excited
about the unique customs, clothes, and conversation we encounter. But
after days of starry-eyed appreciation, our initial enthusiasm begins to
wane. Frustrations with not knowing the language and yearnings for
familiar foods, sights, and sounds begin to surface. Then a deep form
of homesickness can set in. Sometimes in our spiritual lives we can feel
like this world is a foreign country. This is because our true and eternal
home is with God (Hebrews 11:16). Contemplating our true home can
bring renewed hope to our weary lives.

Believers' true homeland is with Christ.

FOR FURTHER READING: *Out of the Silent Planet*
by C. S. Lewis, chapter 21

READ: Romans 1:18–25

Winnable Pagans

Professing to be wise, they became fools, and changed the glory of the incorruptible God into an image made like corruptible man— and birds and four-footed animals and creeping things.
—Romans 1:22–23

In his essay "Is Theism Important?" C. S. Lewis reflects on how unbelievers are open to the gospel. When told by a concerned Christian that England was lapsing back into paganism, Lewis surprisingly responded: "Would that she were. For I do not think it at all likely that we should ever see Parliament opened by the slaughtering of a garlanded white bull in the House of Lords or Cabinet Ministers leaving sandwiches in Hyde Park as an offering to the Dryads." Lewis then goes on to say that a pagan England would be a good thing. For we have seen in history how worshippers of false gods with a conscience heavy with sin will welcome the gospel of Jesus Christ and redemption.

A person who adheres to a non-Christian religion should not be dismissed as unreceptive to Christ. Indeed Paul saw a fruitful witness in evangelizing idolaters. Their practice of placating their gods for forgiveness was an indicator of the need for redemption. Our non-Christian friends should be pointed to Christ as the authentic Redeemer they seek. Religious substitutes are symptoms of a spiritual need that can only be fulfilled in Christ.

Humans are by nature religious creatures who need to be led to the only authentic source of forgiveness and power—the Lord Jesus Christ.

FOR FURTHER READING: *God in the Dock* by C. S. Lewis, "Is Theism Important?"

READ: Ephesians 2:1–10; Philippians 2:1–13

God's Good Works

For we are His workmanship, created in Christ Jesus for good works, which God prepared beforehand that we should walk in them. —Ephesians 2:10

Often we think in terms of our doing good works for God. But C. S. Lewis helps us understand that no authentic act of kindness is ever generated by our hearts alone. Of this, he wrote: "No good work is done anywhere without aid from the Father of Lights."

Whenever we do a good work, behind the scenes is the ever-present God, who places grace in our motives and power in our actions.

But how can Lewis make such a statement? First, he is citing the epistle of James, which reminds us that even our ability to do good works is a gift from God: "Every good gift and every perfect gift is from above, and comes down from the Father of lights, with whom there is no variation or shadow of turning" (James 1:17). Second, he is indirectly drawing on that central principle of the Christian life that the yielded heart and divine empowerment are at work: "Work out your own salvation with fear and trembling; for it is God who works in you both to will and to do for His good pleasure" (Philippians 2:12–13).

God has chosen to work through our wills to find a need and fill it or to find a heart and heal it.

For Further Reading: *Reflections on the Psalms* by C. S. Lewis, chapter 11

READ: Luke 1:26–38

The Virgin Birth

The angel said to her, "Do not be afraid, Mary, for you have found favor with God. And behold, you will conceive in your womb and bring forth a Son, and shall call His name JESUS."

—Luke 1:30–31

C. S. Lewis was adamant in his belief in the virgin birth of Christ: "There was of course unique reasons for it. That time [God] was creating not simply a man but the Man who was to be Himself: was creating Man anew: was beginning, at this divine and human point, the New Creation of all things. The whole soiled and weary universe quivered at this direct injection of essential life—direct, uncontaminated, not drained through all the crowded history of Nature."

Lewis' reflections on the virgin birth can revolutionize the way we see our universe. Imagine all the star clusters that make up the Milky Way. Think back to the first time you looked through a microscope and saw previously invisible tiny creatures swimming in a drop of water. All of creation will someday be remade into something gloriously new. But the starting point for God's redemption of His creation began in the reproductive system of a young Jewish teenager in the first century. The New Creation began in her womb, was born, grew to manhood, died for our redemption, and rose from the grave. The virgin birth is the starting point for the new creation.

The virgin birth is an essential doctrine because that is how the incarnation of Christ took place.

FOR FURTHER READING: *Miracles* by C. S. Lewis, chapter 15

READ: Matthew 11:1–19

Is God in This?

And when John had heard in prison about the works of Christ, he sent two of his disciples and said to Him, "Are You the Coming One, or do we look for another?" —Matthew 11:2–3

We may think that C. S. Lewis followed a direct leading from God in all of his writing. But the reality is that Lewis sometimes had his doubts. In a letter to Don Giovanni Calabria, Lewis asked for prayer as he wrote *Letters to Malcolm: Chiefly on Prayer.* "I invite your prayers about a work which I now have in hand. I am trying to write a book about private prayers. . . . I find many difficulties nor do I definitely know whether God wishes me to complete this task or not."

John the Baptist also experienced doubts about his spiritual mission. Anointed by the Holy Spirit before he was even born, John led a life of self-denial and preparation for his role as harbinger of the Christ (Luke 1:41; Matthew 3:3–4). After he bore witness to Jesus of Nazareth, he realized the Christ must increase while he must decrease (John 3:30). When he was imprisoned by Herod, however, John had doubts about Jesus being Messiah (Luke 7:19–20). Had he fulfilled his mission of announcing the Messiah? Christ did not rebuke John's wavering faith but instead pointed to the signs and wonders that attested to His Messianic ministry (Luke 7:22). When we have doubts, let's go back to Jesus.

*Circumstances may generate doubts,
but God's purposes will prevail.*

FOR FURTHER READING: *Latin Letters of C. S. Lewis*

READ: Revelation 2:1–7

Our First Love

Nevertheless I have this against you, that you have left your first love. —Revelation 2:4

The Christian is often faced with people and things that can become more important than God. This issue of competing affections is a problem not only for adults but also for children. In a letter to a child, C. S. Lewis wrote: "God knows quite well how hard we find it to love Him more than anyone or anything else, and He won't be angry with us as long as we are trying. And He will help us."

In today's reading we see our Lord's response to believers at Ephesus. Although they had remained committed to true doctrine, they were lacking in a matter of the heart. The Ephesian Christians had left their first love. The startling realization that even good things can take priority over Christ in our lives can trouble us. Nonetheless, the God of grace has provided a way back to re-enthrone Jesus Christ as our first love. It comes through confession of sin, repentance of will, and abiding in the Word. But even as we head down this road of restoration, we must always remember that God understands and "He *will* help us."

The first step in keeping Christ as our first love is to confess our sin and yield our will daily to His leading.

FOR FURTHER READING: *Letters to Children* by C. S. Lewis

READ: 1 Samuel 3:1–19; 1 Timothy 4:12–16

Defined by Age?

Therefore, whether you eat or drink, or whatever you do, do all to the glory of God. —1 Corinthians 10:31

Child movie stars, beauty queens, and aging employees all have strong opinions about how their age has affected the way they are treated. For most of us, how old we are will determine in some respect our role in life. Yet C. S. Lewis understood that the real person inside is not defined by age. In his science fiction novel *That Hideous Strength*, we Read: "Youth and age touch only the surface of our lives."

The boy Samuel received his first revelation of God as a child while serving in the tabernacle (1 Samuel 3:1–4). But the boy became a man and anointed two kings of Israel.

Young Pastor Timothy was told, "Let no one despise your youth, but be an example" (1 Timothy 4:12). Timothy did indeed mature and have a fruitful ministry for Christ.

As Paul advanced in age, he referred to himself as "Paul, the aged" (Philemon 1:9). Yet even with that realization, Paul continued to energetically serve the Lord.

In each case it was the trajectory of the spiritual life that counted. Children, young people, and the elderly can all serve the Lord—no matter their age.

We are not defined by our age but by our use of resources for the Lord.

FOR FURTHER READING: *That Hideous Strength*
by C. S. Lewis, chapter 1

READ: Romans 5:1–11

Get Better Not Bitter

Looking diligently lest any man fail of the grace of God; lest any root of bitterness springing up trouble you, and thereby many be defiled. —Hebrews 12:15 (KJV)

In a letter to a friend, C. S. Lewis reflected on how our response to suffering affects the kind of people we become. Some, he observed, were growing and magnificent souls who had offered their suffering to God and therefore had experienced unusual grace. In stark contrast, Lewis had also seen that when people he considered selfish and egotistical experienced pain, suffering seemed to produce resentment, blasphemy, and even greater pride.

It is a theme of Scripture that how we respond to suffering will affect our personal character for good or ill. A positive response to pain can make us resilient and filled with hope (Romans 5:3–4). But indulging in bitterness can poison the soul and even damage others (Hebrews 12:15). Some interpreters see "the root of bitterness" as an attitude of resentment and revenge coming from an imagined or real personal wound. The only solution to such a contaminated heart is to dig it out (Matthew 13:24–30). By heartfelt confession, repentance, and thanksgiving, bitterness can be replaced with gratefulness for the grace of God.

Depending upon our response, a personal injury from another can make us better or bitter.

READ: John 12:1–9

Fragrance of Brokenness

*Then Mary took about a pint of pure nard, an expensive perfume;
she poured it on Jesus' feet and wiped his feet with her hair. And
the house was filled with the fragrance of the perfume.*

—John 12:3 (NIV)

In a letter to a friend, C. S. Lewis reflected on the anointing of Jesus:
"The allegorical sense of her great action dawned on me the other day.
The precious alabaster box which one must break over the Holy Feet
is one's heart. . . . And the contents become perfume only when it is
broken."

Sometimes when we see a believer go through unimaginable suffering, we marvel at the spiritual power and beauty that buoys them
along. Where there should be frantic trauma at a tragic loss, there is a
calm sense of peace. Instead of deep despair over irretrievable loss, we
see a spiritual joy. How can this be? What we are most likely observing
is the Holy Spirit operating according to His job description. He has
been sent into our hearts to comfort us in times of sorrow. Lewis saw in
the record of the woman who anointed our Lord's feet an illustration of
how the human heart can release a wonderful spiritual fragrance only
after it has been broken. God's comfort may be overwhelming at times,
and at other times it may be withdrawn to test us. But in our brokenness the God of all comfort is always near to help.

*Sometimes it is not until we are broken that we can
experience the inner sweetness of the Spirit.*

FOR FURTHER READING: *Letters to an American Lady* by C. S. Lewis

READ: John 12:1–8

Using People

This he said, not that he cared for the poor, but because he was a thief, and had the money box; and he used to take what was put in it. —John 12:6

In *The Magician's Nephew*, we see a pattern of manipulating others. While in her home world of Charn, the wicked Queen Jadis focuses all her attention on the boy Digory, who had awakened her from her enchanted sleep. But when in our world, she shifts her exploitive behavior to Digory's unscrupulous Uncle Andrew. We are told in the story: "I expect most witches are like that. They are not interested in things or people unless they can use them; they are terribly practical."

Manipulation of others is often a characteristic of evil. For more than three years our Lord carried out His public ministry while Judas Iscariot masqueraded as a genuine disciple. One of the few times Judas stood out from the rest was in his self-righteous objection to Mary anointing the feet of Jesus with expensive nard. His complaint was that the money could have been saved and given to the poor. But the biblical writer tells us that his real motive was to keep the money for himself. Judas manipulated others for his own profit (John 12:6). Evil looks for opportunities to use others for its own ends.

The wicked manipulate people,
while the godly minister to them.

FOR FURTHER READING: *The Magician's Nephew*
by C. S. Lewis, chapter 6

READ: Colossians 2:1–15

Rejoice in Sins Forgiven

Having wiped out the handwriting of requirements that was against us, which was contrary to us. And He has taken it out of the way, having nailed it to the cross.   —Colossians 2:14

In a letter to his friend Don Giovanni Calabria, C. S. Lewis wrote, "You write about your own sins. Beware . . . lest humility should pass over into anxiety or sadness. It is bidden us to 'rejoice and always rejoice.' Jesus has cancelled the handwriting which was against us. Lift up our hearts!"

Each of us struggles with an awareness of personal sin. Yet it is important to remember that the cross of Christ is God's master weapon for redeeming and reconciling us to himself. In Paul's letter to the church at Colossi, he makes reference to the clear prohibitions of the law of God that we have all violated in thought, speech, and behavior. Yet this dilemma has been solved by the cross of Christ. There the "handwriting of the ordinances against us were nailed" (see Colossians 2). Because Jesus took the punishment in our place, we were absolved of our guilt and given a new life.

We must appropriately grieve, confess, and repent of our sin. We do this with the realization that our sins were put upon Christ on the cross so we could become righteous and acceptable to God in Him.

The foundation of our walk with Christ is the finished work of Christ on the cross.

FOR FURTHER READING: *The Latin Letters of C. S. Lewis*

Crossroads and Short Cuts

Stand at the crossroads and look; ask for the ancient paths, ask where the good way is, and walk in it, and you will find rest for your souls. But you said, "We will not walk in it."

—Jeremiah 6:16 (NIV)

In his literary essay "The Vision of John Bunyan," C. S. Lewis reflects on the pleasures and pains of life experience amidst the choices we make in life's journey: "Most, I fancy, have discovered that to be born is to be exposed to delights and miseries greater than imagination could have anticipated; that the choice of ways at any cross-road may be more important than we think; and that short cuts may lead to very nasty places."

In our reading today we see that Jeremiah rebuked Judah for listening to false prophecies and living lives of unrepentant sin. In his preaching, the prophet underscores that God's people had passed a pivotal crossroads. There they could have chosen a path back to the ancient ways of obedience and found rest for their souls. Instead they chose to listen to falsehoods and follow their own self-interests. Those shortcuts would soon lead to calamity.

What are you experiencing today? Are you in a happy time, or are you in a place of painful testing? In either case be reminded that the decisions we make will have consequences. Shortcuts will only create more problems.

Life is a series of blessings and testings, and godly choices will lead us into the path of righteousness.

FOR FURTHER READING: *Selected Literary Essays*
by C. S. Lewis, "The Vision of John Bunyan"

READ: Matthew 24:24; 2 Thessalonians 2:3–10;
Revelation 13:11–17

The Dark Tower

*Then the lawless one will be revealed, whom the Lord Jesus will
consume with the breath of His mouth and destroy with the
brightness of His coming.* —2 Thessalonians 2:8

The Dark Tower is an incomplete science fiction manuscript believed
to have been written by C. S. Lewis. Walter Hooper, who was Lewis'
personal secretary, found this unfinished manuscript and edited it as
a short story for publication. It is a dark tale with a possible biblical
connection. *The Dark Tower* begins with a discussion by Cambridge
academics concerning time travel. Using a "chronoscope" (time tele-
scope) to observe "Othertime," they see human automatons controlled
by a tyrant. The plotline of *The Dark Tower* involves the enslavement of
others in a futurist world.

To some readers it could bring to mind the prophecies of the Bible
concerning Antichrist. The Bible tells us that there will be an evil world
leader at the end of the age. He is called "Anti-Christ" or one who stands
against or in place of God's anointed one (2 Thessalonians 2:3–10).
Satan will use this wicked man to control millions and oppose the worship of the one true God. Ultimately, Antichrist will be destroyed by the
Lord Jesus Christ upon His second coming.

*The devil's final attempt to rule our world through
Antichrist will be defeated by the Lord Jesus Christ.*

FOR FURTHER READING: *The Dark Tower* by C. S. Lewis,
edited by Walter Hooper

READ: Matthew 24:36–44

Any Moment Return

Therefore you also be ready, for the Son of Man is coming at an hour you do not expect. — Matthew 24:44

In *The Word's Last Night and Other Essays*, C. S. Lewis gives his own view of the return of Christ: "Precisely because we cannot predict the moment, we must be ready at all moments."

In the history of Christian theology there have been different views concerning the return of Christ. Are we given signs of earthquakes and apostasy before the return of Christ? Or should we be busy about our Father's business, not really fixing our attention on bringing the end of the age? Still another view is the "any moment return of Christ," which uses the blessed hope as a motivation for zeal and lifelong readiness for accountability.

If you were given a task by a supervisor and then left on your own, what would motivate you? If you thought you had all day to get the job done, how would you spend your time? But if you knew that the supervisor might return at any time, might you use your time well? God in His wisdom has given us the "any moment" expectation for His Son's return so that we might be found faithful.

Perhaps today Jesus Christ will return for us.
How should this affect what you do today?

FOR FURTHER READING: *The World's Last Night and Other Essays* by C. S. Lewis, "The World's Last Night"

READ: Mark 7:24–30

The Lost Sheep of Israel

But [Jesus] answered and said, "I was not sent except to the lost sheep of the house of Israel." —Matthew 15:24

In one of his letters, C. S. Lewis reflected on the biblical account of Jesus responding to the Syrophoenician woman. Interestingly, Lewis did not appear troubled by our Lord's seeming aloofness to her as a Gentile. The point Lewis made was "that the Hebrews are spiritually senior to us, that God did entrust the descendants of Abraham with the first revelation of Himself."

The point of the dialogue between our Lord and the Gentile woman who wanted her daughter delivered from a demon is an issue of His Messianic role. For centuries God had given divine revelation and had disciplined His chosen people. In the process He had cultivated an expectation that their Messiah would one day come. When Jesus of Nazareth began His public ministry, that day had arrived. Clearly, His priority was to the lost sheep of Israel. His conversation with the woman from Syrophoenicia illustrates this.

Lewis reminds us that the story ends well: The woman's daughter is delivered. But the point for us is to revere the role the Jews played in our own redemption (Romans 3:1–2).

Jesus Christ is the Messiah of Israel and the Redeemer for all who repent and believe in Him.

For Further Reading: *The Collected Letters of C. S. Lewis,* volume 3

READ: Luke 24:13–35

Not What I Expected

And beginning at Moses and all the Prophets, He expounded to them in all the Scriptures the things concerning Himself.
—Luke 24:27

When Joy Gresham took her two boys David and Douglas to England, their minds were filled with the stories of Narnia. In his book *Lenten Lands*, Douglas Gresham tells of his first encounter with Lewis. The balding man was dressed in well-worn clothes. But beyond the immediate tawdry appearance of the man was the disappointment of his having no visual connection with Narnia: "Here was the man who was on speaking terms with King Peter, with the Great Lion, Aslan Himself. Here was the man who had been to Narnia; surely he should at least wear silver chain mail and be girt about with a jewel-encrusted sword belt. This was the heroic figure of whom Mother had so often spoken? So much for imagery."

During Jesus Christ's ministry on earth, many expected Him to become king of Israel and expel the occupation forces of the Romans (John 6:15). When he was tortured, crucified, and killed, many who followed Him were disillusioned (John 21:3). Yet after the resurrection, those who believed were given a new vision of the Messiah and His kingdom (Luke 24:13–35). He may not have been what they expected, but Jesus was exactly what they needed.

Life is often filled with unexpected experiences, but God can use them to help us grow.

For Further Reading: *Lenten Lands* by Douglas Gresham

READ: Acts 4:1–12

By Another Name

Nor is there salvation in any other, for there is no other name under heaven given among men by which we must be saved.

—Acts 4:12

In *The Voyage of the Dawn Treader*, there is a tearful scene in which Lucy learns from Aslan that she has become too old to return to Narnia. "'It isn't Narnia, you know,' sobbed Lucy. 'It's you. We shan't meet you there. And how can we live, never meeting you?' 'But you shall meet me, dear one,' said Aslan. 'Are -are you there too, Sir?' said Edmund. 'I am,' said Aslan. 'But there I have another name. You must learn to know me by that name. This was the very reason why you were brought to Narnia, that by knowing me here for a little, you may know me better there.'"

Clearly, Lewis is making a connection between the Aslan of Narnia and the Lord Jesus Christ of our own world. Around our multicultural globe Jesus goes by many different names. He is called Íosa in Irish, uJesu in Zulu, Giêsu in Vietnamese, Yeshu in Hebrew, and Iso in Uzbek. Yet each of these designations point to one Person—Jesus of Nazareth, the God Man, born of a virgin, risen from the dead, and coming to redeem heaven and earth (Acts 4:12). One day we will meet him face to face.

> *Although Jesus goes by different names around the world, only the Christ of Scripture can redeem those who place their trust in Him.*

FOR FURTHER READING: *Voyage of the Dawn Treader*
by C. S. Lewis, chapter 16

READ: 2 Peter 3:1–13

Terrible Times

But the day of the Lord will come as a thief in the night, in which the heavens will pass away with a great noise, and the elements will melt with fervent heat; both the earth and the works that are in it will be burned up. —2 Peter 3:10

In a letter to his friend Don Giovanni Calabria, C. S. Lewis wrote, "The times we live in are, as you say, grave: whether 'graver than all others in history,' I do not know. But the evil that is closest always seems to be the most serious . . . Meanwhile, our own security is that the Day may find us . . . fulfilling the supreme command that we love one another."

What troubles you about the time in which we live? Is it the rise of anti-God movements? Perhaps it is the ceaseless threat of terrorism? Whatever your concerns, imagined or real, Lewis' observations about living in terrible times is a good wake-up call. Threats that seem close to us do cause the greater anxiety. But the reminder that our Redeemer is coming back for us should bring comfort to any troubled heart. We may not be living in the last days, but the admonition to love one another as Christ loved us should increase as we see the last days approach (John 13:34–35; Hebrews 10:24–25).

The hope of Christ's return and our mandate to love one another should help us endure any terrible days we may face.

For Further Reading: *The Latin Letters of C. S. Lewis*

READ: Exodus 7:1–3; 9:1–12

God's Tools

For the Scripture says to the Pharaoh, "For this very purpose I have raised you up, that I may show My power in you, and that My name may be declared in all the earth." —Romans 9:17

In his *Preface to Paradise Lost*, C. S. Lewis reflected on how God can use evil to accomplish His will: "Sometimes we can think God is at work in the believer but the devil rules this dark world in which they live. Yet Scripture is filled with examples of how God can use even evil people for his purposes."

When Moses demanded that Pharaoh let the children of Israel be freed from slavery, he met a most obstinate monarch. We are told that Pharaoh hardened his heart and would not let them go (Exodus 9:34–35). Through the stubborn will of this unregenerate man, God would receive glory and His chosen people would be given booty as they left their chains (Exodus 12:36). But an even more stunning example of evil being used by God for good is the death of His own Son. On the day our Lord was crucified, evil seemed to have the final say. But three days later Christ was raised to win our redemption. Even evil men played a part in the purposes of God (Acts 2:22–41).

God can use even the evil of human beings to accomplish His purposes.

FOR FURTHER READING: *A Preface to Paradise Lost* by C. S. Lewis

READ: 1 Corinthians 15:1–11; 2 Peter 1:12–21

Is It True?

For we did not follow cunningly devised fables when we made known to you the power and coming of our Lord Jesus Christ, but were eyewitnesses of His majesty. —2 Peter 1:16

In his essay "Modern Man and His Categories of Thought," C. S. Lewis wrote, "In lecturing to popular audiences I have repeatedly found it almost impossible to make them understand that I recommend Christianity because I thought its affirmations to be objectively true. They are simply not interested in the question of truth or falsehood. They only want to know it will be comforting or 'inspiring' or socially useful."

A similar attitude can be seen today in many people we encounter. Skeptics may give lip service to the admirable moral teachings of Jesus of Nazareth or commend Christian humanitarian efforts. But the eternal truth claims of life after death, sin, and salvation will be met with icy disbelief. One of the major reasons Christians can make these supernatural assertions comes from the historic reliability of the New Testament documents. Lewis understood that there are more Christian manuscripts recording eyewitness accounts than any other documents from the ancient world. And these records paint a portrait of One who claimed to be "the Way, the Truth and the Life." We believe in Christianity because it is true—not just because it may contribute to social good.

Jesus Christ changes lives because He is the Way, the Truth, and the Life.

FOR FURTHER READING: *The New Testament Documents: Are They Reliable?* by F. F. Bruce

READ: Numbers 11:1–9

Longing for the Past

We remember the fish which we ate freely in Egypt, the cucumbers, the melons, the leeks, the onions, and the garlic; but now our whole being is dried up; there is nothing at all except this manna before our eyes! —Numbers 11:5–6

In *Out of the Silent Planet*, Professor Elwin Ransom dialogues with a race of intelligent creatures that live on the planet Malacandra. In response to Ransom's comment about human regret, the extraterrestrial creature Hyoi says, "How could we endure to live and let time pass if we were always crying for one day or one year to come back—if we did not know that every day in a life fills the whole life with expectation and memory and these are that day?"

In our Bible reading today, we see that the children of Israel longed for the past. Although they had been delivered from slavery by mighty miracles, a steady diet of manna in the wilderness did not satisfy their stomach. They missed the herbs, spices, and fresh vegetables of Egypt.

They did not seem grateful for the miraculous food provided each morning. Nor did they fix their minds upon the milk and honey awaiting them in the Promised Land. Often we too can fall into the trap of bemoaning the present and longing for the past. The remedy? Count our blessings and trust in the ultimate provision of God (1 Thessalonians 5:18).

This is the day the Lord has made; we will rejoice and be glad in it. —Psalm 118:24

For Further Reading: *Out of the Silent Planet* by C. S. Lewis, chapter 12

READ: Psalm 13:1–6

Feeling Ignored?

Hear my prayer, O LORD, and give ear to my cry; do not be silent at my tears; for I am a stranger with You, a sojourner, as all my fathers were. —Psalm 39:12

In his book *Letters to Malcolm: Chiefly on Prayer*, C. S. Lewis wrote: "We can bear to be refused but not to be ignored. In other words, our faith can survive many refusals if they really are refusals and not mere disregards. The apparent stone will be bread to us if we believe that a Father's hand put it into ours, in mercy or justice or even in rebuke."

Sometimes we can experience a similar frustration in prayer. In today's reading the psalmist feels anguish and abandonment in his prayers (Psalm 13). Have you ever poured your heart out to a trusted friend only to feel as if you were being ignored? Even with another person in the same room, you can feel completely alone. Connecting and communication are what you need from others. To feel detached indifference is not.

The Bible tells us that "God is love" and that we are "the children of God." Feeling ignored by our heavenly Father is a result of our fallen world and our fluctuating feelings getting in the way. In time, God's response will come, and it will be from the One who loves us with an everlasting love.

I waited patiently for the LORD; and He inclined to me. —Psalm 40:1

FOR FURTHER READING: *Letters to Malcolm: Chiefly on Prayer* by C. S. Lewis, chapter 10

READ: Matthew 6:19–34

Sufficient for the Day

Therefore do not worry about tomorrow, for tomorrow will worry about its own things. Sufficient for the day is its own trouble.
—Matthew 6:34

In one of his letters, C. S. Lewis gives us insight into anxiety management. Having served on the front lines in World War I, he knew something about living with the tensions of imminent threats. So he admonished a worried correspondent with these words: "As one lived in the Front Line 'They're not shelling us at the moment, and it's not raining, and the rations have come up, so let's enjoy ourselves.' In fact, as our Lord said, 'Sufficient unto the day.'"

Our Lord's own instruction is an effective tool for managing worries. Some believers feel that any kind of anxiety is to be avoided. But God gave us the capacity for concern so we might be vigilant in facing threats and keeping our commitments. What our Lord is telling us in Matthew 6:34 is that we should not overwhelm ourselves with what might happen tomorrow. Instead, by faith we should face life's challenges as they come to us by the grace of God. Learning how to trust God in the present is a key factor in matching divine resources with daily needs.

Sufficient grace is always available for facing daily challenges.

FOR FURTHER READING: *The Collected Letters of C. S. Lewis,* volume 3

READ: Psalm 51:1–19

Rationalizing Not Confessing

For I acknowledge my transgressions, and my sin is always before me.
—Psalm 51:3

C. S. Lewis noted that he found a tendency in his own prayer life to rationalize instead of confess sins: "I find that when I think I am asking God to forgive me I am often in reality (unless I watch myself very carefully) asking Him to do something quite different. I am asking Him not to forgive me but to excuse me." One of the great enemies of heartfelt confession is rationalization. The term means "to justify one's behavior with plausible reasons even if they are not true or appropriate." In short, it is making excuses.

In our reading today we have the psalm David prayed when he confessed his sins for having committed adultery with Bathsheba and having her husband killed so she could become his wife. The prayer is characterized by honesty (vv. 1–6), a plea for cleansing (vv. 7–11), and the desire for restoration (vv. 12–19). Although David's sins were very great, his sincere contrition was a characteristic that made him a "man after [God's] own heart" (1 Samuel 13:14). The starting point for confession and forgiveness must be honesty (1 John 1:9).

*God has promised to forgive the sincere
prayer of confession and repentance.*

FOR FURTHER READING: *The Weight of Glory*
by C. S. Lewis, "On Forgiveness"

READ: Deuteronomy 10:12–22; Job 37:23; Psalm 140:12

Protection of the Law

He has shown you, O man, what is good; and what does the LORD require of you but to do justly, to love mercy, and to walk humbly with your God? —Micah 6:8

In his essay "Equality," C. S. Lewis commented on the necessity of righteous laws in society: "Legal and economic equality are absolutely necessary remedies for the Fall, and protection against cruelty." By this he meant that each person should have access to protection under law and fair access to economic opportunities.

Despite the imperfections of civil government, most people would agree that laws are necessary for a just society. But why would Lewis link his argument to the fall of the human race? Because of his Christian faith, he believed that man and woman were created in innocence with an obedient heart toward their Creator. But through the influence of a mighty fallen angel our first spiritual ancestors succumbed to the temptation to choose a path that was independent from their divine Sovereign. Since that time external law has been a necessity to protect the weak and vulnerable from the evil and powerful.

Behind just legislation is a Lawgiver who is "mighty and awesome, who shows no partiality" (Deuteronomy 10:17). The law of God reflects His holy and loving character and must restrain evil and ensure just treatment of others.

In a fallen world righteous laws are necessary to restrain evil and protect the innocent.

FOR FURTHER READING: *Present Concerns* by C. S. Lewis, "Equality"

READ: Matthew 17:1–2; Mark 9:1–10; 1 Corinthians 15:51–53

Putting on Splendor

His clothes became shining, exceedingly white, like snow, such as no launderer on earth can whiten them. —Mark 9:3

What must it have been like to see the Lord Jesus reveal His glory on the Mount of Transfiguration? To see His face, hands, and even His garments shine with divine glory must have filled the disciples with awe and wonder.

Theologians have different views about this divine preview of glory. Some feel it is exclusively a radiance that belongs to Jesus Christ and was the disclosure of the glory He had with the Father before becoming a man (John 17:5). But other scholars think this is a preview of the glory we will share with Christ in eternity (1 John 3:2).

But no matter how this glory plays out in eternity future, we can be sure that the believer will put on a splendor suited to that new world. C. S. Lewis wrote: "For if we take the imagery of Scripture seriously, if we believe that God will one day give us the Morning Star and cause us to put on the splendour of the sun, then we may surmise that both the ancient myths, and the modern poetry, so false as history, may be very near the truth of prophecy." Imagine the splendor!

*Some day we will receive a new indestructible body
that will radiate with the glory of God.*

FOR FURTHER READING: *The Weight of Glory*
by C. S. Lewis, "The Weight of Glory"

READ: Ephesians 5:22–33

The Mystery of Love

This is a great mystery, but I speak concerning Christ and the church. Nevertheless let each one of you in particular so love his own wife as himself, and let the wife see that she respects her husband. —Ephesians 5:32–33

Romance novels and popular films promote the idea of someone finding a "soul mate" or "the right one" based on feelings. Then it is assumed that finding the right mate will result in that feeling being sustained for a lifetime. Sadly, this idealized assumption has led many to divorce court.

In *Mere Christianity*, C. S. Lewis saw that the initial euphoria of romance cannot be sustained for a lifetime: "Love as distinct from 'being in love' is not merely a feeling. It is a deep unity, maintained by the will and deliberately strengthened by habit; reinforced by (in Christian marriages) the grace which both partners ask, and receive, from God."

Our reading for today is taken from Paul's inspired teaching on Christian marriage. Marriage is a reciprocal relationship. The husband is exhorted to provide sacrificial care for the benefit of his spouse. In return the wife is to show respectful cooperation in her role as help-meet. Together they illustrate the mysterious relationship between Jesus Christ and His bride, the church. This kind of love will endure.

Romantic love can only be sustained through shared caring in changing circumstances.

FOR FURTHER READING: *Mere Christianity* by C. S. Lewis, Book 3, chapter 6

Spiritual Rebellion

I will ascend above the heights of the clouds, I will be like the Most High. —Isaiah 14:14

Some of the arguments against the evidence for intelligent design in nature almost seem ludicrous. Outspoken atheists look at the complex and interrelated process of living things and say that the "appearance" of design is an "illusion."

In *A Preface to Paradise Lost*, C. S. Lewis explains why spiritual rebellion leads to intellectual problems: "A creature revolting against a creator is revolting against the source of his own powers—including even his power to revolt. . . . It is like the scent of a flower trying to destroy the flower. As a consequence the same rebellion which means misery for the feelings and corruption for the will, means Nonsense for the intellect."

The first revolt against the Creator happened aeons ago through Lucifer, who chose to be "like the Most High" (Isaiah 14:12–21; Ezekiel 28:14–15). Satan's spiritual rebellion then spread to the human race (Genesis 3). But this terrible insurrection can come to an end in any human heart that submits to the Redeemer Jesus Christ as Savior and Lord (John 1:12; 3:16; Philippians 2:11). At that point, God will redeem the mind as well as the soul.

Rebelling against the Source of truth leads to confusion.

FOR FURTHER READING: *A Preface to Paradise Lost* by C. S. Lewis

READ: Isaiah 43:1–7; John 5:28–29

When Christ Calls Your Name

Do not marvel at this; for the hour is coming in which all who are in the graves will hear His voice. —John 5:28

When a man and woman are in love, the sweetest sound to their ears is the other saying their name. In the love relationship between Christ and His bride, the church, it's even sweeter when the Savior calls out one's name. C. S. Lewis described this in *Prince Caspian* when Lucy hears Aslan calling out to her: "Feeling like the voice she liked best in all the world was calling her name."

The New Testament contains many references to the Lord Jesus calling to believers in a way that is transforming. Our Savior will one day call to each believer—raising them from the ashes of death to a glorified resurrection body: "Do not marvel at this; for the hour is coming in which all who are in the graves will hear His voice" (John 5:28). In Revelation, we see Christ also prophecy: "I will give him a white stone, and on the stone a new name written which no one knows except him who receives it" (Revelation 2:17). The identity of each believer is intimately tied in with Christ the Redeemer in the language of redeeming love.

When God calls to us, it indicates His ownership and our grateful obedience.

FOR FURTHER READING: *Prince Caspian* by C. S. Lewis, chapter 10

READ: Matthew 13:47–52

The Dragnet

But seek first the kingdom of God and His righteousness, and all these things shall be added to you.   —Matthew 6:33

C. S. Lewis understood that an authentic believer in Christ has chosen to seek the kingdom of God instead of some other substitute: "If you have not chosen the kingdom of God, it will make in the end no difference what you have chosen instead. . . . We shall have missed the end for which we are formed and rejected the only thing that satisfies."

In our Bible reading today we see that a dragnet can illustrate how God discerns authentic and inauthentic faith. In contrast to a casting net (Mark 1:16, 18), the dragnet was a wide mesh thrown out over a large area. When brought ashore, the expansive content of the dragnet would be examined. Fish would be kept in one pile while another pile of debris would be disposed of. Our Lord's public ministry of teaching and miracles attracted large numbers of both authentic and inauthentic believers. As in other illustrations of the wheat and the tares (Matthew 13:24–30) or the sheep and the goats (Matthew 25:31–46), the genuine followers of the kingdom of God will be revealed at the end of the world. What a comfort to be an authentic follower of Christ!

Seeking the kingdom of God first will have eternal consequences for every human being.

FOR FURTHER READING: *The Weight of Glory* by C. S. Lewis, "A Slip of the Tongue"

READ: Hebrews 11:8–40

Threats to Faith

Who through faith subdued kingdoms, worked righteousness, obtained promises, stopped the mouths of lions, quenched the violence of fire, escaped the edge of the sword, out of weakness were made strong, became valiant in battle, turned to flight the armies of the aliens. —Hebrews 11:33–34

In *Christian Reflections*, C. S. Lewis pointed out helpful insights into the ways threatening circumstances can challenge our faith: "There are things, say in learning to swim or to climb, which look dangerous and aren't. Your instructor tells you it's safe. You have good reason from past experience to trust him. Perhaps you can even see for yourself, by your own reason, that it is safe. But the crucial question is, will you be able to go on believing this when you actually see the cliff edge below you or actually feel yourself unsupported in the water?"

In our Bible reading today, we see real-life threats that most of us will never have to face in our lifetimes. Being fed to lions, burnt with fire, and killed with the sword were each real threats that certain Old Testament saints had to face. But these believers were called of God and found the grace of God sufficient to help them endure until the end. What fearful circumstances challenge your faith today? When fear creeps into our hearts, we need to trust God and move forward.

Despite our misgivings, challenges can be overcome by faith.

FOR FURTHER READING: *Christian Reflections* by C. S. Lewis, "Religion: Reality or Substitute?"

READ: Deuteronomy 6:4–9; Proverbs 22:6; Ephesians 6:4

The Next Generation

*All your children shall be taught by the LORD, and great shall be
the peace of your children.* —Isaiah 54:13

In his essay "On the Transmission of Christianity," C. S. Lewis wisely
pointed out that each generation will pass on to the next only what they
have. Both virtues and vices feed into this educational transmission: "If
we are skeptical we shall teach only skepticism . . . if fools only folly, if
vulgar only vulgarity, if saints sanctity, if heroes heroism."

It has been wisely said, "We cannot pass on to others what we do
not have ourselves." Certainly this is true when it comes to our own
spiritual lives and our children. Kids and teens are keen observers of
hypocrisy versus authenticity. Parents don't have to be perfect, but they
need to be genuine in the way they exhibit how they face life's challenges by faith. This means seeking to cultivate our own spiritual life
before trying to transmit it to others.

Whether we are traveling with family, enjoying recreation at home,
or just engaging in day-to-day activities, we should be on the alert to
cultivate spiritual interest in the next generation. Our formal examination of the Word should be given time to soak in during everyday life
experiences.

*We can't pass on to the next generation
something we do not have ourselves.*

FOR FURTHER READING: *God in the Dock* by C. S. Lewis,
"On the Transmission of Christianity,"

READ: Exodus 3:1–15

Meeting God

And God said to Moses, "I AM WHO I AM." And He said, "Thus you shall say to the children of Israel, 'I AM has sent me to you.'"
—Exodus 3:14

Concerning a personal encounter with God, C. S. Lewis wrote: "To believe that God—at least *this* God—exists is to believe that you as a person now stand in the presence of God as a Person. What would, a moment before, have been variations in opinion, now become variations in your personal attitude to a Person. You are no longer faced with an argument which demands your assent, but with a Person who demands your confidence."

We don't know that much about Moses' upbringing or his personal understanding of God. It seems likely that he was given some kind of input on the God of the Hebrews through his mother, who nursed him in Pharaoh's court (Exodus 2:1–10). We are told that he received a royal education in all the learning of the highly advanced Egyptian culture (Acts 7:22). There might have even been some conflicting ideas in his mind between the one God of the Jews and the many gods of the Egyptians. If so, we can assume that all changed on the day when he met God personally through a supernatural burning bush (Exodus 3:1-15). He stood in the presence of the living God.

As we pray, we should ask that those who hear the gospel will encounter the living God of Scripture.

FOR FURTHER READING: *The World's Last Night and Other Essays* by C. S. Lewis, "On Obstinacy in Belief"

Chivalrous Judges

And when the LORD raised up judges for them, the LORD was with the judge and delivered them out of the hand of their enemies all the days of the judge; for the LORD was moved to pity by their groaning because of those who oppressed them and harassed them. —Judges 2:18

Many of us grew up with fairy tales that told stories of heroic knights and damsels in distress. There is something about slaying a dragon, defeating a dark knight, or rescuing a fair lady from desperate circumstances that still strikes a chord in young hearts.

C. S. Lewis spent his adult life immersed in studying the medieval world—an era that elevated the whole idea of knightly chivalry. Chivalry often exhibited qualities of courage, justice, courtesy, and compassion for the weak. Interestingly, when Lewis studied the book of Judges, he saw a parallel between the medieval knight and the judges who delivered Israel from its oppressors: "The knight errant of medieval romance who spends his days liberating, and securing justice for, distressed damsels, would almost have been, for the Hebrews, a 'judge.'"

Judges were people called by God to deliver Israel from oppressors. Some of the most familiar to our minds were Gideon, Deborah, and Samson. They did not have any political power as rulers, nor did they receive revelation or teach the Law. The role of each of them was to serve as a heaven-sent deliverer.

In a fallen world, the righteous use of force may be necessary to maintain justice.

FOR FURTHER READING: *Christian Reflections* by C. S. Lewis, "The Psalms"

READ: Acts 20:7–12; 1 Corinthians 16:1–2

Attending Church

*Not forsaking the assembling of ourselves together, as is the man-
ner of some, but exhorting one another, and so much the more as
you see the Day approaching.* —Hebrews 10:25

In his essay "Answers to Questions on Christianity," C. S. Lewis tells
how he became a faithful church attender: "My own experience is that
when I first became a Christian . . . I thought that I could do it on my
own. . . . I wouldn't go to the churches and Gospel Halls; and then
later I found that it was the only way of flying your flag . . . . I came up
against different people of quite different outlooks and different education . . . . It gets you out of your solitary conceit."

Some believers have made television their church experience, while
others have adopted an ongoing habit of "church hopping." This is certainly not the biblical teaching on church involvement. The book of
Hebrews warns us about adopting a habit of not going to church. We
are exhorted to faithful attendance at a particular local fellowship so we
can both give and receive. It is a place of mutual spiritual accountability. There we are to stir each other up to love and good deeds (Hebrews
10:24–25). The various people we meet at church help us connect with
others and help us grow spiritually.

*Active and regular involvement in a local church is vital
for our spiritual health and for the benefit of others.*

FOR FURTHER READING: *God in the Dock* by C. S. Lewis,
"Answers to Questions on Christianity"

READ: Deuteronomy 30:1–20

Evil Choices

And if it seems evil to you to serve the LORD, choose for yourselves this day whom you will serve, whether the gods which your fathers served that were on the other side of the River, or the gods of the Amorites, in whose land you dwell. But as for me and my house, we will serve the LORD. —Joshua 24:15

When theologians try to reconcile why bad things happen to good people, they usually work out of two categories. The first is called "natural evil" in which sickness, earthquakes, tsunamis, and other natural disasters wreak havoc on apparently innocent victims. The second category is called "moral evil," and it is directly related to the choices human beings make that bring harm to others. In his book *The Problem of Pain*, C. S. Lewis wisely pointed out that human choice is at the center of much of the trouble we face: "Evil comes from the abuse of free will."

In the garden of Eden, the choices the first members of the human race had to make were simple and few. One was to tend the garden as stewards of God and the other was to not eat of the Tree of the Knowledge of Good and Evil. Since our original parents fell into sin, life has become a lot more complicated. To protect the human race from self-destruction, God provided the law as a reflection of His holiness and a guide to bless relationships, family, business, and society as a whole (Joshua 24:14–15).

Evil comes from the misuse of free will, while blessing comes from choices aligned with God's Word.

FOR FURTHER READING: *The Problem of Pain* by C. S. Lewis, chapter 9

READ: Revelation 7:9–12; 19:5–7

Praise in Heaven

And I heard, as it were, the voice of a great multitude, as the sound of many waters and as the sound of mighty thunderings, saying, "Alleluia! For the Lord God Omnipotent reigns!"

—Revelation 19:6

In commenting on the perpetual praise to God of angels and redeemed humans, C. S. Lewis said in *From Reflections on the Psalms*, "To see what the doctrine really means, we must suppose ourselves to be in perfect love with God—drunk with, drowned in, dissolved by, that delight which . . . flows out from us incessantly again in effortless and perfect expression."

In our Bible reading today, we see a chorale celebration of praise at the Marriage Supper of the Lamb. The sacrificial work of the bridegroom Jesus Christ has been completed in full. And now He will be joined to the bride of all true believers, whom He has made holy and beautiful. Both singing and musical instruments have been used in praising God as reigning ruler of all heaven and earth (Psalm 97:1; 98:5–6). Similar kinds of worship came forth in gratefulness for deliverance (Exodus 15:1–18). Praise is also evoked in contemplation of the last days and the defeat of evil (Micah 4:6–8; Isaiah 52:4–10). Today, lift your heart and voice in worship to God!

Being in love with God evokes a love song that will last for eternity.

FOR FURTHER READING: *Reflections on the Psalms*
by C. S. Lewis, chapter 17

READ: Matthew 17:1–3; 1 Corinthians 4:9; Hebrews 12:1

Communion of the Saints

I saw under the altar the souls of those who had been slain for the word of God and for the testimony which they held. And they cried with a loud voice, saying, "How long, O Lord, holy and true, until You judge and avenge our blood on those who dwell on the earth?" —Revelation 6:9–10

In a letter C. S. Lewis wrote in 1943, he mentioned feeling connected with a Christian friend who had died: "I also have become much acquainted with grief now through the death of my great friend Charles Williams . . . . And I find all that talk about 'feeling he is closer to us than before' isn't just talk. It's just what it does feel like—I can't put it into words."

Lewis was an active member of the Church of England. As an Anglican he held views that some might think Catholic, and he had other convictions that might appear to be Protestant. One belief held by both Roman Catholic and Eastern Orthodox traditions is "the communion of the saints." This doctrine teaches that through "the mystical body" of Christ those who have died and those who are now alive can share in some mutual benefit. Matthew 17:1–3; 1 Corinthians 4:9; Hebrews 12:1; and Revelation 6:9–10 are sometimes offered as support for this relationship between the living and dead in Christ. All may not agree on the interaction between living and dead believers, but all agree that we will share eternity together forever.

Christian friendships are eternal because they are based on Christ's gift of eternal life.

READ: Colossians 2:1–8

Imprisoned Minds

See to it that no one takes you captive through hollow and deceptive philosophy, which depends on human tradition and the elemental spiritual forces of this world rather than on Christ.

—Colossians 2:8 (NIV)

In C. S. Lewis' children's fantasy novel *The Last Battle,* we see a surprising cynical skepticism exhibited by the dwarfs. Once having been duped by the evil ape Shift and a donkey dressed in a lion's skin, they determine to not trust the true lion king Aslan when he appears. While faithful followers of Narnia begin to experience the excitement of the new world Aslan is creating, the dwarfs do not. Aslan explains that their skeptical doubts have created a mental prison from which they cannot escape: "They have chosen cunning instead of belief. Their prison is only in their minds, yet they are in that prison; and so afraid of being taken in that they cannot be taken out."

Similarly, in the first century the Christian congregation at Colossi was in danger of becoming imprisoned by wrong thinking. Paul warned them: "See to it that no one takes you captive through hollow and deceptive philosophy, which depends on human tradition and the elemental spiritual forces of this world rather than on Christ" (Colossians 2:8 NIV). When human beings replace Christian truth with man-made vain speculations, they run the risk of being taken captive and imprisoned in falsehood.

God wants us to be discerning thinkers who keep Christ in the center of our hearts and minds.

FOR FURTHER READING: *The Last Battle* by C. S. Lewis, chapter 13

READ: Daniel 6:1–23

Dangerous Devotions

And in [Daniel's] upper room, with his windows open toward Jerusalem, he knelt down on his knees three times that day, and prayed and gave thanks before his God, as was his custom since early days. —Daniel 6:10

During World War II, Professor C. S. Lewis was asked to address the topic of "Learning in War-Time." Lewis discussed the overwhelming distractions of war for students in an academic setting. During his oral presentation, Lewis said, "The only people who achieve much are those who want knowledge so badly that they seek it while the conditions are still unfavourable. Favourable conditions never come."

The Old Testament prophet Daniel devoted himself to the study of Scripture and a daily discipline of prayer even during unfavorable times. Corrupt politicians had tricked the king into making a decree that no prayers be offered except to his pagan god. The motive for deceiving the king was to place Daniel in harm's way and remove his influence over the king. Their plan initially worked, though God would eventually deliver the prophet. And Daniel maintained his spiritual disciplines to the one true God despite the risk (Daniel 6:1–23).

Lewis would live through two world wars, and it is clear from his life he valued learning and spiritual growth in spite of danger. We too should seek the Lord at all times, even if doing so is risky.

Growing in the Lord through Bible study and prayer becomes more essential when we face dangers.

FOR FURTHER READING: *The Weight of Glory* by C. S. Lewis, "Learning in War-Time"

READ: 2 Kings 22:1–20

Correcting Our Assumptions

Then Hilkiah the high priest said to Shaphan the scribe, "I have found the Book of the Law in the house of the LORD." And Hilkiah gave the book to Shaphan, and he read it.   —2 Kings 22:8

C. S. Lewis said, "Every age has its own outlook. It is especially good at seeing certain truths and specially liable to make certain mistakes. We all, therefore, need the books that will correct the characteristic mistakes of our own period. And that means the old books. . . . The only palliative is to keep the clean sea breeze of the centuries blowing through our minds, and this can be done only by reading old books."

In today's reading, we see how the ancient writings of the Scripture corrected false assumptions. Josiah (640–609 BC) was a child when he began his reign in Judah. After he had been on the throne for eighteen years, he began to repair the temple and in its rubble found a copy of Scripture. When it was read aloud, Josiah tore his robe in repentance for the sins it exposed. He immediately inquired of the Lord and began reforms to conform his rule to the Word of God. As a result, he was blessed with peace and prosperity. The ultimate guide for correcting our lives is the ultimate old book—the Word of God.

Our unquestioned assumptions need to be challenged by Scripture.

FOR FURTHER READING: *St. Athanasius: On the Incarnation*, "Introduction" by C. S. Lewis

READ: Psalm 46:10; Isaiah 12:1–6

Enjoying God

For from the rising of the sun even unto the going down of the same my name shall be great among the Gentiles; and in every place incense shall be offered unto my name, and a pure offering: for my name shall be great among the heathen, saith the LORD of hosts.
—Malachi 1:11 (KJV)

In *Reflections on the Psalms*, C. S. Lewis writes: "The Scotch catechism says that man's chief end is 'to glorify God and enjoy Him forever.' But we shall then know that these are the same thing. Fully to enjoy is to glorify. In commanding us to glorify Him, God is inviting us to enjoy Him."

It seems that so much of the Old Testament commands our adoration of the living God. Does this mean that the Creator and Redeemer actually needs our affirmation? This is hardly the case. We are told to glorify God because we celebrate Him as the source from which all goodness flows.

When we seek to glorify God, we find ourselves in that happy state for which we were created. Just as a beautiful sunset or a peaceful pastoral scene points to the majesty of the Creator, worship projects our souls even deeper into a spiritual union with Him.

God does not need our praise. We do. By basking in His presence, we drink in the joy of infinite love and exult in the One who stooped low to redeem and restore us. Our future prospect is to enjoy Him forever!

> *The chief end of man is to glorify God and enjoy him forever.* —Westminster Catechism

FOR FURTHER READING: *Reflection on the Psalms* by C. S. Lewis, chapter 17

READ: Matthew 7:15–20; 1 Timothy 4:1–5; 2 Peter 2:1–3

Uncorrected Error

Now the Spirit expressly says that in latter times some will depart from the faith, giving heed to deceiving spirits and doctrines of demons. —1 Timothy 4:1

"Every uncorrected error and unrepentant sin is, in its own right, a fountain of fresh error and fresh sin flowing on to the end of time." This statement by C. S. Lewis seems to be a bit of an overstatement. But is it? Heresy takes on a life of its own. Disturbingly, its false teaching can be passed down from one generation to another. This flow of error "to the end of time" is the legacy of teaching not anchored to the Word of God.

In 1 Timothy 4, Paul tells us that in the latter days there will be an increase in false teaching. The source of this heresy is deceiving spirits. The word *deceiving* is from the Greek word *planet* for "wandering, roving, misleading." Unlike fixed stars, planets were called "wanderers" by the ancients because they moved on their own in the night sky. False teaching has wandered from God's truth. The best way of recognizing a counterfeit dollar bill is to know what an authentic one looks like. The same is true of spiritual truth. We are better able to discern false teaching when we keep ourselves immersed in the Word of God.

Though we must show kindness to members of cults, we should always stand firm on God's truth, which was "once for all delivered to the saints" (Jude 1:3).

FOR FURTHER READING: *The Problem of Pain*
by C. S. Lewis, chapter 4

READ: Acts 7:51–58; 26:1–23

B. C.

"They cast him out of the city and stoned him. And the witnesses laid down their clothes at the feet of a young man named Saul."
—Acts 7:58

The book *All My Road Before Me* records the diary entries of C. S. Lewis as a young atheist at Oxford. It shows the life of C. S. Lewis B. C. (Before Christ). The back cover tells us: "The life of the young C. S. Lewis was filled with contemplations quite different from those of the mature Christian apologist and well known author and his early diary—begun when he was twenty-three—provides readers an excellent window on his formative world." Both Lewis' domestic and academic challenges at the time give us greater insight into those works he would write after becoming a Christian.

Life change in Christ bears witness to divine transformation. Wouldn't it be fascinating to have a window into the life of Saul of Tarsus? We know that this self-righteous Pharisee who once opposed Christ would one day yield to Him as Savior and Lord. But what characterized his life before that transformation? What was Saul's pre-Christian education like? How did his friends and colleagues influence his thoughts and life direction? Because of Christ, the Saul who stood in agreement with Stephen's bloody murder would later become the apostle Paul who proclaimed Stephen's gospel.

The story of a believer's life before Christ testifies to the grace of God.

FOR FURTHER READING: *All My Road Before Me* by C. S. Lewis, *Introduction*

READ: Psalm 8:1–9

Triumph of Humanity

For as in Adam all die, even so in Christ all shall be made alive.
—1 Corinthians 15:22

Regarding the deity and humanity of Christ, C. S. Lewis said this in his book *Reflections on the Psalms*: "We stress the Humanity too exclusively at Christmas, and the Deity too exclusively after the Resurrection; almost as if Christ once became a man and then presently reverted to being simply God. We think of the Resurrection and Ascension (rightly) as great acts of God; less often as the triumph of Man. The ancient interpretation of Psalm 8, however arrived at, is a cheering corrective."

Psalm 8 certainly does describe God's love for humanity. It begins with an exaltation of the name of God (v. 1). A reference to the helplessness of nursing babies and enemies shows the weakness of those who choose to follow their own way (v. 2). The psalmist turns his eyes to the heavens above as he ponders why God should visit such a small creature as man (vv. 3–5). The psalm then shows man's relationship to creation as vice regent over this world (v. 6). Finally, the psalmist returns to praising God's name. Centuries later God would become a man and provide a way of uplifting a fallen race to glory.

*Through Christ, God has made possible
the lifting up of humanity.*

FOR FURTHER READING: *Reflections on the Psalms*
by C. S. Lewis, chapter 19

READ: Psalm 4:7; Acts 14:17; 1 Timothy 6:17–19

Creator of Pleasures

In Your presence is fullness of joy; at Your right hand are pleasures forevermore. —Psalm 16:11

In C. S. Lewis' book *The Screwtape Letters*, a senior devil advises a junior one on tactics for temptation. In their minds, God is the "Enemy" and the damnation of a human soul is the ultimate good. Let's eavesdrop on their conversation: "Never forget that when we are dealing with any pleasure in its healthy and normal and satisfying form, we are, in a sense, on the Enemy's ground. I know we have won many a soul through pleasure. All the same, it is His invention, not ours. He made the pleasures; all our research so far has not enabled us to produce one. All we can do is to encourage the humans to take the pleasures which our Enemy has produced, at times, or in ways, or in degrees, which He has forbidden."

Sometimes the Christian life is viewed as boring, while worldly activities are where the fun is. Yet Screwtape's comments remind us that our God is the creator of pleasures. At His right hand "are pleasures forevermore" (Psalm 16:11), and He has given us "richly all things to enjoy" (1 Timothy 6:17). It is through obeying the living God that we find lasting satisfaction.

Reflect on all of the good pleasures you experience through the day that are gifts from God.

FOR FURTHER READING: *The Screwtape Letters* by C. S. Lewis, Letter 9

READ: Genesis 24:1–27

Patches of Godlight

The LORD has led me on the journey. —Genesis 24:27 (NIV)

Have you ever been in a place of confusion only to encounter a startling touch of God's reality? Maybe it came from an insight from God's Word or through a prompting of the Spirit in prayer. Or perhaps it was an unexpected "coincidence" that gave you direction just when you needed it.

In *Letters to Malcolm: Chiefly on Prayer*, C. S. Lewis refers to this kind of phenomenon as "patches of Godlight." "Any patch of sunlight in a wood will show you something about the sun which you could never get from reading books on astronomy. These pure and spontaneous pleasures are 'patches of Godlight' in the woods of our experience."

Abram's servant was sent to find an appropriate bride for Isaac, the son of promise. If anyone was in need of a "patch of Godlight," it was this conscientious servant. After a long journey and with fears of making a mistake, the servant asked for God's leading. Later he joyously reported to his master: "The LORD has led me" (Genesis 24:27). Do you need God's touch and leading? Watch for "patches of Godlight."

In your faith journey today, watch for evidences of God.

FOR FURTHER READING: *Letters to Malcolm: Chiefly on Prayer*
by C. S. Lewis, chapter 17

READ: Isaiah 40:1–8; 1 Peter 1:22–25

Starting from Scratch?

The grass withers, the flower fades, but the word of our God stands forever. —Isaiah 40:8

What if every time you tried to cook a special dish in the kitchen, you started from scratch? With no instruction from anyone else and having no cookbook to guide you, you were forced to invent a tasty meal? More likely than not, your finished entrée would range from mediocre to awful. Why? Because many who have come before us have used trial and error to establish a method of success. You would not have the advantage of their experiences.

The same could be said for what is true and right in how we live. C. S. Lewis made this observation: "The process of living seems to consist in coming to realize truths so ancient and simple that, if stated, they sounded like barren platitudes. They cannot sound otherwise to those who have not had the relevant experience: that is why there is no real teaching of such truths possible and every generation starts from scratch."

God's recipe for spiritual health and satisfaction can be found in His inspired writings—the Bible. Through it we have both the ingredients and directions to guide our lives. We don't have to start from scratch.

Moral principles are extensions of God's holy character and not created by man.

For Further Reading: *The Collected Letters of C. S. Lewis*, volume 2

Demanding Our Rights

Who, being in the form of God, did not consider it robbery to be equal with God, but made Himself of no reputation, taking the form of a bondservant, and coming in the likeness of men.
—Philippians 2:6–7

In *The Screwtape Letters*, C. S. Lewis talks about how the process of demanding our own rights can lead to spiritual problems: "Whatever men expect they soon come to think they have a right to: the sense of disappointment can, with very little skill on our part, be turned into a sense of injury."

In the familiar story of the prodigal son, the father's gracious reception of his wayward younger son makes the older son angry. He protests that preparing a sumptuous banquet for the one who squandered his inheritance hardly seems appropriate (Luke 15:29). Then with a decided sense of injury he complains that the father has never even given him a party with his friends (v. 30). The older brother feels his rights have been violated, and he resents it.

In contrast to this, the Bible tells us of one who yielded His rights out of a heart of compassion. The Lord Jesus Christ in eternity past possessed all the privileges of divine Sonship. Yet we are told that He voluntarily took on the role of a servant for our redemption (Philippians 2:5–11). With that in mind, how vital is it that we demand our rights?

When demanding our rights consumes us, we can grow bitter and be filled with resentment.

FOR FURTHER READING: *The Screwtape Letters* by C. S. Lewis, Letter 30

READ: Psalm 139; Jeremiah 1:1–5

For This I Was Born

The word of the LORD came to me, saying: "Before I formed you in the womb I knew you; before you were born I sanctified you; I ordained you a prophet to the nations." —Jeremiah 1:4–5

C. S. Lewis at the Breakfast Table and Other Reminiscences records Lewis' view of his life purpose: "I was not born to be free—I was born to adore and obey." In the Bible we sometimes find individuals who knew they were called from birth. Jeremiah recorded God's statement: "Before I formed you in the womb I knew you; before you were born I sanctified you; I ordained you a prophet to the nations" (Jeremiah 1:5). David reflected on the part God played when he was formed in the womb (Psalm 139:13; 1 Samuel 16:13). Then in the New Testament we see that Paul connected his calling to his birth process (Galatians 1:15). Every time we see a new little life brought into this world, there is always the possibility of a special calling.

This is true of every believer in Jesus Christ. Before the creation of the universe or the beginning of life on this world, God looked forward in time and saw you. The divine heart beat with love for you and chose you to be a redeemed son or daughter endowed with a call to love and serve the Creator.

Each believer is called of God to live a life of praise and obedience to our Creator and Redeemer.

FOR FURTHER READING: *C. S. Lewis at the Breakfast Table and Other Reminiscences,* edited by James T. Como

READ: Psalm 63:1–11; 119:145–152

Grudgings and Kindlings

My eyes are awake through the night watches, that I may meditate on Your word. —Psalm 119:148

In answering a letter asking about a devotional time, C. S. Lewis commented on emotions versus will. He set up a contrast between begrudging the necessary time and the spark of spiritual kindling that warms our hearts when we make time: "'Grudging' tho' a nuisance need not depress us too much. It is the act of *will* . . . that God values, rather than the state of our emotions—the act being what we give Him, the emotions what He gives us (usually, I think, indirectly thro' the state of our body, health etc., tho' there are direct kindlings from Him too . . .)."

The psalmist sought times of prayer and spiritual reflection both in the morning and at night. But at either time we might feel an apathy that resists taking the time. God understands this human weakness and looks at our wills—not our emotions—in seeking Him out. As we look to God, His Spirit will bring spiritual "kindlings" to eventually overcome our initial "grudgings." As we seek to meet with God, our will should lead the way.

God is more concerned with our choices than how we feel when we make them.

For Further Reading: *The Collected Letters of C. S. Lewis,* volume 2

READ: Esther 3:1–4:14

Behind the Scenes

Yet who knows whether you have come to the kingdom for such a time as this? —Esther 4:14

In C. S. Lewis' fantasy novel *The Horse and His Boy*, Aslan tells the orphan boy Shasta that he, the great lion, had been there to help him under different disguised identities: "I was the lion who forced you to join with Aravis. I was the cat who comforted you among the houses of the dead. I was the lion who drove the jackals from you while you slept. I was the lion who gave the horses the new strength of fear for the last mill so that you should reach King Lune in time. And I was the lion you do not remember who pushed the boat in which you lay, a child near death, so that it came to shore where a man sat, wakeful at midnight, to receive you."

Esther is an example of a Bible story in which God is at work behind the scenes. Although this inspired book never mentions God directly, theologians have recognized that in its plot line the invisible hand of Providence is at work. Today we too can be confident that the invisible is God at work behind the scenes.

God is our refuge and strength, a very present help in trouble. —Psalm 46:1

FOR FURTHER READING: *The Horse and His Boy* by C. S. Lewis, chapter 11

READ: Acts 2:14–32

Not a Patent Medicine

This Jesus God has raised up, of which we are all witnesses.
—Acts 2:32

In his essay "Man or Rabbit?" from the book *God in the Dock*, C. S. Lewis tells us we should accept Christianity because it is true, not because it will make us feel better. He clarifies that the truth claims about Christ are not a patent medicine. Instead, they are tenants about ultimate reality: "If Christianity is untrue, then no honest man will want to believe it, however helpful it might be: if it is true, every honest man will want to believe it, even if it gives him no help at all."

Sometimes in our zeal to have people respond to the gospel, we make appeals to its meeting of human needs, such as the relief of a guilty conscience or the promise of lasting peace. But the authentic message that must be preserved in sharing the good news of Christ is an account of unshakable truths. God is holy and man is sinful and needs redemption (Romans 3:23; 6:23). Jesus Christ died on the cross and rose from the dead to atone for our sin (1 Corinthians 15:1–5). Finally, we must respond to Christ as Savior and Lord by faith (John 1:12).

*We believe the historic Christian faith because it is true,
not just because it meets an emotional need in us.*

FOR FURTHER READING: *God in the Dock*
by C. S. Lewis, "Man or Rabbit?"

READ: Galatians 5:16–17; 1 John 1

Filled with God

And do not be drunk with wine, in which is dissipation; but be filled with the Spirit. —Ephesians 5:18

In a letter to his assistant Walter Hooper, C. S. Lewis advised him to reduce his preoccupation with sins or virtues and to instead yield his heart to be filled with God's presence: "When the sun is vertically above a man, he casts no shadow: similarly when we have come to the Divine meridian our spiritual shadow . . . will vanish. One will thus in a sense be . . . a room filled by God." Being filled with God's Spirit means being full of God's spiritual light.

The themes of walking in the light and walking in the Spirit are central to the New Testament. John tells us that as we confess our sin and walk in God's presence, we have fellowship with Him and one another (1 John 1:7–9). And Paul, in his letter to the Ephesians, exhorts believers not to be drunk with wine but instead be filled with God's Spirit. Likewise, in his Galatian epistle, Paul assures us that walking in the Spirit is our best safeguard against sin (Galatians 5:16–17). We are to be filled with God's Spirit, whose spiritual light should flow over into others.

Let's get our eyes off ourselves and yield our hearts to God's spiritual light.

READ: Mark 2:13–17

Soul Repair

[Jesus] said to them, "Those who are well have no need of a physician, but those who are sick. I did not come to call the righteous, but sinners, to repentance." —Mark 2:17

C. S. Lewis was an active member of the Church of England. Central in this church's liturgy is *The Book of Common Prayer*. One day Lewis encountered a man who did not agree with the statement: "But thou, O Lord, have mercy upon us, miserable offenders." The layman told Lewis he knew he was imperfect but would not say he was a "miserable offender."

After reflecting on this thought, Lewis wrote an essay entitled "Miserable Offenders." He concluded that the actual term might not easily translate to the modern mind. But it nonetheless included a sobering reality about our sinful condition if Christ is not brought in to deal with it: "Whether we feel miserable or not . . . there is on each of us a load which . . . will send us from this world to whatever happens afterwards, not as souls but as broken souls."

When Jesus spent time with the sinners and outcasts of society, the self-righteous criticized Him for it. They did not think themselves sick and so were not in need of a physician. In order for us to receive the grace of God and be made whole, we must first admit we are in need of repair.

The first step toward being repaired is to admit we are broken.

FOR FURTHER READING: *God in the Dock* by C. S. Lewis, "Miserable Offenders"

READ: Ecclesiastes 1:1–18

God Shaped Vacuum

Then I looked on all the works that my hands had done and on the labor in which I had toiled; and indeed all was vanity and grasping for the wind. There was no profit under the sun.
— Ecclesiastes 2:11

As a young man, C. S. Lewis struggled with his atheism. After his conversion to Christianity, Lewis found that a terrible spiritual vacuum had been filled with the person of Jesus Christ. In *The Weight of Glory*, Lewis spoke of how this affected his heart: "The sense that in this universe we are treated as strangers, the longing to be acknowledged to meet with some response, to bridge some chasm that yawns between us and reality, is part of our inconsolable secret. And surely . . . the promise of glory means good report with God, acceptance by God, response, acknowledgement, and welcome into the heart of things."

A term used for spiritual emptiness is *existentialism*, which emphasizes the isolation of the individual and the meaninglessness of life. Along with this view is the terrible realization that if there is no God, then any moral choice is permitted. Although the word may not always be used, its troubling philosophy can be seen in novels, films, and other media. Some have attributed to Pascal this remarkable quote: "In every man is a God-shaped vacuum which can only be filled with Jesus Christ." Certainly each Jesus follower can attest to its truth.

To be without Christ is to be spiritually empty, to be with Christ is to be full.

FOR FURTHER READING: *The Weight of Glory*
by C. S. Lewis, "The Weight of Glory"

READ: Psalm 145:1–21

The Creator's Due

Every day I will bless You, and I will praise Your name forever and ever.
—Psalm 145:2

In *Christian Reflections*, C. S. Lewis wrote: "One of the things my conscience tells me is that if there exists an absolutely wise and good Person . . . I owe Him obedience, specially when that Person, as the ground of my existence, has a kind of paternal claim on me, and, as a benefactor, has a claim on my gratitude."

Lack of gratefulness can be one of the most annoying behaviors we encounter. When a husband goes "beyond the call of duty" in accomplishing a "honey do" list, he expects his spouse's thanks. Sometimes teens can be so self-absorbed that they seem to forget all the sacrifices their parents made to provide for them. And at work the supervisor who seems to be blind to the employee who puts in a lot of extra effort can be demotivating.

As God looks from heaven at the human race, we might ask, "How does God feel about the billions of people who rarely acknowledge His provision and care?" (see Romans 1:21). Certainly, the committed Christian should guard against ungratefulness and give the Creator His due. We are destined to live to the praise of God's glorious grace (Ephesians 1:3–14).

Let us give thanks to the Lord for His creation, redemption, and glory!

For Further Reading: *Christian Reflections* by C. S. Lewis, "Christianity and Culture"

READ: 2 Corinthians 3:1–18

Gazing at God

But we all, with unveiled face, beholding as in a mirror the glory of the Lord, are being transformed into the same image from glory to glory, just as by the Spirit of the Lord. —2 Corinthians 3:18

In *The Great Divorce*, C. S. Lewis wrote: "There is but one good; that is God. Everything else is good when it looks to Him and bad when it turns away." What does it mean to turn our gaze toward God?

In Paul's second letter to the church at Corinth, he develops the theme of gazing at God. In Exodus we read of Moses looking on the radiant presence of God and the supernatural glow his face took on from the experience (Exodus 34:35). The radiance was so great that he put a veil over his face when he was talking to the Israelites. Paul contrasts this to unbelieving Jews of his day who had a veil over their hearts so they could not receive the glorious reality of Jesus as Messiah (2 Corinthians 3:15). But for the believer in Christ this spiritual blindness has been removed. As a result, we are able to experience the direct revelation of God's glory and are transformed by it (v. 18). To turn our gaze to God is to be transformed into His image by the Spirit.

As we look into Scripture to see Christ, we find ourselves becoming like Him.

FOR FURTHER READING: *The Great Divorce* by C. S. Lewis, chapter 4

READ: Romans 3:1–12

Avoiding God

There is none who understands; there is none who seeks after God.
—Romans 3:11

Secular society has made up its mind to marginalize the Christian faith. Secularists from dawn to dusk find creative ways of avoiding God. C. S. Lewis put together a list of "God avoidance" strategies that help the sons of Adam and daughters of Eve hide from their Maker: "Avoid silence, avoid solitude, avoid any train of thought that leads off the beaten track. Concentrate on money, sex, status, health, and (above all) on your own grievances. Keep the radio on. Live in the crowd. Use plenty of sedation. If you must read books, select them very carefully. But you'd be safer to stick to the papers. You'll find the advertisements helpful; especially those with a sexy or a snobbish appeal."

For the follower of Christ who wants to make contact with God, a simpler and more satisfying strategy can be followed: Go to the pages of Scripture, find a solitary place, and—like Jesus—pray and listen to our heavenly Father (Mark 1:35). Redeemed sons and daughters of Adam and Eve have open access to a loving Creator who delights in being the center of their lives.

What we fill our minds with will determine
if we are seeking God or avoiding Him.

FOR FURTHER READING: *Christian Reflections*
by C. S. Lewis, "The Seeing Eye"

READ: Job 2:1–11

Refining Fire

But He knows the way that I take; when He has tested me, I shall come forth as gold.   —Job 23:10

In writing on the ancient history of the Jews, C. S. Lewis pondered how suffering purified their faith: "The lesson taught in the Book of Job was grimly illustrated in practice. . . . But the astonishing thing is that the religion is not destroyed. In its best representatives it grows purer, stronger, and more profound. It is being, by this terrible discipline, directed more and more to its real centre."

The suffering visited upon the people of God does have a corporate dimension, but the experience is also personal. When Job lost his wealth, children, reputation, and health, he recognized these losses as a refining fire: "But [God] knows the way that I take; when He has tested me, I shall come forth as gold" (Job 23:10). The dross, rock, and soil that hide the precious metal of faith must fall away, eventually revealing its precious content. Peter would echo the principle that suffering purifies our faith: "that the genuineness of your faith, being much more precious than gold that perishes, though it is tested by fire, may be found to praise, honor, and glory at the revelation of Jesus Christ" (1 Peter 1:7).

Problems can purify our faith and,
as a result, God gets the glory.

FOR FURTHER READING: *Reflections on the Psalms*
by C. S. Lewis, chapter 4

READ: John 20:11–18

Splendor from Brokenness

Mary Magdalene came and told the disciples that she had seen the Lord, and that He had spoken these things to her. —John 20:18

Mary Magdalene had been at the foot of the cross and heard the sobs of Jesus' mother, whom she tried to comfort. There was most likely some reminiscing about the marvels of His teaching and the miracles that flowed from His hands. The promise of a wonder-working Messiah had been dashed in a gruesome miscarriage of justice.

Later, as Mary Magdalene kneeled in anguish at the empty tomb, the angels asked, "Woman, why are you weeping?" Mary responded, "Because they have taken away my Lord and I do not know where they have laid Him" (John 20:13). Then she turned around and saw a man. When he called her by name, she knew it was Jesus and shouted, "Rabboni," meaning "Teacher." Before her stood not the mangled remains of a torture victim but the radiant new body that the resurrection had brought. Brokenness had been replaced with splendor. C. S. Lewis wrote: "There are also all sorts of things in our own spiritual life where a thing has to be killed, and broken, in order that it may then become bright, and strong, and splendid." Splendor comes from brokenness.

God will transform our broken lives into trophies of grace to His glory.

FOR FURTHER READING: *God in the Dock*
by C. S. Lewis, "The Grand Miracle"

READ: Matthew 21:28–32

Fruitful Repentance

A man had two sons, and he came to the first and said, "Son, go, work today in my vineyard." He answered and said, "I will not," but afterward he regretted it and went. —Matthew 21:28–29

In a letter, C. S. Lewis wrote of a positive aspect to repentance: "God will use all repented evil as fuel for fresh good in the end."

In the parable of the two sons, Jesus explained how saying "no" to God could be redeemed when a decided "yes" follows in heartfelt repentance. The son who initially disobeyed his father's command to work in the field eventually felt bad about this response and ultimately obeyed him. In contrast, the other son gave a verbal agreement but then chose to not do what his father had asked him to do.

Jesus then asked His listeners, "Which of the two did the will of his father?" And they answered, "The first." Those who heard our Lord's parable understood that repentance could lead to a greater good. The son who initially said, "No" and then felt his conscience moving him to obey had his character strengthened. The tasks he ultimately agreed to do were an asset to his dad's farming enterprise that day. Similarly, our initial response to disobey can be replaced by the choice of fruitful obedience.

An impulse to disobey God can be replaced with the choice to obey Him.

FOR FURTHER READING: *The Collected Letters of C. S. Lewis*, volume 2

READ: Matthew 14:22–33; James 1:6–7

Faith and Doubt

He did not waver at the promise of God through unbelief, but was strengthened in faith, giving glory to God, and being fully convinced that what He had promised He was also able to perform.
—Romans 4:20–21

Addressing the issue of faith and doubt, C. S. Lewis wrote the following: "Believe in God and you will have to face hours when it seems *obvious* that this material world is the only reality; disbelieve in Him and you must face hours when this material world seems to shout at you that it is *not* all" (*Christian Reflections*).

The president of a leading evangelical seminary once told the students the true story of a hardened atheist who was at breakfast with his young family. As the unbeliever ate his meal, he looked over at his baby daughter's tiny little ear and marveled. The soft pink contours of cartilage and skin formed a perfect receptor to sound from the outside world. He paused for just a few moments and speculated that her tiny ear looked like it had been designed by someone. Then he scoffed at the idea and pushed himself back into the comfort of his secular view of life. The seminary president then told the students: "Either you are a believer who is sometimes plagued by doubt or you an unbeliever who is plagued by faith." Which sounds like the better path?

Although our faith may ebb and flow with our changing circumstances, we can trust God in life's journey.

FOR FURTHER READING: *Christian Reflections*
by C. S. Lewis, "Religion: Reality or Substitute?"

READ: Genesis 1:27; 3:1–6; Psalm 8:1–9

Greatness and Fallenness

What is man that You are mindful of him, and the son of man that You visit him?   —Psalm 8:4

When young Prince Caspian is told he will become king of the newly liberated Narnia, he is filled with feelings of inadequacy. To these misgivings, the great lion Aslan reminds him of his ancestry, which should provide a healthy pride balanced by humility: "You come of the Lord Adam and the Lady Eve," said Aslan. "And that is both honour enough to erect the head of the poorest beggar, and shame enough to bow the shoulders of the greatest emperor on earth. Be content."

Look into the human heart, and you will find a similar balance in understanding our capacities for good and evil. We each possess marvelous capacities for creativity, conscience, and caring because we are made in God's image. But because we are all fallen creatures who have rebelled against our Creator, we have tendencies toward selfishness and doing harm to others.

But there is hope through redemption in Christ. By feeding on God's Word and being filled with His Spirit, we can become more like sons and daughters of God until the process is finally completed in glory (Romans 8:28–30).

> *We are honored to be made in God's image and should be humbled by our need for redemption.*

FOR FURTHER READING: *Prince Caspian*
by C. S. Lewis, Chapter 15

READ: Matthew 24:1–35

Move with the Times?

*Heaven and earth will pass away, but My words will by no means
pass away.* —Matthew 24:35

To look back on the flow of events in human history is to see changes
in clothes, customs, and ideas. Today especially we are asked to adapt
to every innovation in technology. We don't write letters like we used
to; instead, we e-mail or text others. Trying to find our destination no
longer requires a map but a smartphone. And once we have adapted to a
new way of communicating and keeping informed, newer innovations
demand a new learning curve.

This appeal to "move with the times" also has an impact on the
assumptions we hold and the ethics that guide our lives. Some things
that society considered wrong a generation ago are promoted as good
and healthy today. What is a Christian to do when faced with such
moral pressures?

C. S. Lewis also felt pressured to accept the values of his time. He
responded to this pressure by saying, "We must at all costs not move
with the times. We serve One who said, 'Heaven and Earth shall move
with the times, but my words shall not move with the times.' " The latest
opinion poll does not define right and wrong. The Word of God does.

*All physical reality in heaven and in earth will someday be
removed, yet Jesus Christ's words will stand indestructibly.*

For Further Reading: *God in the Dock*
by C. S. Lewis, "Christian Apologetics"

READ: Deuteronomy 31:6; Joshua 1:7–9;
1 Chronicles 28:20; Isaiah 41:10–13

Testing Point

Be of good courage, and He shall strengthen your heart, all you who hope in the LORD. —Psalm 31:24

When *The Screwtape Letters* was written, the threat of Nazi Germany was on the horizon. C. S. Lewis was highly qualified to write on the thoughts and feelings of people during wartime. As London endured aerial bombardment by German planes, Lewis used the reverse psychology of the character Screwtape to give the English people courage and hope.

One helpful idea set forth is the value of courage and how it relates to other Christian virtues. Screwtape explains to the younger demon Wormwood: "This, indeed, is probably one of the Enemy's motives for creating a dangerous world—a world in which moral issues really come to the point. He sees as well as you do that courage is not simply one of the virtues, but the form of every virtue at the testing point. . . . Pilate was merciful till it became risky."

This is a valuable lesson for us. Chastity. Temperance. Charity. Diligence. Patience. Kindness. Humility. These can only be successfully acted upon if we are faithful even when we are being threatened. For example, showing protective kindness to someone who is being bullied can put us at risk. Courage is required to show this kind of love.

We need to ask God for courage to do the right thing even when we face threatening circumstances.

FOR FURTHER READING: *The Screwtape Letters*
by C. S. Lewis, Letter 29

READ: Exodus 18:1–27

Divine Delegation

Moreover you shall select from all the people able men, such as fear God, men of truth, hating covetousness; and place such over them to be rulers of thousands, rulers of hundreds, rulers of fifties, and rulers of tens. And let them judge the people at all times.
—Exodus 18:21–22

God certainly does not need our help. But it appears that He delegates tasks to us for our own benefit. C. S. Lewis observed: "For [God] seems to do nothing of Himself which He can possibly delegate to His creatures. He commands us to do slowly and blunderingly what He could do perfectly and in the twinkling of an eye. . . . We are not mere recipients or spectators. We are either privileged to share in the game or compelled to collaborate in the work."

Delegation became a necessity in Moses' ministry. As Israel traveled to the Promised Land, Moses was obliged to mediate interpersonal conflicts. At times it became a burden. But when his father-in-law, Jethro, suggested that Moses delegate the minor cases to qualified leaders and take the difficult cases for himself, this solved the problem. The leadership and the followers were both happy!

God has called us to a "partnership in the gospel" (Philippians 1:5 NIV). Each of us possesses at least one spiritual gift given for the benefit of others (Romans 12:3–8; 1 Corinthians 12:1–11; Ephesians 4:7–16; 1 Peter 4:10–11). Spiritual gifts are God's way of delegating His tasks to us.

As subjects of Christ's eternal kingdom, each of us has been given something to do.

FOR FURTHER READING: *The World's Last Night and Other Essays* by C. S. Lewis, "The Efficacy of Prayer"

READ: Mark 4:26–29

A Seed in Waiting

For the earth yields crops by itself: first the blade, then the head,
after that the full grain in the head. —Mark 4:28

C. S. Lewis knew a thing or two about gardening, so it was natural for him to use the metaphor of a planted seed to represent our spiritual expectations for future glory. In a letter, he told his correspondent: "Think of yourself just as a seed patiently waiting in the earth; waiting to come up a flower in the Gardener's good time . . . . We are here in the land of dreams. But cock-crow is coming. It is nearer now than when I began this letter."

Do you remember being introduced as a kid to the wonders of growing seeds? Tiny seeds were placed in the moist soil and then covered over and gently watered. We were told to wait. Then a week or so later we were astonished to see tiny green shoots coming out of the ground. Jesus used the word picture of the growing seed to describe spiritual receptivity to the gospel. The Word of God planted in the receptive heart will result in future glory. The divine seed within us will some day yield its fruit of a glorified body in a radiant new world. In the meantime, the Great Gardener does His work.

God has planted His divine seed in the believer
with great expectations of future glory.

For Further Reading: *The Collected Letters of C. S. Lewis,* volume 3

READ: Matthew 18:2–4; 19:13–14

Through Children's Eyes

Then Jesus called a little child to Him, set him in the midst of them, and said, "Assuredly, I say to you, unless you are converted and become as little children, you will by no means enter the kingdom of heaven." —Matthew 18:2–3

In the preface to his first Narnia Chronicle, C. S. Lewis said to Lucy Barfield: "I wrote this story for you, but when I began it I had not realized that girls grow quicker than books. As a result you are already too old for fairy tales, and by the time it is printed and bound you will be older still. But some day you will be old enough to start reading fairy tales again. You can then take it down from some upper shelf, dust it, and tell me what you think of it. I shall probably be too deaf to hear, and too old to understand a word you say, but I shall still be your affectionate Godfather, C. S. Lewis."

Lewis believed that childhood wonder could be reacquired after we had grown but that cynicism cut people off from the grand stories of the past. Jesus told us how we could renew that childlike thinking: "Assuredly, I say to you, unless you are converted and become as little children, you will by no means enter the kingdom of heaven" (Matthew 18:3). It appears that God wants us to have the critical mind of an adult and the open heart of a child.

God wants our minds in fighting trim but our hearts trusting as a child.

FOR FURTHER READING: *The Lion, the Witch and the Wardrobe* by C. S. Lewis, Dedication

READ: Proverbs 9:1–10

Iron Sharpens Iron

As iron sharpens iron, so a man sharpens the countenance of his friend. —Proverbs 27:17

In his book *C. S. Lewis: Memories and Reflections*, John Lawlor remembers what it was like to be tutored by Lewis as a student at Oxford: "As for me, I passed from dislike and hostility to stubborn affection, and then to gratitude for the weekly bout in which no quarter was asked for or given."

In military history the phrase "give no quarter" referred to not taking prisoners when an enemy wanted to surrender. It implied a fight unto the death. In the academic world the phrase came to mean a determination to win an argument at all costs. Lewis learned this kind of rigorous argument from his own tutor William T. Kirkpatrick, whom he affectionately referred to as "The Great Knock."

Proverbs 27:17 encourages the challenge of refining mind and character between trusted friends. When one piece of iron is skillfully rubbed against another, the edge becomes sharper with every stroke. In a similar way, believers can sharpen the mind and the spirit of each other by engaging in challenging conversation. We can all grow through discussion and critical thinking as we strive to grow more like Christ.

Christian dialogue can be a dynamic source for personal growth.

FOR FURTHER READING: *C. S. Lewis: Memories and Reflections*
by John Lawlor, Part 1: Memories

READ: John 21:1–25

Shame: The Final Word?

Then [Peter] began to curse and swear, saying, "I do not know the Man!" Immediately a rooster crowed. And Peter remembered the word of Jesus who had said to him, "Before the rooster crows, you will deny Me three times." So he went out and wept bitterly.
—Matthew 26:74–75

It was morning and the designated leader of the twelve disciples had fished all night without success. Then from the shore he heard someone suggest he put out his net on the other side of the boat. When he did that, the net almost broke with the enormous catch of fish, and Peter knew it was the Lord who had made the suggestion (John 21:3–7).

After the awestruck disciples had eaten a meal with their risen Lord, Peter was pulled aside for a private conference. Earlier Peter had reneged on his promise to face death with Christ and had actually denied Him three times. Now the guilt of his cowardly act must have overwhelmed him and taken away any hope of ever serving the Lord. But after Christ confronted Peter's love for Him, an astounding second chance was offered. On the day of Pentecost, Peter's anointed preaching of the gospel resulted in three thousand souls coming to faith in Christ (Acts 2:41). C. S. Lewis said, "I sometimes think that shame, mere awkward, senseless shame, does as much towards preventing good acts and straightforward happiness as any of our vices can do." No matter what the sin, shame does not have to have the final word.

The God of grace is also the Lord of the second chance.

FOR FURTHER READING: *A Grief Observed* by C. S. Lewis

READ: Psalm 91:1; Matthew 6:1–34

The Secret Place

But you, when you pray, go into your room, and when you have shut your door, pray to your Father who is in the secret place; and your Father who sees in secret will reward you openly.
—Matthew 6:6

Jesus exposed the hypocrisy of the Pharisees, who loved to show off spiritually (Matthew 6:5).

The Pharisees loved to pray standing in a public place for the visibility it afforded. The word used for *standing* implies "taking an upright posture for a long time." And *street* is the Greek term for "a wide thoroughfare." In other words, a Pharisee would sometimes stand in a major travel area so the maximum number of people could see him praying. Christ pointed out that they did this in order to "be seen of men." And because of this, they sought and obtained in their prayer posturing spiritual recognition from others. This is not a picture of honest, heartfelt intercession but of spiritual grandstanding.

The lesson we can draw from this passage is clear. We should avoid the ego inflation that comes with parading one's spirituality for the applause of others. Instead, we should look for a private place to commune with our heavenly Father. C. S. Lewis said, "It is always possible that Jesus Christ meant what He said when He told us to seek the secret place and to close the door."

Our spiritual walk should not be on stage for others to see but in a prayer closet to receive the grace we need.

FOR FURTHER READING: *The Secret Place* by Lyle Dorsett, Preface

READ: Matthew 7:7; Mark 11:24; John 15:7;
Hebrews 11:6; James 5:7; 1 John 3:22

Prayer Log

I will praise You, for You have answered me. —Psalm 118:21

C. S. Lewis observed how we can fail to take note of answered prayer: "One simply fails to notice how many of one's intercessory prayers have been granted—never notices how the list of *Thank-yous* grows & perhaps outstrips the list of mere *Pleases.*"

Some believers set up a prayer log in which they note the date when a prayer request was given and the time when it was answered. In this way they monitor answered prayer, which can become a real incentive for trusting God for other needs. In contrast there are people of faith who take a more "in the moment" approach to intercession and may pray even more often but without the paperwork. Yet they mentally have ways of keeping track of God's faithfulness.

Whatever our respective styles of intercession, keeping an eye on answered prayer is important. Otherwise we may fall into the trap of ignoring the "thank-yous" while letting our "pleases" pile up. "In everything give thanks; for this is the will of God in Christ Jesus for you" (1 Thessalonians 5:18).

*Logging answered prayer can build
our faith in the Great Provider.*

READ: Matthew 7:1–5; James 4:11–12

Fault Finding

Judge not, that you be not judged. For with what judgment you judge, you will be judged; and with the measure you use, it will be measured back to you. —Matthew 7:1–2

Whose sins do you think about? C. S. Lewis said, "Those who do not think about their own sins make up for it by thinking incessantly about the sins of others." Today's key verses illustrate this point well.

In the ancient Jewish mind, the day of God's judgment often carried the idea of a measuring scale. Therefore, when Christ preached against a critical spirit, He warned that the same standard critics exacted on others would be brought down upon them. Our Lord's word picture of a speck in our neighbor's eye and a beam in our own illustrates how our own faults seem minor to us while those of others appear sizable.

When Jesus spoke of removing the beam from one's eye, He was likely referring to a procedure of eye surgery that caused pain but was therapeutic. Likewise, self-examination and correction of our own faults can also be painful. But this is necessary if we want to develop a humble estimation of ourselves and a balanced and gracious attitude toward others. If we are not vigilant in self-scrutiny, we can fall into the trap of becoming critics of others.

When we start with our own shortcomings, we are less likely to be overly critical of others.

For Further Reading: *God in the Dock* by C. S. Lewis, "Miserable Offenders"

READ: Acts 15:36–40; 2 Timothy 4:9–16

A Second Chance

Get Mark and bring him with you, for he is useful to me for ministry.
—2 Timothy 4:11

Near the end of his life, the apostle Paul composed a final inspired letter. His last requests are insightful. He reflected on those who had deserted him and those who had remained faithful to him in the cause of Christ. Interestingly, he asks for John Mark to be sent to him. The irony is that Paul and Mark had a stormy history. When Paul and Barnabas were preparing to revisit the churches they'd planted on their first missionary journey, a sharp disagreement erupted between the two over Mark (Acts 15:36–40). Mark had deserted them during the first missionary journey, and Barnabas wanted to include him on this next mission trip. Paul would not trust a second time someone who had shirked his responsibilities as Mark had. Later, Mark had somehow redeemed himself in Paul's eyes—so much so that Paul was now asking for his help in ministry in the final hours of his life.

A soured relationship was made sweet through renewed responsibility and a second chance. C. S. Lewis said, "It does one good to see the fine side of people we've always seen the worst of." Who deserves a second chance from you?

> *When we cast others in the role of villain, we can*
> *ask God to help us see some good in them.*

For Further Reading: *The Collected Letters of C. S. Lewis,* volume 1

In His Steps

For to this you were called, because Christ also suffered for us, leaving us an example, that you should follow His steps.
                                                                —1 Peter 2:21

Is there such a thing as perfect Christianity? C. S. Lewis addressed that when he said, "A perfect practice of Christianity would, of course, consist in a perfect imitation of the life of Christ. . . . It means that every single act and feeling, every experience, whether pleasant or unpleasant, must be referred to God."

First Peter 2:21 contains wonderful insights on the topic of imitating Christ. The word *example* is a Greek word used for teaching writing to pupils. The letters were written down for the students, who would carefully trace the letters to insure a growing mastery of the writing process. The word translated *follow* is taken from the world of painting. An apprentice would make changes in his work by following the help of a guide. The term translated as *steps* is better rendered *tracks* or *footprints*. The master has broken the path, and we follow the tracks left behind.

This principle is reflected in John's statement: "He who says he abides in Him ought himself also to walk just as He walked" (1 John 2:6). Lewis understood that this requires bringing our actions and feelings to God in following the Master's lead.

We become more like Christ as we see His life in Scripture and yield our daily lives to His indwelling Spirit.

FOR FURTHER READING: *God in the Dock*
by C. S. Lewis, "Answers to Questions on Christianity"

READ: Job 1:1–2:10

God's Hammer

*Then the L*ORD *said to Satan, "Have you considered My servant Job, that there is none like him on the earth, a blameless and upright man, one who fears God and shuns evil?"* —Job 1:8

Watching construction workers building a house can be a noisy experience. The sound of multiple hammers pounding nails into joints, beams, and cross bars can really make a racket. If we turn our attention to the building of the Christian's spiritual life, we notice that God sometimes choses to use "hammers" to make us into a more sturdy structure that is well pleasing to Him.

Living a righteous life is no protection against the mighty blows of suffering that come our way. Sometimes it is the enemy who is behind them. Godly Job exhibited a life that was so morally and spiritually exemplary that it became the focus of a dialogue between God and Satan. To test Job's motives, God gave Satan permission to send a series of calamities that did great harm to Job's family, possessions, and health. Yet before the story is over, Job is tested and comes forth as gold (Job 23:10). The terrible sufferings inflicted on Job by the devil were used by God to refine Job's faith in God's sovereignty. Reflecting on Satan's activity, C. S. Lewis wrote, "Satan is without doubt nothing else than a hammer in the hand of a benevolent and severe God."

God uses even evil for good, and He can
employ pain to perfect our faith.

READ: 3 John

Letter to a Child

I have no greater joy than to hear that my children walk in truth.
—3 John 4

The year was 1963, and C. S. Lewis was in ill health. Nonetheless, he took time to respond to the letter of a child named Philip. Complimenting the boy's fine written expression, Lewis also said he was delighted that Philip understood that in the Narnia Chronicles the lion Aslan represented Jesus Christ. The next day, November 22, 1963, C. S. Lewis died at his home at The Kilns, Oxford, England. This was only one week before his 65th birthday.

The New Testament also records an older person giving encouragement to younger ones. In old age, the apostle John sent a letter to his own spiritual children. In it we see the joy of a more mature believer encouraging his younger disciples to take baby steps in following Christ: "I have no greater joy than to hear that my children walk in truth" (3 John 4).

Encouraging spiritual understanding in the next generation should be the desire of all mature believers. A note of appreciation, a word of encouragement, disciplined intercession, or a bit of advice can all be things that help others on their spiritual journey.

> *Do you know a younger believer who*
> *might need some encouragement?*

FOR FURTHER READING: *C. S. Lewis' Letters to Children,*
edited by Lyle W. Dorsett and Marjorie Lamp Mead

READ: Matthew 28:19–20; Acts 1:4–8; 2 Corinthians 5:12–21

Renaissance Man

Now then, we are ambassadors for Christ, as though God were pleading through us: we implore you on Christ's behalf, be reconciled to God. —2 Corinthians 5:20

C. S. Lewis was most definitely a "Renaissance man." The term refers to a master of many subjects. Some said of him that he had read everything and remembered everything he read. This is certainly an overstatement. But Lewis was gifted in devouring a multitude of books and retaining their essence. Lewis loved the medieval period and demonstrated facility in multiple languages. Deeply familiar with the intellectual heritage of the Greco-Roman world, he also distinguished himself in the study of English literature.

Yet with all this scholarly interest, C. S. Lewis sometimes sounded very narrow-minded. In one essay, he wrote: "The glory of God, and, as our only means to glorifying Him, the salvation of human souls, is the real business of life." How could Lewis immerse himself in such vast learning and still have a single focus such as the salvation of souls? The most likely explanation is that he realized the human soul is eternal and will live on long after our material world has come to an end (2 Corinthians 5:12–21; Revelation 21). That makes salvation absolutely essential—no matter who you are.

Our personal interests matter, but we must always keep our eyes on eternal values.

FOR FURTHER READING: *Christian Reflections* by C. S. Lewis, "Christianity and Culture"

READ: Psalms 6:1–10; 30:1–12

Blinded by Tears

Weeping may endure for a night, but joy comes in the morning.
—Psalm 30:5

As C. S. Lewis mourned the death of his wife, Joy, he observed, "You can't see anything properly while your eyes are blurred with tears." Those who have experienced deep grief can relate to those who spend extended time weeping. One woman grieving the loss of her son said, "I have cried enough tears to float a boat." Another man who was going through an unwanted divorce told a confidant: "I was worried about my tear ducts giving out. There has been so much continual crying."

Psalm 6:6 describes this flood of tears: "I am weary with my groaning; all night I make my bed swim; I drench my couch with my tears." Crying is usually accompanied by sighs. And when weeping continues for an extended time, it can cause emotional and even physical exhaustion. The psalmist feels as if he is afloat on a sea of tears.

But God is the one who attends us during the highs and the lows. It is He who comforts us when we weep, and it is He who will send new joys to fill our lives (Psalm 30:5).

Weeping may endure for a night, but joy comes in the morning. —Psalm 30:5

For Further Reading: *A Grief Observed*
by C. S. Lewis, chapter 1

READ: Romans 7:1–8:1

Prone to Wander

For what I am doing, I do not understand. For what I will to do,
that I do not practice; but what I hate, that I do. —Romans 7:15

In 1757 Pastor Robert Robinson, at the young age of 22, wrote a hymn that is still familiar to many: "Come Thou Fount of Every Blessing." In this enduring song of praise, he captures an inner reality for all believers: "Prone to wander, Lord, I feel it, prone to leave the God I love; here's my heart, O take and seal it, seal it for Thy courts above." These lines clearly reveal a dark secret we all struggle with. Even if we have been redeemed, the influence of our sin nature can cause us to stray from the path of righteousness.

C. S. Lewis gave his input on this common struggle: "To find that one's emotions do not 'come to heel' and line up as stable sentiment in conformity with one's convictions is simply the facts of being fallen, and still imperfectly redeemed, man. We may be thankful if, by continual prayer and self-discipline, we can, over years, make some approach to that stability. After all, St. Paul, who was a good deal further along the road than you and I, could still write Romans, chapter 7." We are all prone to wander, so we must let our Father seal our hearts.

Prayer, Bible study, discipline, and accountability to
others can help us in our proneness to wander.

For Further Reading: *Christian Reflections*
by C. S. Lewis, "Christianity and Culture"

READ: Psalm 55; 1 John 3:19–21

Forgiving Ourselves

For if our heart condemns us, God is greater than our heart, and knows all things. —1 John 3:20

It is a serious mistake to not forgive ourselves when God has already forgiven us. C. S. Lewis suggested as much in a letter he wrote to a Miss Breckenridge in 1951. He said that failing to do so is "almost like setting ourselves up as a higher tribunal than [God]." But Lewis understood that absolving oneself of guilt is a common problem.

Thankfully, 1 John 3:20 provides God's solution to this inner conflict. Pangs of remorse can trouble our hearts years after we have committed a serious sin. No two believers have identical consciences or the exact response to personal transgressions. Some are overly perfectionistic while others may need to grow in sensitivity to sin. The Greek word translated as *condemn* in this verse means "to declare guilty," "to name for punishment," or "to cause to find sin." Fortunately, "God is greater than our heart" (1 John 3:20). Because God is perfect love and holiness as well as being omnipresent and omniscient, He knows the true picture of our guilt. We don't. More importantly, God has the basis by which He can respond graciously to our dilemma and grant forgiveness. In short, it is the redemptive word of His Son on the cross (2 Corinthians 5:21).

Our conscience is not always an accurate monitor of our moral decisions. But the God of grace revealed in Scripture is.

FOR FURTHER READING: *The Collected Letters of C. S. Lewis,* volume 3

READ: 1 Corinthians 7:1–40

Just My Opinion

Now concerning virgins: I have no commandment from the Lord;
yet I give judgment as one whom the Lord in His mercy has made
trustworthy. —1 Corinthians 7:25

During the Easter season of 1945, C. S. Lewis delivered a paper to an assembly of Anglican priests and youth leaders meeting together in Wales. The purpose of his message was to equip clergy for the important work of defending the truth of Christianity. In his presentation Lewis made an important distinction between one's individual views and the claims of the Christian belief system: "When we mention our personal opinions, we must always make quite clear the difference between them and the Faith itself."

In today's reading we see Paul making a distinction between the direct commands of Scripture and one's personal opinion. In a persecuted church waiting for the return of Jesus Christ, the question of marrying or remaining single became an issue. Paul admits that he has "no commandment from the Lord" on this subject. This would be a clear imperative handed down to Christ's disciples while on earth or a revelation given directly to Paul. Instead, the apostle gives his own "judgment" on the matter. The Greek word means "opinion or one's personal view on the matter." Paul makes a distinction between the commands of Scripture and his own opinions. It's a distinction we need to recognize as well.

It's important that we discern the difference
between Scripture and personal opinions.

For Further Reading: *God in the Dock*
by C. S. Lewis, "Christian Apologetics"

READ: Acts 15:36–40; 23:1–5; 2 Corinthians 10:1–6

Anger Management

"Be angry, and do not sin": do not let the sun go down on your wrath.
—Ephesians 4:26

"Reasonableness and amiability (both cheerful 'habits' of the mind) are stronger in the end than the . . . spleen," suggested C. S. Lewis. "To rail is the sad privilege of the loser." In the medieval period various organs of the body were believed to store certain "humours," which affected someone emotionally. The spleen was considered to contain anger. From this we get the phrase to "ventilate your spleen," which means to express anger verbally and to relieve inner turmoil.

Some of us have more of a temper than others. At times the apostle Paul had an anger problem. When John Mark deserted Barnabas and Paul on their first missionary journey and then later asked to be reinstated, "a sharp disagreement" arose between the two apostles. Later, when Paul stood before the high priest, rather than turning the other cheek when struck in the face he called the high priest "a whitewashed wall" (Acts 23:3).

In many ways, Paul's lapses into anger should give us hope for managing our own anger. Few of us have never had an anger outburst we haven't regretted. It is important to practice reasonableness instead of "venting our spleen." (See 2 Corinthians 10:1–6.)

Each of us should be on guard in how we express anger.

FOR FURTHER READING: *Selected Literary Essays*
by C. S. Lewis, "Addison"

READ: Acts 2:25–32; 5:29–32; 1 Corinthians 15:3–8; 2 Peter 1:16

No Middle Way

Sanctify them by Your truth. Your word is truth. —John 17:17

In his essay "Man or Rabbit?" C. S. Lewis demands that the reader make a decision about the truth or falsity of the Christian faith: "Here is a door, behind which, according to some people, the secret of the universe is waiting for you." Lewis then goes on to say that an honest response to this claim will bring about one of two responses. Either someone will devote his or her life to serving this great secret or to exposing it as a hoax. There really is no middle ground.

Certainly the apostle Paul was convinced of the truth concerning the claims of Christ. Originally a Pharisee who zealously persecuted the followers of Christ, he encountered the living Christ on the road to Damascus and all of that changed. Paul came to see the reality of Jesus as Messiah fulfilled in prophecy, attested by miracles, and witnessed to by Christ's resurrection. Saul the persecutor had become Paul the apostle to the Gentiles. Today many want to remain neutral about the claims of Christ. But our Lord did not leave this alternative open to us. Either we are for Christ or against Him. There is no middle way.

*Each person must make a decision about
the truth claims of Jesus Christ.*

FOR FURTHER READING: *God in the Dock*
by C. S. Lewis, "Man or Rabbit?"

READ: Daniel 4:28–37

Pride's Punishment

Now I, Nebuchadnezzar, praise and extol and honor the King of heaven, all of whose works are truth, and His ways justice. And those who walk in pride He is able to put down. —Daniel 4:37

In *The Horse and His Boy*, we read of a noble from the country of Calormen. His name is Rabadash, and he is filled with pride. Leading an army to invade Archenland, Rabadash is defeated and taken captive. King Lune wishes to grant him mercy, but all Rabadash does is swear vengeance on the kind king. Aslan intervenes and turns Rabadash into a donkey. Although Aslan gives Rabadash stipulations to regain his humanity, Rabadash's people will first see him as a donkey. Rabadash the Great becomes a byword among his people: "Rabadash the Ridiculous."

In Daniel we read of a monarch with a similar ego problem. At the apex of his reign, Nebuchadnezzar gave himself credit for everything he saw: "Is not this great Babylon, that I have built for a royal dwelling by my mighty power and for the honor of my majesty?" (Daniel 4:30). Then a great voice from heaven proclaimed divine discipline for his arrogance. Nebuchadnezzar began living in the wild and eating grass like an animal. Finally, after several years God mercifully restored his sanity. Out of gratitude for this mental restoration, Nebuchadnezzar publicly praised the God of heaven and warned others of the consequences of pride.

The Scriptures teach that pride comes before a fall.

FOR FURTHER READING: *The Horse and His Boy*
by C. S. Lewis, chapter 15

READ: 1 Corinthians 12:12–31

Parliament of Owls

There is neither Jew nor Greek, there is neither slave nor free, there is neither male nor female; for you are all one in Christ Jesus.
—Galatians 3:28

Have you met Glimfeather? He is a talking owl that appears in C. S. Lewis' book *The Silver Chair*. Glimfeather mixes English and owl-like "hoo" sounds when he talks. After conferring with a parliament of his fellow owls, he assists Jill and Eustace in looking for the lost Prince Rilian. Lewis' ability to portray convincing animal characters is one of the many reasons the Narnian tales continue to win new readers with the passage of time.

Some animals have acquired amusing group names. Here are just a few: a dazzle of zebras; a pitying of turtle doves; a tower of giraffes; a troop of monkeys; a float of crocodiles; a leap of leopards; a murmuration of starlings; an army of frogs; a cackle of hyenas; a pride of lions; a scourge of mosquitoes; a parliament of owls; and a convocation of eagles. And this is only a short list! God delights in giving us a wonderful diversity of life on our planet.

The principle of diversity may also be seen in the church—the body of Christ around the world. Believers in Christ reflect differences in language, customs, and physical appearance. Yet each is part of an eternal family made up "of every tribe and tongue and people and nation" (Revelation 5:9).

God delights in an eternal family of all kinds, and so should we.

FOR FURTHER READING: *The Silver Chair* by C. S. Lewis, chapter 4

READ: Genesis 39:1–6; 41:1–57

Life Witness

And [Joseph's] master saw that the LORD was with him and that the LORD made all he did to prosper in his hand. —Genesis 39:3

Concerning spreading the gospel in a hostile secular society, C. S. Lewis said, "We must attack the enemy's line of communication. What we want is not more little books about Christianity, but more little books by Christians on other subjects—their Christianity latent." Not many of us are called to write a book, but all of us are telling a story with how we live. Our faith may be latent but not silent.

In the Old Testament we never see Joseph writing a book. But his dynamic faith was visible though not always spoken. Serving effectively in the house of Potiphar, Joseph was recognized as one with whom the Lord was at work. Later, when he was unjustly put in prison, even there he earned a platform of credibility. When Joseph was finally given an opportunity to openly share his faith through the interpretation of dreams, Pharaoh exclaimed that God was with him. Likewise for us, there is a time to show God's reality by how we live and other times when we should openly share spiritual truths.

Wherever we work, our latent faith should show a distinctive difference to God's glory.

FOR FURTHER READING: *God in the Dock* by C. S. Lewis, "Christian Apologetics"

READ: Acts 26:1–30

We Need to Talk

For if I preach the gospel, I have nothing to boast of, for necessity is laid upon me; yes, woe is me if I do not preach the gospel!
—1 Corinthians 9:16

"Christianity is not merely what a man does with his solitude," wrote C. S. Lewis. "It tells of God descending into the coarse publicity of history and there enacting what can—and must—be talked about."

The unlikely duo of Paul and Jonah provide us with a fascinating parallel in struggling with telling others about God's truth. Saul of Tarsus actually fought against the gospel until he met Jesus personally on the road to Damascus (Acts 22:6–10). Jonah was commanded to preach God's Word to a people he personally hated, the Ninevites. But despite the fact that both Paul and Jonah initially opposed telling others God's truth, the Lord finally had His way with them.

For many of us, the call to tell others about our faith can make us feel ill at ease. Wouldn't it be safer just to respect the privacy of others and avoid religion altogether?

But each of us has a platform through which we can and ought to share the gospel with friends, relatives, and neighbors. And we have the Lord's promise to empower His message of God's love (John 3:16; Acts 1:8).

Some may feel religion is a private matter, but the gospel is something that must be talked about.

FOR FURTHER READING: *God in the Dock* by C. S. Lewis, "The Founding of the Oxford Socratic Club"

READ: Acts 2:41–47

Christian Camaraderie

By this all will know that you are My disciples, if you have love for one another. —John 13:35

Hugo Dyson was an authority on Shakespeare, and J. R. R. Tolkien was a professor of Anglo-Saxon literature. As younger men, the two would dialogue with their atheist friend Jack Lewis. When Lewis finally became a Christian, the deep friendship among the three was made even stronger by their shared faith in Christ. These comrades in faith were joined with others to make up the Inklings, an informal literary group that took turns critiquing each other's writing projects. Lewis later reflected: "Dyson and Tolkien were the immediate human causes of my conversion. Is any pleasure on earth as great as a circle of Christ friends by a good fire?"

The foundation of Christian friendship lies in the shared experience of redemption in Christ. The newborn church in Jerusalem met in homes, celebrated the Word and prayer, and showed love that flowed out to others in the community (Acts 2:46–47). It was the spiritual reality they shared that caused their fellowship to grow in quality and outreach. Even today, Christian camaraderie finds its foundation in a converted heart, which kindles the flame of Christ within.

A shared Christian faith provides the deepest level of friendship known to the redeemed.

READ: Joshua 22:1–34

What Are Your Motives?

What treachery is this that you have committed against the God of Israel, to turn away this day from following the LORD, in that you have built for yourselves an altar, that you might rebel this day against the LORD? —Joshua 22:16

Nothing is quite as helpful in discerning an apparent indiscretion by another person as learning the person's motive. C. S. Lewis said this about motives: "We are doubles full of faults and do not shun criticism, provided such criticism is based on an understanding of our aims. You may not agree with these aims—though I hope that you will—but do not blame a man for making slow progress to the North when he is trying to get to the East."

We can be quick to criticize what people say or do without understanding what lies behind their words or actions. Think of the times you have made judgments about someone without understanding his or her motives.

After the allotment of territories to various tribes in the Promised Land, the tribes on the east bank of the Jordan built an altar. The rest of Israel misunderstood this as an act of apostasy against the centralized religious faith of their nation. Israel gathered for war until a wise leader named Phineas intervened by asking the reason for the altar. Then he learned that it was a memorial altar constructed to teach the children their kinship with the other tribes. This realization defused the conflict immediately. An earlier "motive check" would have prevented this problem.

We should be slow to judge when we do not know a person's motives.

FOR FURTHER READING: *Rehabilitations, and other Essays* by C. S. Lewis, "The Idea of an English School"

READ: Genesis 1:28; 2:19; Exodus 23:5; Deuteronomy 22:6–7; 25:4

Cruelty to Animals

A righteous man regards the life of his animal, but the tender mercies of the wicked are cruel. —Proverbs 12:10

C. S. Lewis loved both pets and animals in the wild. He often encountered animals on his many walking tours. He was horrified by animal abuse, and he even wrote on the subject. In the essay "Vivisection," Lewis wrote: "In justifying cruelty to animals we put ourselves also on the animal level. We choose the jungle and must abide by our choice."

Proverbs 12:10 tells us that the person with spiritual integrity has concerns that reach beyond himself and his immediate family. He is also attentive to the needs of his pets and livestock. In our key verse today "regards the life of his animals" might be better rendered "cares for the needs of" or "knows the soul" of his beast. Often each pet has a unique emotional response to family members. Also, their basic needs of food, water, and exercise come into play. Righteous people care for the needs of animals while the wicked abuse them through cruelty and neglect. As good stewards of God's good earth, we should show respect to the animal kingdom: "The righteous knows the soul of his beast."

The Scriptures admonish us to show kindness to the animals entrusted to our care.

FOR FURTHER READING: *God in the Dock*
by C. S. Lewis, "Vivisection"

READ: Colossians 2:1–15; Hebrews 2:1–18

Victory Over Death

Forasmuch then as the children are partakers of flesh and blood, he also himself likewise took part of the same; that through death he might destroy him that had the power of death, that is, the devil. —Hebrews 2:14 (KJV)

In his book *Miracles*, C. S. Lewis expressed his view on this matter: "Human death is the result of sin and the triumph of Satan. But it is also the means of redemption from sin, God's medicine for man and His weapon against Satan."

Since the fall of our first spiritual parents in an idyllic garden, the fear of death has hung over every member of the human race. Because Satan understood this, he and his minions have exploited this dread to influence people to wrong moral choices for self-preservation. This morbid fear of death held people in bondage until God provided the solution. Near the end of Jesus' public ministry on earth, He began to tell His disciples that soon He would be betrayed and then killed by evil men. But on the third day, He would rise from the dead (Mark 8:31). Christ's victory over death took away the devil's power over human beings. Through His death and resurrection, Christ disarmed all principalities and powers and triumphed over them (Colossians 2:14–15). Because of that, we have victory over death!

Satan used death to banish humans from God's presence, but Christ's victory over death made a way for them to become children of God.

FOR FURTHER READING: *Miracles* by C. S. Lewis, chapter 14

READ: Matthew 23:1–23

What Matters

Woe to you, scribes and Pharisees, hypocrites! For you pay tithe of mint and anise and cummin, and have neglected the weightier matters of the law: justice and mercy and faith. These you ought to have done, without leaving the others undone. —Matthew 23:23

As a student of culture, C. S. Lewis had an opinion about the education system of his day. He wrote: "All schools, both here [in England] and in America, ought to teach far fewer subjects and teach them far better." That observation still has value. In our age of Internet inclusivism and global sensitivity, our focus can be so broad in its sweep that we tend to neglect the weightier things. We may have casual acquaintance with many subjects but not a deep engagement with a few. Someone has wisely said, "Everyone's responsibility is no one's responsibility." In a similar way, to focus on everything is to focus on nothing. The old adage "Jack of all trades and master of none" applies here.

In our study of Scripture, our focus matters. But what might be considered things of more weight than others? Our Lord scolded the Pharisees for becoming experts in the Mosaic Law while missing the most important aspects of the Law. The Pharisees were preoccupied with the minutia of obedience to tithing to the extreme—while at the same time neglecting what Jesus said was "the weightier things of the Law," namely, justice, mercy, and faith. When we study the Bible, we should consider what matters: fair play, a forgiving attitude, and trusting God.

When we study Scripture, let's keep our focus
fixed on the things that matter.

FOR FURTHER READING: *C. S. Lewis' Letters to Children,*
edited by Lyle W. Dorsett and Marjorie Lamp Mead

READ: Matthew 27:32–50

"Eli, Eli, Lama Sabachthani?"

And about the ninth hour Jesus cried out with a loud voice, say-ing, "Eli, Eli, lama sabachthani?" that is, "My God, My God, why have You forsaken Me?" —Matthew 27:46

C. S. Lewis' portrait of the evil scientist Weston in *Perelandra* has been described as the most realistic depiction of a demon-possessed man ever written. When Professor Ransom tries to prevent Weston from persuad-ing the Perelandra Eve to disobey her creator, a shocking scene ensues. An evil intelligence inside Weston claims that he was at the foot of the cross when Jesus was executed. Then he shouts, "Eli, Eli, lama sabach-thani!" Ransom recognizes the quote from the New Testament, but then a chill goes down his spine when he realizes that Weston spoke the orig-inal Aramaic from memory. He was quoting what he personally heard Christ say from the cross. As the story continues, Ransom calls Weston the "unman" because a fallen angel was directing his words and deeds.

Sometimes the stark reality of our Lord's death can become all too familiar. But through re-addressing this story, as did Lewis, with evil clearly depicted, we gain a new appreciation for what our Lord went through to purchase our salvation. We see anew the glorious victory that came when He rose from the dead.

The demonic world was decisively defeated at the cross of Jesus Christ.

FOR FURTHER READING: *Perelandra* by C. S Lewis, chapter 12

READ: 1 Corinthians 3:9–15; 2 Corinthians 5:1–11

Purgatory?

For we must all appear before the judgment seat of Christ, that each one may receive the things done in the body, according to what he has done, whether good or bad. —2 Corinthians 5:10

C. S. Lewis' belief in purgatory is controversial. The idea of purifying fire after death to prepare the believer for heaven is repugnant to Protestants because of the lack of scriptural evidence to support it. Ironically, Catholics are also put off by Lewis because he rejected the Catholic view of purgatory, calling it a "Romish doctrine." So, if Lewis disagreed with both camps, what was his view? Lewis felt Cardinal John Henry Newman's poem "The Dream of Gerontius" best expressed what happens to the believer after death. The gaze of love between Redeemer and creature give the one being purified endurance to withstand a final cleaning process before entering heaven.

Perhaps both Christian traditions can provide a few points of consensus. We can all agree that Christ paid the penalty for our sin on the cross. But we also need to be reminded that Christ will scrutinize our lives with His burning gaze. Paul had a reverential fear of standing before the judgment seat of Christ, and so should we. "Knowing, therefore, the terror of the Lord, we persuade men" (2 Corinthians 5:11).

*Every believer will someday stand before
the judgment seat of Christ.*

FOR FURTHER READING: *Letters to Malcolm: Chiefly on Prayer* by C. S. Lewis, chapter 20

READ: John 9:1–41

Your Story

One thing I know: that though I was blind, now I see.

—John 9:25

In *Spenser's Images of Life*, C. S. Lewis wrote: "Just as a lobster wears its skeleton outside, so the characters in Romance wear their character outside. For it is their story, that is their character."

Although Lewis was speaking in terms of literary characters, his words can apply to us. In many ways each of us has a story that should be apparent to others. During His three-year public ministry, the Lord Jesus Christ was a controversial figure. The religious leaders of the day found His message of grace and social contact with sinners too much to stomach. Then when Christ gave sight to a man who had been born blind, this miracle became an illustration of spiritual blindness versus spiritual sight.

When the Pharisees told the man healed of his blindness that Jesus was a sinner, the man said, "Whether He is a sinner or not I do not know. One thing I know: that though I was blind, now I see" (John 9:24–25). Because Christ has touched our lives, we need to be open to share our story of His marvelous, life-changing presence.

Each of us has a story to share about how Christ has changed us.

FOR FURTHER READING: *Spenser's Images of Life*
by C. S. Lewis, chapter 9

READ: Isaiah 43:1–19

Living in the Present

Do not remember the former things, nor consider the things of old. Behold, I will do a new thing, now it shall spring forth; shall you not know it? I will even make a road in the wilderness and rivers in the desert. —Isaiah 43:18–19

In C. S. Lewis' book *Out of the Silent Planet,* when the evil scientist Weston and his accomplice Devin kidnap Professor Elwin Ransom and take him to another planet, Ransom is able to escape captivity. The fugitive then encounters various races, which have not fallen into sin as we have. In one conversation with extraterrestrials, Ransom learns how fickle human beings can be when they long for the past. "And how could we endure to live and let time pass if we were always crying for one day or one year to come back—if we did not know that every day in a life fills the whole life with expectation and memory and that these are that day?"

The problem of living in the past is addressed in Scripture. When Isaiah spoke to the Jews returning from the Babylonian captivity, he recognized their tendency to focus on happier days of past blessing (Isaiah 43:18–19). But the prophet now called them to a renewed expectation of God's provision in the present and ultimately a place of eternal bliss in the Messianic kingdom. Living in the past can dull our senses and prevent us from clearly seeing the wonderful blessing of the present.

Let's look for God's provision in the present and not focus on happier days in the past.

For Further Reading: *Out of the Silent Planet*
by C. S. Lewis, chapter 12

READ: Genesis 1:1–31

In the Beginning

By faith we understand that the worlds were framed by the word of God, so that the things which are seen were not made of things which are visible. —Hebrews 11:3

As C. S. Lewis reflected on the first verse of the Bible, he wrote: "No philosophical theory which I have yet come across is a radical improvement on the words of Genesis, that 'In the beginning God made Heaven and Earth.'"

Bible teacher Warren Wiersbe holds a similar view: "No scientist or historian can improve upon, 'In the beginning God . . . .' This simple statement refutes the atheist, who says there is no God; the agnostic, who claims we cannot know God; the polytheist, who worships many gods; the pantheist, who says that 'all nature is God'; the materialist, who claims that matter is eternal and not created . . . . God's personality is seen in this chapter, for He speaks, sees, names, and blesses."

The Word of God tells us that the universe did not come into existence by blind chance. Instead, it was willed into existence by a personal God. Later, that same deity would reveal himself to succeeding generations and then become a man and step into human history. Ultimately, He would pay the penalty for sin and rise from the dead—leading the way to a new creation yet to come. But it all started with these four words: "In the beginning God."

The story of our universe begins with God and will receive a new beginning with God.

FOR FURTHER READING: *Miracles* by C. S. Lewis, chapter 4

READ: Luke 18:9–14

Pride and Prayer

And the tax collector, standing afar off, would not so much as raise his eyes to heaven, but beat his breast, saying, "God, be merciful to me a sinner!"　　　　　　　　　—Luke 18:13

In first-century Judea, the person often considered beyond reproach was the Pharisee. Conversely, the villainous members of society were tax collectors who collaborated with the Romans and skimmed off the top for personal gain.

This is why the parable of the Pharisee and the tax collector (Luke 18:9–14) was so shocking to the listeners' ears. The Pharisee, smug in his self-righteousness, cited the many commendable deeds he had done. Yet the tax gatherer showed signs of deep regret for his transgressions and begged God for mercy. Our Lord told His listeners that the humility of the tax collector had been met with divine forgiveness while the pride of the Pharisee left him unforgiven. C. S. Lewis said, "All men alike stand condemned, not by alien codes of ethics, but by their own, and all men therefore are conscious of guilt." But it is possible for a self-righteous person to deceive himself into ignoring his conscience.

Maintaining a healthy conscience requires times of reflection, confession, repentance, and—when necessary—restitution for those wronged (Exodus 22:7; 1 John 1:1–10). In prayer, let's discover and reject any pride in our lives.

Although everyone has a conscience, its moral health depends on the attention given it.

FOR FURTHER READING: *The Problem of Pain* by C. S. Lewis, Introduction

READ: Psalm 63:1–11

Christian Liturgy

*So I have looked for You in the sanctuary, to see Your power and
Your glory.* —Psalm 63:2

In *Letters to Malcolm: Chiefly on Prayer*, C. S. Lewis commented on interacting with the worship service: "Novelty, simply as such, can have only an entertainment value. And they don't go to church to be entertained. They go to *use* the service, or, if you prefer, to *enact*. Every service is a structure of acts and words through which we receive a sacrament, or repent, or supplicate, or adore."

Christian liturgy varies greatly among Christian churches. High-church traditional services follow an ancient and elaborate series of rituals. Prior to Vatican II, the Roman Catholic Church conducted its religious ceremonies in Latin in solidarity with the "one universal catholic church." Those of us who attend Protestant churches are often part of a low-church tradition. Here the order of service has been chiefly designed with a clear focus on the preaching of the Word of God. Nonetheless, even the most fundamentalist Protestant churches have their own simplified liturgy, which is often quite predictable. No matter whether we attend high church or low, we should come to the worship service to praise God and receive spiritual nourishment.

*Church worship services may vary, but we
should align our hearts with the church
we attend in order to both give and receive.*

For Further Reading: *Letters to Malcolm: Chiefly on Prayer*
by C. S. Lewis, chapter 1

READ: 1 Corinthians 11:17–34

Symbol of Sacrifice

In the same manner [Jesus] also took the cup after supper, saying, "This cup is the new covenant in My blood. This do, as often as you drink it, in remembrance of Me." —1 Corinthians 11:25

A stained-glass window in Saint Mark's Church, Gillingham, England, portrays a stunning image entitled *A Pelican in Her Piety.* The carved, colored glass depicts a majestic mother pelican piercing her breast with her beak so blood can spill into the mouths of her hungry chicks.

In medieval times, observers would see a pelican feeding her young and mistake the red stain of fish in her pouch for the mother pelican giving her own blood to feed her young. Despite this misunderstanding, the mother pelican became a powerful symbol in the medieval mind of Christ's redeeming blood shed for us.

C. S. Lewis, who specialized in medieval studies, understood the stature that pelicans merited in the Middle Ages. Correspondingly, in *The Magician's Nephew*, Lewis included them as part of the retinue attending the first coronation of King Frank, the first royal sovereign of Narnia. Lewis also included pelicans in the war efforts of strategic Narnian battles. But the takeaway value for the believer today is to see how the symbol of the pelican can serve as a reminder of the sacrifice of Jesus Christ for our redemption.

Jesus Christ shed His own blood to redeem us from the power and penalty of sin.

FOR FURTHER READING: *The Magician's Nephew* by C. S. Lewis, chapter 14

READ: Isaiah 43:16–21; 58:11; John 7:37–39

Irrigating Blessings

For the land which you go to possess is not like the land of Egypt from which you have come, where you sowed your seed and watered it by foot, as a vegetable garden. —Deuteronomy 11:10

In *Reflections on the Psalms*, C. S. Lewis used the illustration of irrigation to speak about the channel we dig with our lives through obedient behavior: "When we carry out our 'religious duties,' we are like people digging channels in a waterless land, in order that when at last the water comes, it may find them ready. I mean, for the most part. There are happy moments even now, when a trickle creeps along the dry beds; and happy souls to whom this happens often."

When the children of Israel were in bondage in Egypt, their responsibilities varied. Interestingly, they were not exclusively pyramid builders as is so commonly thought. In reality, some worked as field hands. In Deuteronomy 11:10, we see an interesting reference to God contrasting the Israelites' field irrigation work in Egypt with the promise of seasonal rain in the land flowing with milk and honey. The Jews were being promised that their future earthly home would have adequate rain so that the drudgery of irrigation would not be necessary. Similarly, we can learn from this that acts of obedience in following God create channels that can direct blessings from heaven when they are given.

Obedient Christian habits open channels for blessing.

FOR FURTHER READING: *Reflections on the Psalms* by C. S. Lewis, chapter 9

READ: Deuteronomy 6:10–12, 8:18; Psalm 24:1; 2 Corinthians 9:6–11

Giving Back

Give, and it will be given to you: good measure, pressed down, shaken together, and running over will be put into your bosom. For with the same measure that you use, it will be measured back to you. —Luke 6:38

In *Mere Christianity*, C. S. Lewis commented on believers' giving and their relationship with their heavenly Father: "If you devoted every moment of your whole life exclusively to [God's] service, you could not give Him anything that was not in a sense His own already."

Small children can be adorable in their attempts to give back to their parents. A little girl may ask her father for some money so she can buy him something for Christmas. Dad grants her request while Mom takes her shopping for Daddy's special present. On Christmas morning the child's eyes are glued to her father as he opens up the carefully wrapped item she bought him. The little girl then squeals with delight as her father showers her with praise for such a "wonderful gift." Dad knows, however, that it was his money that bought his present. Just the same, he delights in receiving it from his child.

The same principle is true in giving back to the Lord's work. There is not anything we give that was not originally given to us by God. It is our heart, not the gift, that is important.

Giving back to God involves resources He has graced us with in the first place.

FOR FURTHER READING: *Mere Christianity*
by C. S. Lewis, book 4, chapter 11

READ: Genesis 28:10–22

Spiritual Prompts

And Jacob awaked out of his sleep, and he said, "Surely the Lord is in this place; and I knew it not." —Genesis 28:16 (KJV)

The church calendar and its iconic locations were important to C. S. Lewis. "It is well to have specifically holy places," he said, "and things, and days, for, without these focal points or reminders belief . . . will soon dwindle into a mere sentiment."

The Bible is filled with examples of special places of spiritual encounter with God. One night Jacob slept and was given a vivid dream in which angels ascended and descended from heaven on a ladder. God then verbally confirmed the passing of the covenant from Abraham and Isaac to Jacob. When Jacob awoke, he realized he had had a divine encounter and set up a spiritual reminder by naming that place Bethel, or house of God (Genesis 28:19).

For those in denominations that follow the Christian calendar, many spiritual prompts can be seen throughout the year. And for those of us who do not have these set reminders, we can find other ways of recalling God's faithfulness. Christmas and Easter can be wonderful times to reflect upon the gift of God in Christ Jesus and His redemption for all who believe.

Whatever our background, each of us can find spiritual prompts to help us connect with God throughout the year.

A church calendar can help us to recall God's faithfulness.

For Further Reading: *Letters to Malcolm: Chiefly on Prayer* by C. S. Lewis, chapter 14

READ: Psalm 119:89–104

Burrowing in Books

How sweet are Your words to my taste, sweeter than honey to my mouth!
—Psalm 119:103

The longest psalm in the Bible is Psalm 119. Containing an expansive 176 verses, this psalm compares the Word to silver and gold for its precious value. It also says the Word provides a lamp to guide our paths and is honey because of the sweetness it brings to the spirit.

Unfortunately, in the twenty-first century the steady rise of technology in communication has a tendency to shorten our attention span and oversimplify our minds and hearts. When looking at a thick book these days, a likely response might be: "Of making many books there is no end, and much study is wearisome to the flesh" (Ecclesiastes 12:12).

But earlier generations discovered the lasting joys that come from burrowing into books of real length and substance (Jeremiah 15:16). Careful in his attention to Scripture and prayer, C. S. Lewis also spent extended time engaged in digesting the written word. He once said, "You can never get a cup of tea large enough or a book long enough to suit me." We need to ask God to boost our attention spans and then spend extended time in His Word—the Bible.

Let's take unhurried time to reflect on the ultimate, life-transforming Book.

FOR FURTHER READING: *God in the Dock*
by C. S. Lewis, "On the Reading of Old Books"

NOVEMBER 30

READ: Psalm 119:73–80; 1 Peter 2:21–24

The School of Pain

I know, O LORD, that Your judgments are right, and that in faithfulness You have afflicted me. —Psalm 119:75

In his book *The Problem of Pain*, C. S. Lewis observes, "God whispers to us in our pleasures, speaks in our conscience, but shouts in our pains: It is His megaphone to rouse a deaf world." Suffering often helps us to redirect our focus from immediate circumstances to listening to how God is working in our lives. Business as usual is replaced by a spiritual schoolroom of instruction.

In the Old Testament, we read that the psalmist believed every affliction has been permitted by a faithful and loving God (Psalm 119:75). Isaiah the prophet exhorted the people of God to view suffering as a refining process. Only when the dross is melted away do we see the precious gold that resides within (Isaiah 48:10).

But we have not been left alone in our experience of pain. God himself took on human form and drank deeply from the cup of suffering. It is the faithful obedience of Jesus Christ that gives heartfelt meaning to the believer who is hurting (1 Peter 2:21–24).

What pain are you experiencing? How might it help you grow in your walk with God? Remember, our Lord himself attended the school of pain, and He understands.

Christ has suffered—leaving us an example to follow.

FOR FURTHER READING: *The Problem of Pain*
by C. S. Lewis, Introduction

READ: Galatians 1:11–24

The Reluctant Convert

But they were hearing only, "He who formerly persecuted us now preaches the faith which he once tried to destroy."
—Galatians 1:23

Do you have friends or loved ones who oppose your Christian beliefs? C. S. Lewis' conversion illustrates how they may still be graciously drawn to Christ. In his autobiography, *Surprised by Joy*, Lewis writes of his journey from atheist to Christian: "In the Trinity Term of 1929 I gave in, and admitted that God was God, and knelt and prayed: perhaps, that night, the most dejected and reluctant convert in all England. . . . But who can duly adore that Love which will open the high gates to a prodigal who is brought in kicking, struggling, resentful, and darting his eyes in every direction for a chance of escape?" Lewis went on to become a great proclaimer of Christianity.

Similarly, Saul of Tarsus encountered the risen Christ on the road to Damascus (Acts 9). There he was transformed from a persecutor of the church into a zealous proclaimer of the gospel. The Christian community was astonished to learn: "He who formerly persecuted us now preaches the faith which he once tried to destroy" (Galatians 1:23).

This same God can reach reluctant skeptics today. Keep praying and keep proclaiming Jesus.

*Keep praying for the conversion of your
unbelieving friends and loved ones.*

FOR FURTHER READING: *Surprised by Joy*
by C. S. Lewis, chapter 14

READ: Job 23:12; Psalm 19:7–11; 1 Peter 2:1–3

Happiness Fuel

Your words were found, and I ate them, and Your word was to me
the joy and rejoicing of my heart; for I am called by Your name,
O LORD God of hosts. —Jeremiah 15:16

Unless we drive semi-trucks for a living, the fuel we need for our cars is probably gasoline and not diesel. In fact the fuel industry and local gas stations have designed different-sized fuel pumps to keep inattentive customers from putting the wrong fuel in their cars, which could ruin an engine. A well-tuned car filled with the right kind of gasoline, though, is a joy to drive.

Reflecting on the spiritual journey of human beings, C. S. Lewis drew a parallel between fuel for the soul and the source of human happiness: "God designed the human machine to run on Himself. He Himself is the fuel our spirits were designed to burn, or the food our spirits were designed to feed on. There is no other."

We feed upon God by immersing ourselves in His Word and being filled with His Spirit (Ephesians 5:18; Colossians 3:16). This does not occur, however, without having to deal with temptation or struggle. We overcome those things by making God the priority, which helps us recapture the fellowship that was lost when the human race fell into sin. Fellowship with our Redeemer is the fuel our souls were designed to run on.

God designed the human spirit to run on God
as its fuel. Imitations just won't work.

FOR FURTHER READING: *Mere Christianity*
by C. S. Lewis, book 2, chapter 3

READ: Exodus 3:1–20; Acts 7:22

Second Best

Now Moses was tending the flock of Jethro his father-in-law, the priest of Midian. And he led the flock to the back of the desert, and came to Horeb, the mountain of God. —Exodus 3:1

Do you sometimes feel that your lifelong dream has shattered and there is no hope of repair? If so, you would be joining the surprisingly large number of people who live a life they think is second best.

As strange as it might seem, C. S. Lewis' writing career could be considered his "second best." Originally, Lewis had fervently wanted to be a poet. However, his two works of poetry, *Dymer* and *Spirits in Bondage*, met with disappointing sales.

Later, after his conversion, Lewis' drive to write was rechanneled into a creative flurry of prose writing on Christian themes. *Time* magazine put Lewis on its cover and featured his writing of *The Screwtape Letters*. His apologetic work *Mere Christianity* would earn its place as a classic in Christian apologetics. And his Narnia Chronicles would become widely read by children and adults alike. Many C. S. Lewis scholars believe that Lewis was able to write compelling articles and stories because of his poetic use of words.

God used Lewis' broken dream as a foundation for a dynamic future. In a similar way, Moses' desire to bring relief to his people (Exodus 2:11–15) was interrupted by a 40-year career as a shepherd, which prepared him to lead the people of God in the wilderness according to God's plan (3:1). Like Lewis and like Moses, you can find God's leading.

God can use what we may think is second best
as a platform for greater fruitfulness.

For Further Reading: *Surprised by Joy* by C. S. Lewis, chapter 8

READ: Luke 19:1–10

Our Ultimate Rescue

For the Son of Man has come to seek and to save that which was lost. —Luke 19:10

During World War I, an American fighting unit serving in France was trapped. Surrounded by enemy troops, their last hope of rescue was a little carrier pigeon named Cher Ami (French for "Dear Friend"). Released by the soldiers and carrying a note with their location strapped to his leg, the bird took off. Wounded by enemy gunfire, Cher Ami flew twenty-five miles to deliver the message. Although the pigeon succumbed to those wounds, it saved the lives of two hundred men.

Is it possible for us to learn from one of God's brave little creatures? Cher Ami died while carrying a vital message of hope—despite the danger. In the same Great War but in another location, a young British officer was also in desperate need of rescue (of the spiritual kind). The difference was that he did not know it. Young Lieutenant Clive Staples Lewis would be wounded and sent back home to recover. A few years later he would personally encounter the Redeemer who would ultimately save him. After this life-changing experience, Lewis dedicated his life to proclaiming our ultimate rescue.

> *When we share the gospel with others, we are proclaiming the only hope of eternal rescue.*

For Further Reading: *Surprised by Joy*
by C. S. Lewis, chapter 7

READ: Acts 17:1–15; 2 Peter 1:19–21; Revelation 22:18–19

Scripture Interpreting Scripture

These were more fair-minded than those in Thessalonica, in that they received the word with all readiness, and searched the Scriptures daily to find out whether these things were so. —Acts 17:11

Have you ever been called a "Berean"? It's quite an honor! It means you would agree with C. S. Lewis in his view of the unity and value of Scripture: "I take it as a first principle that we must not interpret any one part of Scripture so that it contradicts other parts, and specially we must not use an apostle's teaching to contradict that of Our Lord."

The Jewish community in Berea was open to the gospel of Paul—but not without a clear understanding of Scripture. We are told that they "searched the Scriptures daily" (Acts 17:11) to test his gospel against multiple passages in the Old Testament. In the ancient world the term translated as *search* was used in courts of law to refer to how attorneys would scrutinize context, motive, and multiple sources in a case. This is what the Jews in Berea did when they checked Paul's gospel with Scripture. Most likely this process led many to believe in Jesus as Messiah. A community of faith carefully cross-checking Scripture can provide both fruitful evangelism and encourage spiritual growth. Bible study should never be exclusively a solo experience (2 Peter 1:20). Are you a Berean?

The Scriptures have an internal unity because their ultimate author is God the Holy Spirit.

FOR FURTHER READING: *The Collected Letters of C. S. Lewis*, volume 3

READ: John 1:1–14; Hebrews 1:1–4

God Incognito

The secret things belong to the LORD our God, but those things which are revealed belong to us and to our children forever, that we may do all the words of this law. —Deuteronomy 29:29

In reflecting on the presence of God in our world, C. S. Lewis made an interesting comment about God being incognito: "We may ignore, but we can nowhere evade the presence of God. The world is crowded with Him. He walks everywhere incognito. And the incognito is not always hard to penetrate. The real labor is to remember, to attend. In fact, to come awake. Still more, to remain awake."

The word *incognito* means "having one's true identity hidden or assuming a different one." When the term is used today, it has a range of meanings. It can be used of an administrator who disguises as a visitor to a factory to evaluate employee efficiency. Or it can even be used of a spy in deep cover in a foreign country. In each case the identity of the person is veiled.

In what ways does God "walk everywhere incognito"? A starter list might be as follows: through the beauty of His handiwork in creation; in the voice of conscience, which guides our moral choices; in the spiritual conversations we have with others about films we see and books we read. Look for God, even when you can't "see" Him.

Although God is often incognito,
He is never absent from our lives.

FOR FURTHER READING: *Letters to Malcolm: Chiefly on Prayer* by C. S. Lewis, chapter 14

READ: Judges 4:4–24

Women Warriors

Then Deborah said to Barak, "Up! For this is the day in which the Lord has delivered Sisera into your hand." —Judges 4:14

In the Narnia Chronicles, C. S. Lewis does not exclude girls and women from having roles in battles. Susan becomes accomplished with a bow and arrow. Lucy tends the wounded with a magic cordial.

History records women warriors who were less subtle in battle. In AD 60 a major rebellion took place in the Roman colony of Britannia. The king of the Iceni Celtic tribe died—leaving no male heir to rule. Roman monetary gifts and tax agreements formerly given to the king were then withdrawn by a greedy Roman tax collector. Outraged by this unjust treatment, Boudica became a warrior queen who rallied tens of thousands of Celts to fight the Romans in an attempt to regain their liberty.

God's Word also records instances in which women were assertive for a just cause. One is Deborah, who was both a prophetess and judge. When the military leader Barak seemed indifferent to his duty, Deborah took the initiative: "Up! For this is the day in which the Lord has delivered Sisera into your hand." This helped galvanize a mighty army and brought victory for the Lord's people (Judges 4:4–24). Thank God for women warriors.

*Life's challenges may require all of us
to be assertive for the right.*

For Further Reading: *The Lion, the Witch and the Wardrobe*
by C. S. Lewis, chapter 17

READ: Psalm 25:1–11

Keeping Time

Lead me in Your truth and teach me, for You are the God of my salvation; on You I wait all the day. —Psalm 25:5

The majestic chimes of London's Big Ben clock are familiar to many. But did you know that the original chimes had words to match each note? The melody is taken from Handel's *Messiah* oratorio section: "I Know That My Redeemer Liveth." And the lyrics written for the clock have a time significance:

*All through this hour
Lord, be my guide
And by Thy power
No foot shall slide.*

As David faced the challenges of life, he sought the Lord's help one day at a time: "Lead me in Your truth and teach me, for You are the God of my salvation, on You I wait all the day" (Psalm 25:5). Wanting to be a teachable follower of Yahweh, David looked to his Redeemer for direction. His heart's desire was to wait on God in dependent faith throughout the entire day.

In *The Screwtape Letters*, C. S. Lewis reinforces this biblical idea of time: "The Future is, of all things, the thing least like eternity. It is the most temporal part of time—for the Past is frozen and no longer flows, and the Present is all lit up with eternal rays."

*To maintain a regular spiritual focus, let each
new hour be a reminder to pray.*

FOR FURTHER READING: *The Screwtape Letters*
by C. S. Lewis, Letter 15

READ: Joshua 1:1–18

Life's Battlefield

You therefore must endure hardship as a good soldier of Jesus Christ. —2 Timothy 2:3

World War I has been ranked by many as one of the deadliest conflicts in human history.

On November 11, 1918, a ceasefire was observed on the eleventh hour of the eleventh day of the eleventh month. During that historic moment, millions around the world observed the discipline of silence while they reflected upon the war's terrible cost in loss of life and human suffering. That generation hoped "the Great War" as it was called would truly be the "war that would end all wars"—and that everyone could get back to normal life.

While still in his teens, Jack Lewis served in the trenches of this catastrophic war. Yet, years later, when World War II loomed on the horizon, his Christian faith made him remarkably grounded. Addressing students at Oxford, Lewis reminded them: "War creates no absolutely new situation: it simply aggravates the permanent human situation so that we can no longer ignore it. . . . We are mistaken when we compare war with 'normal life.' Life has never been normal." Life often feels like a battlefield, yet our Great Commander Jesus Christ stands ready to guide us through the conflict.

Conflict is inevitable, but God's grace is sufficient in facing it.

For Further Reading: *The Weight of Glory*
by C. S. Lewis, "Learning in War-Time"

READ: Matthew 6:19–21; 13:45–46

Earthbound

For Demas has forsaken me, having loved this present world, and has departed for Thessalonica. —2 Timothy 4:10

Let's return to C. S. Lewis' *The Screwtape Letters* today. In writing about how to compromise Christian commitment, Screwtape tells Wormwood: "The truth is that the Enemy [God], having oddly destined these mere animals to life in His own eternal world, has guarded them pretty effectively from the danger of feeling at home anywhere else. That is why we must often wish long life to our patients; seventy years is not a day too much for the difficult task of unraveling their souls from Heaven and building up a firm attachment to the earth."

In our key verse today we see Paul lamenting that his colleague Demas deserted him because of his love for this present world. The root meaning for *love* here is *esteem* or *value*. In Demas' value system the allure of this present world is at the top of the list. He has become earthbound instead of heavenly minded. Ironically, he had a past of faithful service with Paul (Philemon 24; Colossians 4:14). The life lesson Demas' choice offers is that even faithful service for Christ can end when affections for the things of this world eclipse a heart for God.

Each day we should renew our affections for Christ's eternal kingdom through confession, prayer, and reflection on His Word.

FOR FURTHER READING: *The Screwtape Letters*
by C. S. Lewis, Letter 27

READ: Psalm 119:89–96; Matthew 24:35; 1 Peter 1:25

Changing Tide of Fashions

And there arose another generation after them, which knew not the LORD, nor yet the works which he had done for Israel.
—Judges 2:10 (KJV)

The news media, the latest books, and the film industry often view ideas held even fifty years ago as obsolete. C. S. Lewis objected to this, saying that he didn't agree with "rejecting something . . . simply because it happens to be out of fashion in your own time. . . . For our own age, with all its accepted ideas, stands to the vast extent of historical time much as one village stands to the whole world."

When we consider our own age as the only enlightened one, we make the mistake of thinking our own time is right in everything it holds and all other times are wrong when they disagree with us. Fortunately for the believer, the Bible can be a firm foundation amidst the changing tide of fashion. Although the Bible recognizes the reality of human social change, it is inflexible about its claim about eternal truths (Isaiah 40:8; Malachi 3:6). God's holy love and the need for redemption will never go out of fashion. This is why when a generation seeks to do everything that is right in its own eyes, a call back to God's truth must be given (Judges 21:25; Matthew 3:2).

Our evangelistic methods should adapt to a new generation, but the message must always remain the same.

FOR FURTHER READING: *Studies in Medieval and Renaissance Literature* by C. S. Lewis, "Edmund Spenser"

READ: Genesis 1:20–3:24

A New Species

And they heard the sound of the LORD God walking in the garden in the cool of the day, and Adam and his wife hid themselves from the presence of the LORD God among the trees of the garden.

—Genesis 3:8

Scientists tell us that hundreds of new species of flora and fauna are discovered each year. In an article titled "Undiscovered Species," the website *Current Results* makes these claims: "Each year scientists record another 18,000 new species of plants and animals."

When God created life on our planet, He filled it with an astonishing variety of animal and plant life. And when he fashioned the first man and woman, God proclaimed this creative masterpiece "good." Then the Creator set our first human parents over this world as caretakers. The only prohibition given to the young couple was not to eat of the Tree of the Knowledge of Good and Evil. When Adam and Eve both transgressed the command of God, they became a different kind of human being. They were no longer innocent bearers of the divine image but depraved creatures with a bent to disobey God and harm one another.

Of the fall of man, C. S. Lewis said, "A new species had sinned itself into existence." Man the holy had become man the sinner in need of redemption. Our only hope lies in the atoning work of Jesus Christ (John 3:16; Romans 6:23).

We are sinners in need of redemption.

FOR FURTHER READING: *The Problem of Pain*
by C. S. Lewis, chapter 5

READ: Matthew 4:1–11

Tempted in All Points

For we do not have a High Priest who cannot sympathize with our weaknesses, but was in all points tempted as we are, yet without sin.
—Hebrews 4:15

Of Christ's example in resisting temptation, C. S. Lewis said, "We never find out the strength of the evil impulse inside us until we try to fight it: and Christ, because He was the only man who never yielded to temptation, is also the only man who knows to the full what temptation means—the only complete realist." The Lord Jesus is a hardened veteran in the fight against sin.

In reading Matthew's account of the temptation of Christ, we might wonder how anyone could resist the rewards offered for acting independently from God. Yet in every case, our Lord used the Word of God to resist the evil one's seductions to sin. When we take an honest look at our own proneness to sin, we might lose heart. But this is the remarkable ministry of Jesus Christ. We are told that He "was in all points tempted as we are, yet without sin" (Hebrews 4:15). And this experience with all kinds of temptations qualifies Christ to be supremely understanding with the temptations we face. He is the Great High Priest who can "sympathize with our weaknesses."

Jesus is always present to give grace in forgiveness and help to obey.

FOR FURTHER READING: *Mere Christianity*
by C. S. Lewis, book 3, chapter 11

READ: Matthew 25:1–46

End of the World

*For you yourselves know perfectly that the day of the Lord so comes
as a thief in the night.*   —1 Thessalonians 5:2

Matthew 25 gives us three stirring images of Christ's return. The parable of the ten virgins illustrate how each believer should be prepared for the Lord's return at any time (vv. 1–13). The parable of the talents tells how each believer will be held accountable for the use of resources given as a steward of the King (vv. 14–30). And finally, the parable of the sheep and goats speaks of how final judgment will reveal the authentic believer by the compassion for "the least of these My brethren" (vv. 31–46).

So, what did C. S. Lewis say about the glorious truth of the return of Christ? "The doctrine of the Second Coming is deeply noncongenial to the whole evolutionary or developmental character of modern thought. We have been taught to think of the world as something that grows slowly towards perfection, something that 'progresses' or 'evolves.' . . . [The Second Coming] offers no such hope. . . . It foretells a sudden, violent end imposed from without; an extinguisher popped onto the candle, a brick flung at the gramophone, a curtain rung down on the play—'Halt!'"

Indeed, the end is coming. Be ready.

*We are called to live our lives in view of
the ultimate day of reckoning.*

FOR FURTHER READING: *The World's Last Night and Other Essays*
by C. S. Lewis, "The World's Last Night"

READ: Mark 6:45–52

Hardened Hearts

But Pharaoh hardened his heart at this time also; neither would he let the people go. —Exodus 8:32

When we hear the idea of a hardened heart in Bible study, more often than not Pharaoh of Egypt comes to mind. After promising to release Israel from bondage to follow Moses, Pharaoh changed his mind and hardened his heart (Exodus 8:32; 9:12).

Unexpectedly, the same idea of hardening one's own heart is used of our Lord's disciples. Following the extraordinary miracle of the feeding of the five thousand with just five loaves and two fishes, the disciples encountered a terrible storm at sea. Seeing Jesus walking on the water, they were terrified until Jesus calmed them with His words. We then read these words: "For they had not understood about the loaves, because their heart was hardened" (Mark 6:52).

Having seen the miraculous multiplication of loaves and fishes, they failed to let this expand their openness to see other supernatural acts like walking on water or stilling the storm. C. S. Lewis said, "A naturalistic Christianity leaves out all that is specifically Christian." The purpose of seeing the miraculous in Scripture is so that our hearts will be softened to expect God to do even greater things. How is your heart?

Our attitude toward miracles in the Bible must not be selective. We may not believe one and disbelieve another.

FOR FURTHER READING: *Miracles* by C. S. Lewis, chapter 10

READ: Philippians 4:10–20

Childlike Contentment

I know how to be abased, and I know how to abound. Everywhere and in all things I have learned both to be full and to be hungry, both to abound and to suffer need. —Philippians 4:12

In C. S. Lewis' science fiction novel *That Hideous Strength*, Jane, a restless young woman, comes into contact with an older Christian couple: Mr. and Mrs. Denniston. Initially, it is their attitude toward England's changing weather that shows her how the two have grown into the art of contented living: "'We both like Weather. Not this or that kind of weather, but just Weather. It's a useful taste if one lives in England.' 'How ever did you learn to do that, Mr. Denniston?' said Jane. 'I don't think I should ever learn to like rain and snow.' 'It's the other way round,' said Denniston. 'Everyone begins as a child by liking Weather. You learn the art of disliking it as you grow up. Haven't you ever noticed it on a snowy day? The grown-ups are all going about with long faces, but look at the children—and the dogs? *They* know what snow's made for.'"

We can learn something from the delight of children. As we grow in our faith, we can take on a childlike delight in the changing life experiences God brings our way. Learning to appreciate the little things is a first step toward being satisfied with the bigger ones.

Through observing children we can learn to appreciate our present circumstances.

FOR FURTHER READING: *That Hideous Strength* by C. S. Lewis, chapter 7

READ: Genesis 2:16–17; 3:1–6; 1 John 2:15–17

Sinful Curiosity

So when the woman saw that the tree was good for food, that it was pleasant to the eyes, and a tree desirable to make one wise, she took of its fruit and ate. She also gave to her husband with her, and he ate. —Genesis 3:6

In *The Magician's Nephew*, we read about Digory and Polly encountering the dead world of Charn and seeing a bell with this inscription:

Make your choice, adventurous Stranger,
Strike the bell and bide the danger,
Or wonder, till it drives you mad,
What would have followed if you had.

Polly urges the two of them to flee this terrible temptation. But Digory insists on ringing the bell—with devastating results. The terrible Queen Jadis is awakened and eventually follows them into Narnia bringing evil into that newly created world. Sinful curiosity has disastrous consequences.

When the mother of the human race looked at the forbidden fruit, her thoughts were filled with curiosity. The taste played on her physical appetites. The beauty of the fruit was an aesthetic vision. The promise to provide intelligence appealed to her vanity. Eve reached out, took the fruit, ate it, and gave it to Adam—who ate as well. When wondering about what a certain sin might be like, we can be assured that it will bring negative consequences (1 John 2:15–17).

Sinful curiosity has resulted in drug addiction, illicit affairs, and a multitude of other destructive behaviors.

FOR FURTHER READING: *The Magician's Nephew* by C. S. Lewis, chapter 4

READ: 1 John 1:1–10

Transparent Prayers

And there is no creature hidden from His sight, but all things are naked and open to the eyes of Him to whom we must give account.
—Hebrews 4:13

Sometimes when we come before God, we may think we ought to sanitize our words and camouflage our inner struggles. We think of a perfectionistic version of the Christian we "ought to be" and gauge our conversation with our heavenly Father accordingly. Regarding being transparent in prayer, C. S. Lewis said, "We must lay before Him what is in us, not what ought to be in us."

The Bible sets a premium on honest communication with God. The psalms are replete with raw emotions that arise out of disappointments and struggles. Psalms 69, 109, and 137 are all examples of prayers that expose raw wounds of personal injury presented before the God of justice. The psalmist doesn't hide his hurts but openly exposes them to God's listening ear.

The lengthy record of Job's painful cries to heaven also show how being transparent in prayer is the real pathway toward authentically encountering God (Job 38–40). In reality, God always sees what we are experiencing (Hebrews 4:13). So why should we try to put on a façade when talking with Him?

God wants us to be authentic about our struggles and meet Him at our point of honest need.

For Further Reading: *Letters to Malcolm: Chiefly on Prayer* by C. S. Lewis, chapter 4

READ: John 16:33; Romans 5:1–5; 2 Corinthians 12:7–10;
1 Peter 4:12–19

Tribulation in Particular

*And lest I should be exalted above measure by the abundance of
the revelations, a thorn in the flesh was given to me, a messenger
of Satan to buffet me, lest I be exalted above measure.*
—2 Corinthians 12:7

In a letter to his lifelong friend Owen Barfield, C. S. Lewis wrote of
a particular tribulation that causes us the most distress: "The real difficulty is, isn't it, to adapt ones steady beliefs about tribulation to this
particular tribulation; for the particular, when it arrives, always seems
so peculiarly intolerable."

The apostle Paul suffered in many different ways for the Savior.
Physical torture, being stoned and left for dead, shipwrecked in the sea,
and other hardships accompanied him in his tireless witness for Christ.
He accepted these sufferings as part of his calling. But there was one
tribulation in particular that drove him to beg for relief. Three times
Paul asked the Lord to take it away. But it was revealed to him that in
weakness God's power is perfected (2 Corinthians 12:7–10).

Suffering in general is not the problem. What sometimes gets to
us is a "particular tribulation" that brings repeated pain, makes us feel
weak, or saps our strength. It is here that we most need God's grace. In
this prism of pain, God's power can be perfected.

*When a particular trial hurts us, it is the place
where God's grace can be most evident.*

READ: Luke 8:4–14

Conversion Distractions

Those by the wayside are the ones who hear; then the devil comes and takes away the word out of their hearts, lest they should believe and be saved.
—Luke 8:12

Have you ever shared your faith with a receptive seeker only to find distractions erupt unexpectedly? A baby starts crying, there is a knock at the door, or the seeker seems preoccupied with some other thought. Whenever the gospel is shared, fallen angels are not far away. In one of his letters, C. S. Lewis wrote, "I think that all Christians have found that [the Devil] is very active near . . . the eve of conversion: worldly anxieties, physical comforts, lascivious fancies, doubt, are often poured in at such junctures. . . . But Grace is not frustrated."

Whenever the gospel is shared, the spiritual atmosphere is not neutral. God the Holy Spirit is present to convict of sin, of righteousness, and of judgment (John 16:8). God the Son continues to seek and save the lost (Luke 19:10). And God the Father is overseeing the outworking of redemption, which was decided upon before the foundation of the world (1 Peter 1:20–21). Yet Satan will not take this lying down. He hates God, so he seeks to frustrate any attempt God makes to redeem fallen creatures who are made in His image (Luke 8:12). Rejoice, though. In all of this, grace is not frustrated.

In the plan of God, the gospel will prevail despite any opposition from fallen angels or evil men. Keep sharing the gospel.

FOR FURTHER READING: *The Collected Letters of C. S. Lewis,* volume 2

READ: Philippians 2:12–18; Revelation 21:1–5

Walking in the Light

But the path of the just is like the shining sun, that shines ever brighter unto the perfect day. —Proverbs 4:18

On June 8, 1942, C. S. Lewis preached a sermon called "The Weight of Glory" at a church in Oxford. He spoke of how his Christian faith uniquely altered his perspective on life's journey: "I believe in Christianity as I believe that the sun has risen: not only because I see it, but because by it I see everything else."

Proverbs 4:18 makes a remarkably similar statement. "But the path of the just is like the shining sun, that shines ever brighter unto the perfect day." During the night, we stumble in the dark and lose our way. But as the sun rises, more light is shed on our path so we see with growing clarity. This is the spiritual light that illuminates the path of the believer.

In the New Testament, John exhorts us: "If we walk in the light as He is in the light, we have fellowship with one another, and the blood of Jesus Christ His Son cleanses us from all sin" (1 John 1:7). Here we see that when we stumble, cleansing is available through Christ's atonement. What matters is that we keep our eyes on the path and grow in righteousness. Walking in the light gives us growing visual clarity.

Growing in righteousness gives us greater clarity in seeing reality and goodness.

FOR FURTHER READING: *The Weight of Glory* by C. S. Lewis, "The Weight of Glory"

READ: Matthew 28:1–6; Luke 2:10–15

Fear Not

And the angel said unto them, Fear not: for, behold, I bring you good tidings of great joy, which shall be to all people.
—Luke 2:10 (KJV)

It is marvelous to observe angels at work during our Lord's ministry on earth. In preparing the way for Christ's forerunner, John the Baptist, Zacharias is told by an angel to "fear not" but to expect his aged wife Elizabeth to conceive a child (Luke 1:13). When the Virgin Mary is told by the angel Gabriel of the miraculous conception to take place in her womb, she is also told to "fear not" (Luke 1:30). Then on a hillside as shepherds grazed their sheep, an angel appears to announce the birth of the Christ (Luke 2:10). To calm them at the supernatural vision, the angel tells the shepherds to "fear not." Finally, at the open tomb where Jesus' dead body had been placed, an angel tells the women who had come to embalm the body, "Fear not." Christ's body was not there, because He had risen from the dead (Matthew 28:5–6).

In a letter, C. S. Lewis observed, "I believe no angel ever appears in Scripture without exciting terror: they always have to begin by saying, 'Fear not.'" Why not fear? Because of the good news!

When "supernature" invades our natural world through God's heavenly agents, we are told to "fear not."

READ: Genesis 39:1–20; 1 Peter 3:13–17

Unjust Punishment

For what credit is it if, when you are beaten for your faults, you take it patiently? But when you do good and suffer, if you take it patiently, this is commendable before God. —1 Peter 2:20

In a letter to his brother concerning Joseph's unjust treatment as recorded in Genesis 39, C. S. Lewis speculated on why Joseph was only put in prison—and not executed—after Potiphar's wife accused him of attempted rape. With a master having the power of life and death over his slaves, killing Joseph would have seemed more likely the penalty. But certainly the young Hebrew slave had made a positive impression on Potiphar, and we don't know that his wife's promiscuous nature surfaced only here. Lewis wondered, "How often had [Potiphar] heard similar stories from her before?"

We don't know Potiphar's real motivation. But we can be certain that Joseph was treated with great injustice. The Scriptures do not promise believers they will never experience injustice. Indeed, we are told we should not be surprised when we experience persecution for doing the right thing. In businesses, at school, and in other areas of involvement, our righteous behavior is a challenge to those who do not wish to live that way. Peter tells us that we glorify God when we are treated unjustly for doing the right thing (1 Peter 3:13–17).

Life is often filled with unexpected experiences, but God can use them to help us grow and glorify Him.

FOR FURTHER READING: *The Collected Letters of C. S. Lewis,* volume 2

READ: John 15:9–17

Choosing or Chosen?

You did not choose Me, but I chose you and appointed you that you should go and bear fruit, and that your fruit should remain, that whatever you ask the Father in My name He may give you.
—John 15:16

In C. S. Lewis' book *The Silver Chair*, we find a fascinating illustration about coming to faith. Eustace and Jill have called to Aslan, who responds by bringing them to Narnia to fulfill an urgent mission. Interestingly, the great lion Aslan tells them: "You would not have called to me unless I had been calling to you."

In *Surprised by Joy*, Lewis writes of his own conversion: "The odd thing was that before God closed in on me, I was in fact offered what now appears a moment of wholly free choice . . . I say, 'I chose,' yet it did not really seem possible to do the opposite."

It is popular these days to refer to receptive unbelievers as "seekers" who only need to be pointed to Christ. Yet it is the testimony of Scripture that it is God who actively draws people to himself through Christ. Jesus said, "No one can come to Me unless the Father who sent Me draws him" (John 6:44). Although it might seem we come to faith in Christ purely on our own initiative, the reality is that God is calling us to make that decision.

God through Christ calls us to the place of decision.

FOR FURTHER READING: *The Silver Chair*, chapter 1

READ: Luke 2:1–7

God in a Stable

And she brought forth her firstborn son, and wrapped him in swaddling cloths, and laid him in a manger, because there was no room for them in the inn. —Luke 2:7

In *The Last Battle*, we discover something unusual about a stable, which appears to be a gateway to another world: " 'It seems, then,' said Tirian, smiling to himself, 'that the Stable seen from within and the Stable seen from without are two different places.' 'Yes,' said the Lord Digory. 'Its inside is bigger than its outside.' 'Yes,' said Queen Lucy. 'In our world too, a Stable once had something inside it that was bigger than our whole world.' "

In this tale, C. S. Lewis skillfully illustrates the remarkable setting of the incarnation. In a humble stable in first-century Bethlehem, the Son of God who had been conceived in the Virgin's womb entered our world as the baby Jesus. The all-powerful and all-knowing God of the Old Testament had come to reside in the tiny body of a newborn infant. The Lord of glory humbled himself and was born in a stable to grow to manhood and ultimately die and rise again to redeem all who believe (Philippians 2:5–11). The humble beginnings of the incarnation would result in the glorious redemption of our world.

The incarnation is the central miracle of the redemptive story. The Old Testament prepares for it, and the New Testament results from it.

FOR FURTHER READING: *The Last Battle* by C. S. Lewis, chapter 13

READ: 1 Peter 4:12–19

Painful Investment

Therefore let those who suffer according to the will of God commit their souls to Him in doing good, as to a faithful Creator.

—1 Peter 4:19

In a letter to Father Peter Bide, C. S. Lewis made a comment about suffering within the will of God: "We are not necessarily doubting that God will do the best for us: we are wondering how painful the best will turn out to be."

God is in the business of using pain in our lives for our growth and for His glory. But sometimes the discomfort either emotionally or physically can make us question the goodness of God. When this happens, it is important to realize that our pain for seeking to obey God is an investment in eternity that will yield future dividends. When Peter exhorts those of us who suffer to commit ourselves to doing good, he uses an interesting Greek word *paratithēmi*. It is a banking term that means "to give in charge as a deposit." When we suffer within the will of God, we are investing in eternity. God has allowed these painful circumstances to enter our lives, and His just evaluation at life's end will recompense us for our endurance. Painful investments do hurt, but they will be rewarded in the end.

Suffering for our faith builds character and invests in our eternal reward.

For Further Reading: *The Collected Letters of C. S. Lewis,* volume 3

READ: John 11:1–44

For Crying Out Loud

Jesus wept. —John 11:35

Should we cry? In one of his preserved letters, we read that C. S. Lewis talked about the benefit of crying out loud to express emotion: "By the way, don't 'weep inwardly' and get a sore throat. If you must weep, weep: a good honest howl! . . . Aeneas and Hector and Beowulf, Roland and Lancelot blubbered like schoolgirls, so why shouldn't we?"

"Jesus wept" is famous for being the shortest verse in the Bible. But it by no means is without deep meaning. The context is Christ seeing the despair Mary and Martha were experiencing at the death of their brother Lazarus. As he started toward the sealed tomb, our Lord was overwhelmed with emotion. The Greek word is *dakruo,* which means "to tear up." Later in the book of Hebrews we are reminded that as our Great High Priest, Jesus Christ is able to identify with our hurts and weaknesses unlike any other (Hebrews 4:15). As both the Old and New Testaments bear witness, there is something therapeutic about letting our emotions out through weeping (Psalm 30:5; 2 Corinthians 2:4; Philippians 3:18). When we cry, Jesus weeps with us.

The Bible tells of many people who both wept and rejoiced.

READ: Job 42:2; Psalm 135:5–7; Isaiah 46:9–10;
John 3:8; Ephesians 1:11

Not a Tame Lion

See, the Lion of the tribe of Judah, the Root of David, has triumphed.
— Revelation 5:5 (NIV)

In *The Lion, The Witch and the Wardrobe*, Mr. Beaver helps us understand the unpredictable nature of Aslan. After Aslan defeats the White Witch and then leaves, Mr. Beaver says, "He'll be coming and going . . . One day you'll see him and another you won't. He doesn't like being tied down—and of course he has other countries to attend to. It's quite all right. He'll often drop in. Only you mustn't press him. He's wild, you know. Not like a tame lion."

This marvelous illustration of Christ in another world provides insight into the sovereignty of God. Like the wind, His Spirit blows where it wills (John 3:8). As the Almighty, He does what He chooses in heaven and earth (Psalm 135:6). By His omnipotent power, Christ does as He pleases (Isaiah 46:10). And with His sovereign will our Lord guides the universe (Job 42:2; Ephesians 1:11).

The God of Scripture made known in Jesus Christ is not a cosmic bellboy who rushes to our every need. Instead, He is a wise and sovereign Lord who deals with His creation and the redeemed often in mysterious ways.

God is not under our control, but we are to be under His.

FOR FURTHER READING: *The Lion, the Witch and the Wardrobe*
by C. S. Lewis, chapter 17

READ: 1 Corinthians 12:1–12

Why Go to Church?

For as the body is one and has many members, but all the members of that one body, being many, are one body, so also is Christ.
—1 Corinthians 12:12

When C. S. Lewis came to faith in Christ, he initially thought he could lead a Christian life through private prayer and study of the Scripture and not have to go to church. He did not care for church hymns. He thought them to be weak both in lyric and music. But as he began to attend a congregation, he soon saw the merit of active participation. He observed such a range of education and vocation in the congregation that his arrogant attitude was challenged and slowly began to disappear. Observing the sincere faith of those who had gathered for worship and to hear the Word of God put things in perspective. Lewis wrote, "It gets you out of your solitary conceit."

Paul tells us of both the diversity and unity we find in the church as the body of Christ (1 Corinthians 12:12). The Holy Spirit brings vitality and refreshment to a complex and interdependent group. It would be chaos for each member to try to work solo or function outside of one's gifts. So a celebration of mutual need and reciprocal ministry is to be recognized and adapted. What a joy to be a part of the celebration!

The Christian life is to be shared with other believers
in Christ through mutual interdependence.

For Further Reading: *God in the Dock* by C. S Lewis,
"Answers to Questions on Christianity"

READ: 2 Thessalonians 3:1–18

The Lost Art of Letter Writing

I, Paul, write this greeting with my own hand. This is the sign of genuineness in every letter of mine; it is the way I write.
—2 Thessalonians 3:17 (ESV)

In our world of technology, much of our communication is almost instantaneous. E-mail, Twitter, smartphones, and Skype encourage messages in quick and short bursts. Yet we could learn something from the low-tech C. S. Lewis, who answered thousands of pieces of correspondence by writing with a pen.

To his friend Arthur Greeves, Lewis wrote, "It is the immemorial privilege of letter-writers to commit to paper things they would not say; to write in a more grandiose manner than that in which they speak; and to enlarge upon feelings which would be passed by unnoticed in conversation."

The apostle Paul conserved the fruits of evangelism by planting churches and later sending them inspired letters to build them up in the faith. One such congregation was in Thessalonica. Believers there were a delight to him as their zeal for their faith had spread throughout the region (1 Thessalonians 1:6–10).

Twenty-first century Christians can learn something from Paul and C. S. Lewis. We do not need to give up electronic forms of communication, but we would do well to relearn the art of letter writing and become more reflective in the ideas we share.

Prayerful and reflective letters can do much to help others. Indeed, much of the New Testament is made up of inspired epistles.

FOR FURTHER READING: *The Letters of C. S. Lewis to Arthur Greeves,* edited by Walter Hooper

READ: 2 Corinthians 10:1–5; Acts 7:20–22; 22:3

Expanding Our Minds

We demolish arguments and every pretension that sets itself up against the knowledge of God, and we take captive every thought to make it obedient to Christ. —2 Corinthians 10:5 (NIV)

Some followers of Christ think we should only read "Christian books." But C. S. Lewis read widely and in a variety of fields. In doing so he was able to "take captive every thought to make it obedient to Christ" (2 Corinthians 10:5). Lewis rejoiced in this process because of the way it expanded his perception of life: "In reading great literature I become a thousand men and yet remain myself. Like the night sky in a Greek poem, I see with a thousand eyes, but it is still I who see. Here, as in worship, in love, in moral action, and in knowing, I transcend myself: and am never more myself than when I do."

The Bible is not an anti-intellectual book. Indeed, it is filled with exhortations to be lifelong learners (Proverbs 1:8–9). Moses received an education as a prince in Egypt (Acts 7:22). Years later, God could use what Moses learned in the Egyptian Academy to mold him into an effective leader. Likewise, Paul was educated under Gamaliel—a top scholar of the day (Acts 22:3). Once he encountered Christ, Paul was able to access all he had learned as the Holy Spirit led him to write Scripture.

Read widely, but find truth in God's Word.

Our educations may vary, but all believers are called to be lifelong learners.

FOR FURTHER READING: *C. S. Lewis, An Experiment in Criticism,* Epilogue

SCRIPTURE INDEX

381